STREETWISE®
BUSINESS
COMMUNICATION

Deliver Your Message with Clarity and Efficiency

Joe LoCicero

Adams Media
Avon, Massachusetts

Copyright © 2007, F+W Publications, Inc.
A Streetwise® Publication. Streetwise® is a registered trademark of
F+W Publications.

Published by Adams Media, an F+W Publications Company
57 Littlefield Street
Avon, MA 02322
www.adamsmedia.com

ISBN 10: 1-59869-066-3
ISBN 13: 978-1-59869-066-8

Printed in the United States of America.

J I H G F E D C B A

Library of Congress Cataloging-in-Publication Data
is available from the publisher

This book is available at quantity discounts for bulk purchases.
For information, please call 1-800-289-0963.

CONTENTS

Dedication

For Dad, who showed me that enlightened communication makes success in business stronger and sweeter.

Acknowledgments

Having worked in publicity, marketing, and advertising, I've had the luck to be aligned with smart, talented stars. I am grateful to Lynn Brockman, who guided me through my first publicity experiences; to Shawn Sites, for her amazing expertise; and to Alison Hill, for an invaluable entrée into entertainment. To Kristy Wylie, thank you for teaching me the importance of bridging business and creativity. I also appreciate those who marvelously contributed examples, inspiration, and goodwill to this book: Carrie Gerlach Cecil, Libby Gill, Melissa Mahoney, P. Jay Massey, Audra Platz, Eileen Spitalny, and Patty Triplett West. This work also reaped rewards from the delightful insights of my editor, Shoshanna Grossman, and the sage wisdom of my agent, Jacky Sach. Finally, my good business practices benefit from a communicative home, and there, I extend love and thanks to my always-engaging wife and two children.

Introduction

When mastered effectively, the art of business communications can build a lucrative, impressive, and respected company beyond imagination. A company that embraces solid communication saves *and* makes time *and* money—the two hottest commodities in the business world. In today's exceedingly fast-paced environment, you have a rich bounty of communication modes at your disposal. Using them to your best benefit takes care, practice, judgment, and finesse. The upside is that because communication is so prevalent in our business activities, you can constantly hone your skills.

Today, in a plethora of media platforms—such as newspaper articles, magazine accounts, television reports, Web sites, and blogs—we can gain enormous insights into how both seasoned executives and starting-out entrepreneurs can use communication to a booming advantage or disastrous disadvantage. Shining examples of corporate success show how using communication wisely can form the sturdy foundation for a company's rise. Conversely, abusing or ignoring communication can be the impetus for an enterprise's downfall.

In all of its formats, communication must constantly, continually, and cleverly work to get—and keep—business. Herein, you'll find the tools to diligently and deftly command communication's rich, varied facets.

Having been fortunate enough to have worked for *Fortune* 500 companies that range from beverage behemoths and hospitality pioneers to world-renowned entertainment studios and beloved icons, I have been integrally involved with a host of communications endeavors, marketing campaigns, and brand launches that achieved astounding, heady results. My career scope has encompassed creating Web sites, scripting speeches, developing press kits, creating commercials, devising direct mail pieces, and polishing presentations. I've been able to parlay that breadth of experience and knowledge into my own entrepreneurial efforts, and to help others launch and succeed in theirs.

Now, in these chapters, you'll learn how to put that expertise to work for your company, garnering attention from intended audiences with keenly crafted communications that will brim with excellent content, take the right tone, and reach the most targeted audience.

While you may easily think of the flashier components of business communications (such as marketing materials), an exceptionally strong skill set is also required to embrace the routine elements that make business survive and thrive on a daily basis: the well-composed e-mail, the respectful thank-you letter, the spot-on business proposal. You'll learn about those, too.

Of course, clear verbal communication is not just a valuable asset, but a downright necessity if your company is to achieve success at regular intervals. Winning meetings, powerful brainstorm sessions, receptive cold calls, and perceptive interviews also must be part of your repertoire.

When you don't take communication's many components seriously, you run the risk of a slew of problems and predicaments. We're all familiar with the e-mail that should have been a phone call (or a face-to-face conversation), the PowerPoint presentation that lost an account, the meeting that wasted everyone's time, or the crisis that spiraled out of control and took a company down with it.

Still, many of us know the joy of securing a magazine spread that sprang from an articulate media pitch, winning business as a result of a sizzling sales letter, outperforming goals by drawing big audiences with a well-executed Web site, and inspiring loyal customers with a vibrant print ad that connects.

If you're not familiar with the kinds of successes that can be readily attained, but you are eager to make them happen, rest assured: This book cogently explains the style and mechanics involved in business communications for both the uninitiated and the experienced. It provides an abundance of instruction and resources for rising stars seeking guidance, while also offering tips and techniques for established businesspersons looking to sharpen skills.

So, dive in. Your business is waiting and yearning for your communication expertise to expand and reap more productive employees, more satisfied clients and customers, and more profitable ventures!

The Art of Effective Communication

PART **1**

Why Is Communication Important to the Small Business Owner?

Whether you realize it or not, communication—not money, not "the big idea," not buzz—represents the most solid core foundation for any business. Without communication, your company would have no blueprint or method to get things going or keep them moving.

In the business world, mastering the art of communication goes beyond sparkling conversation or a well-worded memo. It involves such pivotal situations as laying out the road map to accomplish your business goals, delivering clear messages to employees for peak performance, and reading another person for successful negotiations.

Save Time, Make Money

Has it ever occurred to you that communication is used in every facet of your operation? It begins with how you formulate your entrepreneurial idea and craft your mission statement, and extends to all sorts of endeavors: how you tell your investors what you plan to do, explain to your customers what you can provide them, and even publicize your efforts to generate more business.

When your communication efforts are effective, you can use them to your full advantage to start, maintain, and grow your business. When you do, you save *and* make more time *and* money. And, as a side benefit, you—in that process—ease frustration, eliminate confusion, and avoid mistakes.

Avoid Problems

When you consider the possible problems your business may encounter, most relate to communication. The Web site *Myownbusiness.org* cogently points out such poor communication pitfalls as the absence of a well-thought-out business plan; inadequate research, testing, and focus groups; unprofessional logos, stationery, packaging, ads, or Web sites; poor signage; a staff that hasn't been appropriately trained; poor relationships with vendors; an unfocused marketing plan; and not using the advertising media that works best for your specific business.

Many times, a small business owner will be short on resources—financial and otherwise—making it incumbent upon him or her to use pithy communication to cut clutter, save time, and get a message across.

Unfortunately, business owners and employees can get so wrapped up in simply getting the job done that the methods, and their effectiveness, can get lost in the madness. For instance, securing money for your venture is certainly important, but the way you'll explain, detail, and ultimately persuade depends on how you communicate information about your start-up. Even the seemingly mundane, such as ordering the right size mailing label, requires sound communication skills; the layout of a form, for example, might require all of the specifications, including the label's measurements and the PMS colors of your company's logo. You also need the right size if addresses will be printed on the labels using a laser or inkjet printer.

Poor business communication costs your company in wasted time and lost effort, in clearing up misunderstandings, and subsequently having to redo projects. It can also cost goodwill: if your communication has inadvertently annoyed the recipient, your company suffers by association.

Different Kinds of Communication

In this book, you'll be exposed to a wealth of modes of communication and avenues for it. In delving into each one, you'll ascertain the best ways to produce, use, and distribute business communication, and key your success by understanding the advantages and disadvantages of the different modes.

Part of effective business communication is selecting and mastering the channel you decide to use. Will you leave a voice mail or send an e-mail? Does getting this piece of business mean you should write a proposal? What copy should you include in a direct mail piece? (Of course, discerning which type of communication to use also must be geared to the correct audience, such as customers or employees. You'll learn more about communicating to different audiences in the next chapter.)

What Is Communication?

If communication has such broad parameters, what is communication in a nutshell? Quite simply, it's the passing of information through words, gestures, or messages, spoken or written; and, in that, the interchange of thoughts, facts, and opinions. Primarily, you use communication to:

Inform: to provide information, to give directions, and to educate: describing your product line to a customer, notifying a vendor of a change in method of payment, explaining how a product is used or a task is performed

Inquire: to solicit or collect information: asking for quotes for a service, querying for research about your competition or demographics of your target market

Request: to ask that a certain action be taken: requesting that payment be made, asking that a deadline be met

Persuade: to prompt action: attracting new investors, new customers, or the media, which you hope will cover your company, product, or service

Build relationships: to foster goodwill with prospective and existing clients, customers, employees, and vendors: sending letters of congratulations or thanks, verbally checking in on the phone

The Single Most Important Business Skill

According to the National Federation of Independent Business Web site (*www. nfib.com*), a survey of 1,500 graduates of eighteen full-time MBA programs around the country rated the single most important business skill as one-on-one communication. Further, the MBAs said that only 6 percent of business schools did a "moderately effective" job helping students develop this all-important skill.

Your Communication Trifecta

In deciding what vehicle you'll use for your communication, your first consideration should be content. What is the message or information you're trying to get across? What is the most effective way to make sure your communication is received?

In the business world, communication is accomplished through:

Writing: or using words electronically or on paper to have a record of that message, or to communicate that message visually rather than orally. This type of communication includes a vast range of materials that can propel efforts forward mightily. They can have a longer impact and more lasting effect because they are presented in visual, permanent formats. They include memos, e-mails, letters, thank-you letters, forms, business plans, Web sites, newsletters, direct mail pieces, brochures, sell sheets, catalogs, press releases, advertisements, and PowerPoint presentations.

Speech: or the act of verbally using words to express ideas and thoughts; for example, in conversations and presentations. While the business world may increasingly seek to do business in a written arena, particularly with the proliferation of Web-based businesses and messages, verbal communication still holds sway in many cases. In the verbal arena, business communications include conversations, interviews, voice mails, speeches, and meetings.

Body Language: nonverbal signals or cues that are conveyed through posture, facial expressions, and the like that can be invaluable to the active listener and cognizant speaker in determining—and acting upon—hidden messages.

The Writing that Every Small Business Depends On

In business, writing can prove to be an obstacle (or at the very least, a challenge) that few are eager to regularly tackle. Setting aside time, concentrating on the writing task at hand, and finding the right words are all common excuses for avoidance.

The kind of writing that every small business depends on must be concise, on-message, and descriptive without being wordy. Clear, cohesive messages must coalesce with the image you want your company to project. Solid punctuation, logical wording, and consistent formatting must be the norm. Also, of course, a human approach is a given, and a necessity.

Writing Specifically for Your Business

Business writing occurs in a specific context. The tone, style, diction, and format of the writing you generate are influenced by the type of business you're in, how long you've been in business, and of course, the audience you're targeting and engaging. For instance, a law firm's materials will be different in language and manner than that of a pizzeria's, which will be different from that of an interior decorator's.

Whatever business you're in, business writing emphasizes results. You're urging readers, for example, to invest or to buy. Communication can only be effective if you're willing to excel in the basics: good grammar; an absence of misspellings; editing; and proofing. These mechanics are also instrumental in making sure that ads, marketing pieces, press releases, and other communications contain an effective message.

As you produce and disseminate your communication, be mindful of your core business mission. What do you want employees, customers, and, for that matter, anyone else, to know about your business? What makes your business different? What can you point out with particular pride? Incorporate a sense of this core in all that you write.

A Few Pointers

Eliminate the jargon, empty words, and pretentious phrases that appeal to few, and prize clarity and well-articulated simplicity with a healthy dose of humanity. No one wants to feel that they're reading correspondence that's been mass-produced. Your writing can be professional and still have a human touch. Less is usually more, so try to stay away from too many words or unnecessary adjectives.

Be aware that today, your target audience is most likely bombarded with a barrage of written communications via snail mail, memos, and e-mails. Realistically, you only have a few seconds to grab someone's attention and keep it, so reel in the reader with a clear and articulate opening that keeps attention and interest.

Further, write in a way that values, respects, and addresses the needs of your audience. You may be the best in your business, with the best prices, and also be a great writer, but none of these attributes will matter if the recipients of your correspondence aren't made to feel through your writing that you value them as individuals, customers, or clients. Respect your audience and their intelligence. Use your communication to let them know that what you're providing will serve them well or be beneficial to them, their company, or their lives.

Entrepreneurial Effective Communication Advice

The Web site PROFITguide.com pegs good communication skills as a prerequisite to business success when you take into account all the areas in which communication comes into play: convincing customers of your product benefits, understanding your clients' needs, coaching employees, and resolving conflicts between colleagues. The site reported that a poll of entrepreneurs from fast-growing companies submitted such choice effective communication techniques as these: avoid communication barriers by listening to the other person; plan communications ahead to steer clear of roadblocks; talk to a potential customer as you would a friend; and "proofread, proofread, proofread" any type of written communication before sending it out.

The 10 Cs to Master Communication

Despite communication's intense role in business, miscommunication seems to increasingly be the norm. As the barriers come down for a global marketplace, cross-cultural ties increase, and technology advances at a staggering rate, the propensity to give and receive mistaken messages goes up. It seems that the more ways you can get a message out, the more ways there are for the message to get mixed up.

Understanding that these factors exist and working to master the art of communication represent the easiest ways to get ahead. As you take command of business communication, make sure that, as often as possible, it features these "10 Cs":

1. **Captivating:** Strive to make your message interesting, and you'll command more attention and better responses.
2. **Clear:** Take a focused tack with your communication effort. Don't leave your audience wondering what your intentions or objectives are.
3. **Coherent:** Eliminate the irrelevant and embrace logic to ensure that your message is consistent and on the mark.
4. **Complete:** Be thorough. Don't leave your intended audience with a string of unanswered questions. Work to paint a picture that leaves little to the imagination, but still be economical with words.
5. **Concise:** Use as few words as necessary to convey your information—but don't spare words just to be brief.
6. **Concrete:** Go for specifics and certainty, rather than vagueness and generalities.
7. **Conversational:** Some believe that business communication somehow has to take a loftier tone or be wrapped up in complex words. To the contrary, while it should never be slang-filled, overtly intimate, or contain jargon that some may not understand, it should be easy to follow and pleasant.
8. **Convincing:** Win over the reader or listener with compelling and impelling language that encourages action.
9. **Correct:** You have the responsibility of making sure that your communication is truthful, accurate, and honest.

10. Courteous: Your communication should always convey a professional demeanor. Even correspondence bearing legal ramifications, such as a collection letter, should have a respectful tone.

The Process

Regardless of your kind of business, you must begin your communication with an organized approach that will flow from your writing. While some of these topics will be examined more closely in other chapters, this outline will aid in understanding the direction your writing should take. Realize that the scope, intensity, and importance of your writing project will dictate the time and energy each of these phases demands. For instance, if you're writing a memo about closing early for a holiday, you won't even need to take some of these steps into account. For putting together a marketing campaign, however, you'll need every one of them.

Before you begin your method of communication, consider the following questions and directions:

- Do I know the content of my message?
- Do I know and understand my audience?
- What do I want to accomplish? To answer, define your reason for writing, and your goals; identify the topic; analyze your audience; determine any special circumstances; choose the correct channel of communication; decide the tasks of the writing job; and determine a schedule that runs from start to completion.
- Generate ideas through creative endeavors such as brainstorming and visual maps.
- Gather information through research, being sure to use credible sources.
- Organize your ideas and shape your document, strategically focusing the message for efficiency and impact.
- In the draft stage, compose the document, not worrying about the final order of sentences, paragraphs, and sections. Avoid editing at this phase.
- If possible, take a reasonable break from the material for rethinking and revisions, which involves cutting, replacing, adding, and

rearranging. Solicit feedback from interested parties whose opinions you value, and be open to their remarks.

⊃ Revise, edit, and proofread for strategy, for design and format, for style and structure, and for logic, brevity, flow, tone, grammar, punctuation, and spelling.

Don't Always Have the Write Stuff?

Not a problem. Rather than ignoring your writing needs, find someone who fills the bill and can take those necessary writing chores off of your plate. You can pay by the hour or by the project. While fees can vary widely—from $25 to $200 and more per hour—the job will be done by someone dedicated to the task, helping you get it integrated into your business much more quickly. Looking for a freelance writer? Try *www.asja.com* and the listings on *www.craigslist .org*. Do feel free to ask a freelancer for writing samples to make sure that his or her style and experience are commensurate with your needs.

The Polish of Professionalism

Presentation is key to the perception that you engender.

To ensure that your communication will stand out, make it look professional. It's astounding how many companies don't pay attention to the presentation of their communications. A sure way for your message to get lost is for it to be riddled with misspellings, contain inappropriate language, look sloppy, and take a detrimental tone. With the onslaught of daily communication everyone faces, why bother with pieces that don't even look like they warrant attention?

Oftentimes, your communication doesn't have to be produced on flashy paper, or be wrapped up in an expensive mailing. Simply being presented professionally, succinctly, and accurately will foster confidence. Details matter when it comes to your communications.

The Bathroom Renovators

In 2003, a renovation company watched its sales skyrocket as homeowners took to its promise of having major bathroom remodels completed in two days. However, as the company experienced a steady stream of annual double-digit sales growth, its communication pains became massive, complicated by the fact that it had both on-site work crews and in-office personnel.

The company had a haphazard communication system, consisting of an eclectic mix of phone calls, e-mails, and handwritten documents that shared little in common and often resulted in confusion. Communications regularly broke down, resulting in lost information, double bookings, incorrect parts and materials delivered, unhappy customers, missed "two-day" deadlines and—ultimately—a lower profit margin. An overreliance on mangled phone messages and hard-to-read handwritten notes further damaged the business. Some jobs were managed with Post-it notes attached to original work orders. If a bathroom installer lost a note, or missed a change because he didn't see the note, the time and cost involved to make it good for the customer were painful.

Once the company realized that missing and ineffective communication was at the core of its problems, it put a new communication system in place, setting up new formats and guidelines for e-mails, messages, memos, and forms. The upshot: sales and profit margins increased because deadlines were met; communication propelled, rather than hindered, the business.

That polish extends to verbal communications as well. Be sure to have a professional, articulate staff to answer your phones, as well as professional-sounding outgoing voice-mail messages on both your office and cell phones.

Ensure that you're projecting the success that you and your company deserve.

Be Small, Look Big

A 2004 National Commission on Writing survey of business leaders asserted that good writing served as a "gatekeeper," meaning that poor writing skills might prevent a business from reaching its potential—or at least climbing to the next level of success.

A company's size should never be an excuse for lazy writing or communication. Too often, the leaders of a smaller company might think their business can be forgiven for laxity; expectations are lowered because of its size. If that's the case, think how you'll attract more business by exceeding expectations.

Don't let poor communication diminish your company's stature. Instead, take advantage of the fact that proper communication from your company will make your business benefit by appearing more accessible and amenable to new business.

Matters of Credibility

Polish and projection in communication point to the next level: building your credibility. Your company's outward expressions of professionalism can definitely bring trustworthiness. Obviously, customers, investors, and the like want to do business with a company they trust.

Further, you'll attract more of the types of people and companies you'd like to do business with. Think about the kinds of companies you like to, or want to, work with. What about the ones you're proud to patronize? What sets them apart?

To get business, you should be cognizant of projecting and presenting an image that attracts potential customers and clients. The manner and method of your communication show potential clients and customers that you're worthy of their trust and ultimately their business.

As a side benefit, that credibility goes a long way with your employees, too—keeping them happy, proud to serve your company, and on the lookout for ways to improve business, satisfy customers, and increase profits.

Take a look at the following two customer notices and decide which company you would rather do business with.

Obviously, Exhibit B is much more adept at effectively and humanely conveying its information and, in so doing, seems more interested in keeping a customer. Besides containing incomplete information, poor punctuation, misspellings, and nonsensical sentences, Exhibit A seems intent—if unwittingly—on sounding accusatory and building mistrust.

EXHIBIT A

TO CUSTOMER:
IMPORTANT NOTICE!!!!!
THIS IS THE ONLY BILL YOU WILL RECIEVE FOR THE PARKING GARAGE PASS ANNUAL FEE.
IF IT IS NOT RECEIVED BY NOVEMBER 10, YOUR GATE CARD SERVICE WILL BE INTERRUPTED. **NO EXCEPTIONS.** IF YOU DON'T RESPOND AND INTERRUPTION OCCURS, A $30 CHARGE WILL BE ASSESSED. PLUS YOU WILL N OT BE ALBE TO GET IN THE GARAGE.
DON'T' LET THIS HAPPEN TO YOU!
EVELYN
310/555-4689
PAY NOW!!!!!

EXHIBIT B

Dear Mr. Landingham:
November 1 marks the annual renewal for your parking garage pass. Your past business has been greatly appreciated, and we look forward to serving you in the future.
A payment of $75 is due no later than November 10. Please note that if payment is received after this date, you will incur a $30 reprogramming fee for the parking garage gate card, and daily entry into the garage may be interrupted.
Please don't hesitate to contact us at 310/555-4689 if you have any questions or concerns regarding this bill.
Thank you again for your business.
Sincerely,
Evelyn Humphries
Account Manager

The Profitable Effects on Your Bottom Line

English, which is spoken by 700 million people around the world, is the language of diplomacy, finance, science, technology, and business. So, clearly, mastering communication allows you to effectively reach, sell and relate to a worldwide audience of customers for commerce. In the business world, the bottom line is money; communicating well saves—and makes—it.

Consider this recent headline in a business publication: "Poor Communication Skills Could Be Costing Your Business Millions." Now that you're aware of communication's multifaceted ways, could that headline apply to your business?

Communication: Your Not-So-Secret Weapon

With an onslaught of new businesses starting each year, you must do your best to continue differentiating your own from the competition or, if you're a pioneer in your field, consistently positioning yourself outside the pack. In either case, communication is your not-so-secret weapon in doing so. According to a recent report from the Small Business Administration, half of the businesses that opened in 2004 will be closed by 2009. In five years, more than half of those new businesses will be closed.

You can lift your business out of obscurity and distinguish it from the others with such communication efforts as conducting intense market analysis, developing your major sales advantage, and identifying your prime opportunities for sales and growth.

Make Your Company Thrive

If you think your business may be in a rut, not as profitable as it should be, or slow on the growth scale, check out your communication methods. Here are a few questions you might ask yourself:

- ⤷ Does your company logo say enough about your company?
- ⤷ Is the sales component/force trained and well equipped with information about your company?
- ⤷ When was the last time your Web site was updated?
- ⤷ Do you promptly return calls?

● Have you been reluctant to approach the media to publicize your business? Have your media efforts been unproductive?

● How would you rate your business relationships?

● Do meetings brim with accomplishment or agony?

The tentacles of communication run deep and are pervasive, so embrace rather than neglect them. You'll quickly notice that communication infiltrates every aspect of your business. Ask yourself, "Is there an area of my business that needs improving?" There almost certainly is; can you immediately tell how that area is somehow rooted in communication?

You might not have the operating or marketing budget of Coca-Cola or Microsoft, but few companies do. However, a healthy, honest assessment of the way you do business through communication could reap untold rewards. A commitment to mastering the art of business communication can put your company on an entirely different playing field.

▶▶ TEST DRIVE

Now that you've committed to incorporating more effective communication, survey your own needs to answer these questions:

● Have you considered how verbal and written communications are being used in your business?

● Is there a particular area that needs improvement? Do you excel at one more than the other? Are you staying away from some that could help your business but that you haven't mastered?

● Do you have a consistent format for memos and letters?

● Make a list of words you would want a customer to use to describe your company. Now evaluate how well your current communication conveys these descriptors, and specific areas where you want to improve.

Who's Your Audience?
Communicating to the Right One

In your business, you'll need to appeal to different audiences—depending on the content of your message—and each one will require you to modify your approach for the best results. In this chapter, you will learn about identifying your specific audience, and then figuring out the best way to reach them.

Sometimes, you may easily forget that there's an audience out there that you're communicating to. An audience shouldn't be seen as some gray, amorphous blob you're sending words out to, but rather as a clearly defined, intended target. Keeping your audience in mind while you write or speak can help you make sound decisions about the material to include, the order of your ideas, and how best to express your material.

Identify Your Audience

Your first step in communicating to the right people is identifying and analyzing the intended audience. For instance, an investor for your caramel business isn't likely to care about the brand of brown sugar you use, but she would want to know which stores you're approaching for distribution.

Before you launch into any communication, make sure you've clearly, squarely defined your intended audience. Whomever your audience, they all want the same basics: an articulate, clear, and courteous communication. As you're competing with untold amounts of information for your audience's attention, consider their priorities, interests, and needs. You can actually quickly analyze your audience by listing out who will be on the receiving end of your document or communication form, and then enumerating their priorities, interests, and needs.

Have a Plan

Examining each of the audiences discussed in this chapter will give you the opportunity to formulate a plan that allows your business to connect appropriately with them. For each audience examined—employees, customers, vendors, and investors—take time to answer the questions posed to determine how well you're communicating with each one. From there, you should have a framework in which to place a system that applies uniquely to your business.

An Audience Checklist

For the sake of your communication, ask the following questions:

- ⮑ Who is your audience?
- ⮑ What's important to them?
- ⮑ What are they least likely to care about?
- ⮑ What do you want your audience to think or learn from your communication?
- ⮑ What impression do you want to convey?

Then, after you've assessed all of the above components, try spending some time from the perspective of your audience member. This vantage point gives you untold benefits in objectively analyzing the communication to determine whether you've reached them in the best way possible.

Consider the Tone You Take with Your Audience

In your audience analysis, you next need to determine what will be the best way to reach your audience. Communication occurs in such forms as dyadic communication, meaning between two people; public communication, such as in speeches; and small-group communication, which falls in between the previous two (and might include meetings and brainstorming sessions that you conduct in a conference room with your employees).

Really think about the audience you're trying to reach, including their needs, their point of view, and what they'll think and do with the information you're providing. Whatever you're communicating should convey respect and a positive attitude and—at all times—stay away from biased references (regarding gender and race) and prejudiced language.

Whatever audience you're reaching, you should take the tack of tailoring your communication to their perspective, by informing rather than telling, asking rather than demanding and persuading rather than insisting.

In that vein, express ideas, directions, requests and the like in ways that aren't condescending. Take the tone that will foster understanding on the recipients' part, combined with a non-threatening approach. That tack will be more productive because it will make your recipient more prone to take the action you're trying to impel.

Some questions to consider in ensuring that you take the appropriate tone include:

- ➲ Who will read or hear your communication? How will they use this document or conversation?
- ➲ Do they need any information about you? Do you need to establish credibility and trust?
- ➲ What do your readers already know about this topic? What is their level of expertise?
- ➲ What are your readers' attitudes in coming to the communication?
- ➲ Are your tone and word choice appropriate? Are you using a voice of "goodwill" throughout the document?
- ➲ Are your writing style and your document design appropriate both for your business' culture and that of your audience?
- ➲ If your message is negative, have you assessed the readers' level of tolerance to absorb the news?

The Ambassador Effect

Drawing on my background in public relations, I like to encourage start-ups (and sometimes, even well-established companies) to consider the "Ambassador Effect" their words can have on any audience. The messages you generate should always express ideas in a way that creates good public relations for your company. Avoid words and phrases that talk down to the audience and may characterize them as dishonest, careless, or incompetent. You'll find that a positive tack will have a sticking factor whatever your audience—employee, customer, investor—because they'll remember that your communication has a history of being respectful and intelligent, and treats them with courtesy and kindness.

Be Objective

No matter how frustrated you may be with a customer or employee, that feeling should never come across in your writing. Emotion—particularly negative feelings—has no place in business writing. Always strive to be as objective as possible in the information you're laying out and parlaying. For instance, if a client hasn't paid his bills, state your case for payment matter-of-factly. Don't chide or assault.

Engage Your Audience with Precision

In each of your communication instances, you want to engage the audience, either by prompting them to listen, or commanding their attention as they read. Generally, business writing has two objectives: to make people understand you and to prompt them to take some action, whether making a purchase, confirming an order, or thinking good thoughts about your company.

For your readers to understand your message and act upon it, you must be precise so they understand what you mean. If a guessing game ensues, you'll most likely be the loser in it. And remember: those who read your letters, e-mails, faxes, reports, and memos have no opportunity to interpret your body language or tone of voice, as they would in a conversation. So although you should be conversational in your approach, you should speak with clarity, sound word choices, and proper grammar.

Even when it's structured and precise, good writing helps your reader see you as a real person, and treats him or her as one too. Many business writers are tempted to hide behind officious, complex language, using it both to avoid saying what they mean, and because others use it. You don't have to do that, and your writing will be more effective when you don't. In your final assessment of your communication, analyze these components:

➲ Are your points logical and organized? Is the message concise and efficient? Have you used headings and titles to make key points stand out?

➲ Is there additional information to include that ensures clarity in getting your message across?

➲ If you're making a request, is your intention clear to the reader? If you're asking for a response or action, have you set a realistic timetable?

Regarding Internal Communication Between Managers and Employees

Do you have a plan for communicating with employees? If not, you should set one up, focusing on communicating with employees on a regular basis and making sure they're the first to hear about company news; ensuring that they're absolutely certain of how their jobs fit into the company's overall picture and your vision for it; and consistently giving them enough information to speak enthusiastically about the company to family, friends, and acquaintances.

Ways to Communicate

Several employee communication modes are at your disposal, the most pervasive being e-mail. But there are also newsletters, voice mail, video conference calls, walking around, bulletin boards, annual reports, online meetings, lunch discussions, newsletters, and grapevine power. Then, of course, there is the company staple: meetings.

Select your communications vehicle according to the purpose for the communication. A CEO of a large health-care company once said he chooses his meeting venue this way: "I like small groups for listening; I like large groups for maximum impact and clarity of message; and I like one-on-one because you bring out the best in people and are really cultivating their loyalty."

According to Mark Hughes, author of *Buzzmarketing: Get People to Talk About Your Stuff* (Portfolio, 2005), the one thing employees want besides money is communication. He writes, "Great employees save you marketing dollars and great employees accelerate growth."

Most people can describe a boss they didn't connect with. Communication was no doubt at the crux of the disconnect. Perhaps those bosses were "screamers," taking a pitched approach to discussions and doling out assignments. Or they were "mumblers," with an inexact or ambiguous approach, making it difficult to understand what the task to be accomplished actually was. Or maybe they were "noncommunicators," making company goals and opinions about performance a perpetually unsolved mystery.

The Advantages of Good Employee Communication

All of the benefits of setting up proper and working communication channels with employees may not be immediately apparent, but consider the ability to achieve a shared understanding of a company goal, to anticipate problems, to coordinate workflow, to make quicker decisions, to create a unified vision, and to promote products and services to be just a few of the inherent advantages that energize employees, break down barriers to have more productive discussions, and promote more action to attain goals.

When employers take the time to communicate with employees, everyone stays more informed about company progress, mission, and goals. Well-informed employees also signify that customers and vendors are working with a well-oiled machine, so answers, decisions, and purchases are made more quickly and efficiently.

Since working in a positive communicative environment is far more productive, employers who take the time to concentrate on effective communication with their employees will save time and earn more money.

Your Company's Communication System

Before continuing, ask yourself:

➲ Is a system in place for reporting challenges, problems, or difficulties? If not, provide a communications channel to deal with a problem that may immediately occur, and another for receiving continuing feedback at predetermined intervals. For instance, if you have a weekly employee meeting, set aside a few minutes of the scheduled time to address concerns that have popped up during the week.

➲ Do internal meetings "go nowhere," or do they have concrete agendas and goals?

➲ Do internal memos and e-mails seem succinct and to the point, or are they rambling and without purpose?

➲ Are your training materials up to date?

➲ Are employees kept abreast and up to date on changes that could impact them?

➲ Are they kept abreast and up to date on changes that could impact customers, vendors, and investors?

Communication Characteristics to Avoid

In communicating with employees, many of the same guidelines apply that were reviewed for communication overall in Chapter 1. But employees, like all audiences, have specific needs that should be recognized in communicating your messages. Your message should *not* be:

Tardy, ruled by the grapevine. Get your message out there before employees hear it the wrong way, but don't get the information out there just to get it out there. Make sure you've confirmed all your particulars. Concurrently, give employees regular feedback; avoid surprises.

Fuzzy, lost in masked messages. Make sure your communication will be easily understood.

Awkward, hem-and-haw-like. Have your message flow, beginning with your most important information, then fleshed out with details.

Irrelevant. Make sure your message is necessary.

Boring. While a boring communication will be read or heard, your chances for it being followed are better if it's presented in an interesting way. Embellish with details, specifics, or a perky presentation.

The Wrong Vehicle. Don't hide behind an e-mail when a conversation or meeting may be the better route to take.

Other Considerations

In making the time to communicate with employees, brush up on your listening skills. Sometimes, paying attention to tone, inflection, and body language lets you in on a secret; what's not being said may be more important than what's being said.

Also important: criticize in private, praise in public. Have you ever witnessed one of those uncomfortable moments when an employer is disciplining an employee? The experience no doubt left you with a less-than-favorable impression of the employer and the business itself. Take that experience into account when dealing with employees. In the presence of customers, calmly and patiently instruct the employee through the situation. Afterward, in private, discuss the situation with the employee and give pointers on how to handle it differently next time.

Communication's Role in Savvy Customer Service

In this next audience realm, consider your communication's approach in attracting, handling, and keeping customers. Ask yourself:

- Do you easily lose customers?
- Is it difficult to keep customers?
- Do your customers seem satisfied?
- Have you been successful in consistently attracting new customers?
- If appropriate, do you recognize their accomplishments outside of your working relationship?
- How do you communicate with your customers now?
- Do you have a system in place for dealing with complaints?

The first way to examine this audience is to think about how you like being treated in the customer service arena. Whatever business you're patronizing, you want to be treated with respect. And in an age when technology makes it even harder for customers to feel valued, don't lose the human touch—particularly if most of your business is done via technology. Reward them for their loyalty. It doesn't have to be extravagant; a simple token or gesture is sufficient.

Be Available and Listen to Them

Countless businesses lose sales or customers on a daily basis by simply not having means of communication in place. How often have you called a business during or after hours and not gotten a live person, or not even voice mail so that you could leave a message? Certainly, many small businesses are one-person shops, but that doesn't mean that when that person is out, business comes to a standstill. Give the impression that you care and do want to talk with those calling. With cell phones, it's even easier to stay connected to your prospective and current customer base. Even in off hours, a friendly outgoing message giving your hours and, if appropriate, directions to your business could spur a sale.

Know Your Customers

The easiest, best way to communicate with your customers is to know them: their needs, priorities, and demographics. When you've got a handle on these aspects, you'll be more apt and able to tailor messages for them. Depending on your business, you might interact with customers at your store, or via e-mail from your Web site.

Be a Problem Solver

Once they've gotten you, listen to your customers. Aggravation ensues if they have to repeat themselves because someone hasn't been paying attention to them. Let them talk, and show that you're listening by making appropriate responses. Your best chance at keeping customers is by showing your genuine interest. If a problem does arise, make sure that you understand what they're saying, let them know you understand them, and offer suggestions to solve the problem.

As a small business owner, you have the advantage of not having to navigate through layers of a corporation to fix a customer's problem. Let customers know that you've got their best interests in mind and, as such, want to keep them.

Are You Unintentionally Turning Business Away?

Five calls were made to five gardeners. Not one of those calls was answered, nor was there even voice mail so that a message could be left. Those gardeners would have had a shot at a substantial piece of regular business had they left a specific outgoing message on voice mail, saying that they appreciated the call and would be back at the end of the day to return it, or offering a cell phone number where they could be reached immediately. Another option might have been for any or all of them to contract with a telephone answering service, or to use the call-forwarding feature on the phone.

So many options exist to make communicating with customers easy, letting them know that you appreciate their interest in conducting business with you. Have your phone line somehow tended to, and make it a useful business tool.

Relating to Vendors and Other Companies

Keep vendors on your side with some of the same communication qualities that work for your other audiences. In other words, be clear, direct, and courteous with your orders. Make sure the vendors understand your needs and expectations with articulate e-mails and, if appropriate, inclusion on mailing lists for such communications as direct mail pieces from your company.

Even before you first approach a potential supplier, visit the company's Web site or talk to a referral to get information about the vendor and a sense of how it does business. Make sure you're going to the right vendor for your needs. Why waste time in finding out through a long-winded and possibly frustrating personal conversation that the vendor you're approaching isn't actually a fit for your needs?

Inside Track Taking a Cue from a Master Communicator

If you live in a city where there is a Nordstrom department store, it may seem that everyone who regularly shops there has a Nordstrom story. From its founding in 1901, Nordstrom has a legendary policy of customer service that has always been of paramount importance. Nordstrom managers and employees know how to communicate expertly, quickly, and efficiently. On one occasion, a customer who shopped regularly at another upscale chain visited Nordstrom and bought a pair of jeans. Once home, the customer realized an inventory tag had been left on the jeans, rendering them unwearable until it was removed. When the customer called to complain, the store manager wasn't in, but her outgoing message indicated that she would be in her office by noon that day. The manager returned the customer's call shortly after her noon arrival and arrangements were made immediately to have a salesman come to the customer's home and remove the tag from the jeans. An apology note from the manager included sincere thanks for the customer's business as well as gift cards to the in-store espresso bar.

Amazed at the level of service, the customer then wrote a letter to company president Blake Nordstrom, expressing how impressive the service was—and the communication that was integrated into it. Mr. Nordstrom then sent a letter back, thanking the customer for his kind words and support for the store and its employees. The customer quickly switched upscale chain alliances to Nordstrom.

After you begin a relationship with that supplier, keep them in the loop. While you should use timesaving technology for communication, don't forget the personal touch of a phone conversation. That way, if you run into a problematic situation, you've developed a relationship that gives you a track record both you and the vendor can depend on.

Finally, be up-front. If you can't pay on time, don't hide from your vendors. Instead, let your vendors know right away, and work out a payment plan in writing. Once again, this "problem" actually presents an opportunity for the goodwill you nurtured in getting to know them to be very helpful.

> ### Have You Considered a Blog?
>
> Some companies are embracing a new trend of setting up blogs (short for Web logs). On a public Web site, a company exec will create a sort of "professional diary" that gives customers an inside look at the company workings and goings-on. As long as the blog maintains a professional mien, it can serve as a very "in the moment" way to connect with customers and also offers a chance to spotlight important customers, as well as company accomplishments that may attract new customers.

Appealing to Investors

The best way to communicate with investors is to keep them informed. You don't have to overdo it, filling them with minutiae about each tiny advancement, but they should be given regular status reports, keeping them abreast of major accomplishments and obstacles. That kind of ongoing communication with investors can boost opportunities for growth and sales, and mitigate impending problems.

Here again you have an opportunity to engage an "ambassador" who's prone to extol your company's virtues. Make sure that ambassador's prepared with the key messages you've provided.

Key into Investor Know-How

Since experts agree that the biggest mistake entrepreneurs make is ignoring investors, you can move your business forward by being cognizant of that pitfall. Whether your investors are family members, angel investors, or venture capitalists, realize that they became involved with your enterprise for good reasons. They know that when you succeed, they do too. Perhaps they had experience in your business and are eager to help start-ups benefit from their know-how. They're also probably knowledgeable about tapping into other resources, financial and otherwise. Even better, they can smooth out snags your company may run into, and avert disaster more quickly and effectively because of the experience they bring, and the stake they have in your success.

Keep Investors Satisfied

For you to effectively get the expertise your investors can offer, be proactive in engaging them with company developments, milestones, and plans. By all means, don't bog them down with day-to-day operations, but regularly keep them informed.

Understandably, investors want to know that—eventually—they'll be getting a return on their investment. Therefore, habitually present them with numbers. Here, you may need to familiarize yourself with the specifics that they need and care about, such as cash flow and projections. If need be, hire a financial person who can help you articulate such information. (One of your investors may actually be just the person to mentor you in this area; use your discretion when making this decision.)

Sarbanes-Oxley

On the matter of investor relations, now is a good time to have an experienced attorney look over disclosures before you release them to any audience. Even when you have a private company, it's becoming an exceedingly better idea to operate as if you were a public one. In 2002, Congress passed the Sarbanes-Oxley Act (SOX), a sweeping legal overhaul of corporate reporting and securities regulations for publicly traded companies. Two of the Act's provisions apply to private companies (regulations for the destruction of certain documents and retaliation against whistleblowers). Increasingly, private companies are voluntarily opting for the stringent SOX oversight, according to a 2005 survey of 9,000 senior executives and board directors from public and private organizations conducted by Chicago-based law firm Foley & Lardner. By complying with SOX regulations, private companies believed they were making a statement to potential investors that their businesses were well-managed and open to scrutiny.

So that investors can feel in touch, have a company contact in place who can answer questions that may arise. Further, some companies also benefit from a password-protected area on their Web site specifically dedicated to news and developments for investors. Consider making that part of your communication plan as well.

If bad news seeps into your operations or developments, don't ignore it, wish it away, or hope your investors won't find out. While you don't want to dwell on it, do come forward with it in a timely manner, and keep investors posted on its status. Here again, you may unexpectedly receive advice that will help change your course for the better, and investors will undoubtedly appreciate that they've been given a heads-up.

Finally, remember that your investors came on board because of the way you deal with and handle the company. Keep their confidence up with your commitment to communicate with them fairly, knowledgeably, and routinely. You'll quickly see how that approach reaps dividends—financial and otherwise—for everyone concerned.

▶▶ TEST DRIVE

With which audience—employees, customers, vendors, or investors—do you need to improve your communication the most? Once you've selected the audience, conduct this communications audit:

- ➲ What made you say that this particular audience needs help? That is, identify the need: perhaps there has been a surplus of customer complaints, or investors who have withdrawn support.
- ➲ What's one mode you could put in place today to improve communication with this audience? For instance, order a voice mailbox for your office line, start a blog, draft a customer service survey for customers (see Chapter 11 for more information), or initiate a status report for investors.

Style Is in Session

Style is the manner in which you communicate your message. While everyone has his or her own style, you want to make sure that yours does the best possible job and serves you and your company well in the process. Like it or not, right or wrong, some readers deduce personalities of the communicator from their writing style: boring writing equals boring person, lively writing means someone they want to do business with. You can easily make more of an impact with style.

This chapter gives you a brushup on those mechanics that, when faulty, detract from your style, and also explains the enhancements that will make it brim with energy and assertion.

In general, you should ask this of your style: Can you present material in another way that sounds better, is more compelling, and that exudes confidence?

Spelling Rules

Nothing mars business communications like misspellings that pepper a message or a memo. Your credibility instantly takes a hit, and your intended message is given less attention. While misspellings don't equate with low intelligence, they do take away from credence on paper. Before you review these spelling rules, please remember that spelling is notoriously fickle with its rules, and rife with exceptions. While these guidelines will provide a good foundation and common ground, be cognizant of spelling's many configurations.

EI versus IE

The most famous spelling rule is probably "i before e except after c, or if the i-e sounds like ay, as in neighbor and weigh." (However, that doesn't account for words like "foreign," "either," "leisure," "weird," or "height").

Plural Spellings

Making words plural easily causes some communicators to lapse into misspellings. In the case of making words plural, follow these rules:

- For most words ending in consonants, add an *s*.
- For words ending in a vowel and a *y*, add an *s*.
- For words ending in *ch*, *sh*, *s*, *x*, or *z*, add an *es*.
- For words ending in a consonant and a *y*, drop the *y* and add an *ies*.
- For words ending in *f* or *fe*, drop the *f* or *fe* and add *ves*.
- For most words ending in *o*, add *s*.
- For some words ending in *o*, add *es*.
- Some nouns forgo an ending *s*, and instead change their vowel sound when pluralized, such as "man" to "men" or "tooth" to "teeth."
- Some nouns have the same plural as their singular, such as "species" and "fish."
- Some nouns have carryover plural forms from Old English, such as "children."

Suffix Spellings

For spelling words after adding suffixes:

- If a word ends with a silent *e*, drop the *e* before adding a suffix that begins with a vowel.
- Don't drop the *e* when the suffix begins with a consonant.
- When a one-syllable word ends in a consonant preceded by one vowel, double the final consonant before adding a suffix that begins with a vowel. This guideline is also called the 1-1-1 rule: one syllable, one consonant, one vowel.
- When a multi-syllable word ends in a consonant preceded by one vowel, and the final syllable is accented, the same rule holds true: double the final consonant.
- When the final syllable doesn't have the end accent, you usually don't double the consonant, as in "focused," "signaled," or "pardoned."

Other Considerations

→ Words that end with *el*, *le*, *ile*, *al*, and *il*, such as "bottle," "parcel," and "civil," are tricky. There are virtually no rules for words like these; you need to rely on memory and a dictionary.

→ Don't attach *mis-*, *dis-*, *non-*, *un-* and *ir-* to words indiscriminately and interchangeably. When unsure of the prefixes for such words as "organize," "reversible," or "understand," check the dictionary. (The correct words in these three cases are "disorganize," "irreversible," "misunderstand.")

→ Make sure you're pronouncing words correctly. That will eliminate such incorrect spellings as "canidate" for "candidate."

→ Determine whether you routinely misspell the same words or kinds of words, so that you'll be particularly aware of those during your proofreading phase.

→ Spell out numbers zero to nine; ten and above, use the numeral. If numbers within the sentence range among the rules, be consistent, as in "The shipment consists of 3 pairs of skis and 37 pairs of skates."

→ Spell out numbers that start a sentence but, if possible, rewrite the sentences that begin with a number so that they don't start with one.

The Most Important Rules

Double-check and, if necessary, triple-check to make sure you have spelled the names of people and companies correctly. Use official Web sites, the phone book, and business cards as sources for verification.

Don't rely fully on your computer spell checker. Often it will bypass a word that you've spelled correctly, but that is used in the wrong context for the sentence you're writing. For instance, the spellchecker wouldn't flag, "He has excepted our offer," although the correct sentence would be, "He has accepted our offer."

Finally, always have a dictionary nearby—and use it—when you're drafting documents. Not only will it verify spellings, but it also provides you with the information to help out with word choice and vocabulary, two upcoming sections in this chapter.

Don't Let These Common Misspellings Plague Your Writing

In writing, misspellings can happen two ways: words may be spelled right, but are used in the wrong context; or, the spellings are just plain tricky.

Common Usage Challenges

These sets of words, distressingly similar, can shift or confuse the meaning of your sentence. Worse, they easily fool your spell-check feature: from/form, of/or, to/too/two, there/their/they're.

These next sets of words need a little further differentiation. They too are spelled correctly, but writers often confuse their meanings:

- **Accept/Except:** "accept" is to allow; "except" is to exempt
- **Affect/Effect:** "affect" is to influence; "effect" is to cause
- **Advise/Advice:** "advise" is a verb, meaning to counsel; "advice" is a noun, or the substance of the counsel
- **Conscious/Conscience:** "conscious" refers to being aware, while "conscience" is one's moral compass
- **It's/Its:** "it's" is a contraction for "it is"; "its" is a possessive pronoun
- **Than/Then:** "than" is for comparison; "then" is relative to time

This next set focuses on pairings of words that sound alike, but have different meanings:

- **All ready/Already:** "all ready" means that everything or everyone is prepared; "already" means "so soon"
- **All together/Altogether:** "all together" means a group standing as one; "altogether" means "entirely"
- **Anyone/any one:** anyone is a pronoun; "any one" refers to a single, though indiscriminate, thing or person
- **Anyway/any way:** "anyway" is an adverb meaning no matter what; "any way" refers to a single, if indiscriminate method or direction
- **Maybe/may be:** "maybe" means "perhaps"; "may be" is a verb

Common Spelling Challenges

Studies of the most commonly misspelled words have routinely turned up these troublemakers.

As you read over the list, determine how often you're affected by them: accommodate, a lot, all right, business, calendar, committee, commitment, conscientious, consensus, definitely, description, embarrassing, embarrassment, existence, gauge, government, grammar, harass, height, hierarchy, immediately, indispensable, irresistible, maintenance, minuscule, millennium, misspell, necessary, noticeable, occasion, occurred, occurrence, parallel, pastime, perseverance, preceding, privilege, publicly, questionnaire, rhythm, seize, separate, supersede, transferred, unanimous, weird, withhold.

Diction: Selecting the Best Words

When you call upon the right words to convey your meaning, you can make your writing much more powerful. For instance, to say "Executives rebuff hype of long-range, wireless access" packs more of a wallop than "Executives discourage excitement over new wireless technology."

You can immediately perk up your document by selecting the absolute best, most descriptive words that appropriately articulate your thoughts. That doesn't mean calling on multi-syllabic, high-toned words; it just means finding the right ones.

Dissecting Diction

From the outset, make sure you know the goal of your writing and what you're trying to say. Then, after you've written a draft, determine whether you're using clear, descriptive language or if you've included vague words with neutral meaning. To probe further, be certain you know what each word you're using means. And test yourself: Have you found the best word, or just settled for the easiest or most obvious one? In answering that last question, remember that you don't have to find words to impress your reader. In fact, if your sentences aren't making sense or you think you're not using the best words, try to write the sentence in the simplest way possible. You can try that tack by phrasing it as you would in conversation, and then fleshing it out from there.

For instance, "DVD retailers are taking a stance on piracy" becomes much more vivid in the sentence "DVD retailers crack down on piracy."

Add Details

In brightening up the sentence, remember to give your reader the specifics and details that people crave. When details are well presented, they offer your writing untold advantages in keeping your reader interested and encouraged to take the the action you want.

Parallel to Your Tone

Selecting the best words feeds into the tone you've decided to take in your communication. In Chapter 2, you explored tone regarding your audience. You should also take word choice into account regarding the tone of the situation at hand. Is your memo, letter, or e-mail addressing a serious situation or a casual one? Is a formal demeanor necessary, or an informal one?

The language you use can also suggest how important the matter or idea is. "Most important," "major," and "primary" are more emphatic terms than "minor point to consider" or "least important." Further, the amount of space you devote to an idea will correlate to the idea's importance to your reader. Therefore, more detail is expected for more important ideas.

How Do You Find the Right Word?

The right word is out there. You just have to find it. When you're challenged, these five easy strategies can simplify your search:

1. Strive for clarity. Which words would make the purpose of this sentence completely clear?
2. On a tip from the classic and essential *Elements of Style,* by William Strunk Jr. and E.B. White, get rid of "very," "really," "truly," "quite," and "thing" from your writing. If you do, you'll immediately notice how an overreliance on these prevent you from finding words that will do a better job in their place.

3. Use a thesaurus. This resource can never be overrated as an indispensable tool for adding clarity and variety to your writing. You'll find several entries for everyday words that will often be more exact and descriptive than the one you've initially chosen. Still, be cautious: look up the word you want to substitute in the dictionary to avoid misuse.

4. Don't be tempted to use a word just because it sounds better or may make you seem more impressive. Pick one based on its fitting into your sentence and providing the meaning you need.

5. Brainstorm as you write. Try inserting a string of words that you'll come back to. For instance, "That version is too rudimentary/basic/elementary/sophomoric." On reflection, you can pick the one word that's most suitable.

Help in Finding the Right Word

Finding the right word can, no doubt, be difficult. Several valuable books may enrich your writing. Jan Venolia's *The Right Word!: How to Say What You Really Mean* (Ten Speed Press, 2003) doles out specifics on confusing words. S.I. Hayakawa's *Choose the Right Word* (Collins, 2004) is an indispensable guide, particularly for choosing between and among synonyms. Also, of course, Norman W. Schur's omnipresent *1,000 Most Important Words* (Ballantine, 1982) has become a fixture on many writers' bookshelves. Finally, both for finding the right words and fine-tuning your writing style, revisit Strunk and White's famous writing manual *The Elements of Style*, which has gained such a following that it recently spawned *The Elements of Style Illustrated* (Penguin 2005), featuring witty illustrations by fashion artist Maira Kalman.

Enhance Your Vocabulary

It's true that finding the right word is easier when you've got a healthy vocabulary at your disposal. Since a bountiful vocabulary goes hand-in-hand with diction, you'll soon be able to draw on an arsenal of words to get your point across in the most succinct and interesting way that you can. As Mark Twain said in an oft-quoted saying, "The difference between the right word and the almost-right word is the difference between light-ning and the lightning bug." Your propensity for and intensity in prepar-ing effective business communications will benefit exponentially from the on-target messages and audience comprehension a valuable vocabulary can bring.

At first, you may be more comfortable just getting your thoughts down in articulate sentences, using simple language. Then, take a stab at rewrit-ing them using an enhanced vocabulary.

Conventional Means

Be cognizant of how others express themselves. You may have a col-league or employee who seems to not only have a vast vocabulary, but also picks appropriate words at appropriate times. Take a cue from that person's knack for expression and see if you can start calling on words that suit your style.

Subscribe to magazines that serve your industry well. Take particular note of words these use in their articles to describe industry trends, to profile companies, and to discuss controversies. You'll soon start gleaning several words to add to your word armament. Also, venture outside your industry, and read books, articles, and magazines of general interest. The more words you're exposed to, the more you'll know. Read and listen to challenging material so that you'll be exposed to many new words.

When you hear or see an unfamiliar word, look it up. Chances are you'll hear or see it again soon thereafter. Once you've discovered the meaning, try using the word yourself.

Unconventional Methods

Research shows that the vast majority of words are learned from con-text. To improve your context skills, pay close attention to how words are used. Doing a search on a word using Google.com will give you many examples of how that word is used in context. Then, practice the words you've learned. Research shows that you may need ten to twenty repeti-tions to really make it a part of your vocabulary.

You could also invest in a "word-a-day" calendar. Sure, that may seem silly. But as words beget words, you'll find that your curiosity—and your vocabulary—will increase.

Also play word games, like Scrabble, the crossword puzzles, or Boggle. You'll find that you'll open up to even more words. Plus, these can even be played on the computer, so you're not dependent on a partner to play.

For the Best Vocabulary, Stay Current

Some research suggests that some 20,000 words are added to the English language each year. That number may be high, but dictionaries add a still-astonishing 2,500 each year. Some words and phrases, such as "Cyber Monday," "mash-up," "placeshift," "CSI effect," "metrosexual," and "folksonomy," probably weren't even part of your vernacular a few years ago. Stay on top of words that you've heard for the first time. Find out what they mean. Even if it's not a fit for your vocabulary, it may help you understand someone else's communication.

Be careful to steer clear of "buzzwords," which are new yet empty words that sound important and busy for the workplace but are actually vapid and will bring down your writing and intended meanings.

Beware of Homonyms and Malapropisms

Homonyms and malapropisms are two word groups to be cognizant of when preparing communications because they represent wrong word choices that can seriously derail your best efforts to keep the reader on your train of thought.

Homonyms

"Homonyms" has become an umbrella term used for several groups of words: true homonyms, which are words that are spelled or pronounced alike, but have different meanings (a tie for a business suit versus a railroad tie); homographs, which are words that are spelled alike, but have different meanings or pronunciation (as in lead a meeting versus lead in old paint); and homophones, which are words that aren't spelled alike, but sound alike (the sale at a store versus the sail of a ship). Although some may equate homonyms only with the spoken word, they have a way of seeping into our writing because of what we "hear" as we write.

These are some common homonyms to avoid: ad, add; altar, alter; ate, eight; been, bin; bizarre, bazaar; canvas, canvass; cell, sell; complement, compliment; do, due; err, heir; grate, great; higher, hire; idle, idol; might, mite; morning, mourning; one, won; overdo, overdue; passed, past; plain, plane; pole, poll; pore, pour; principal, principle; rap, wrap; sew, so; soared, sword; team, teem; wait, weight; weather, whether; wood, would.

In each of these preceding pairs, can you easily determine how confusion or unintentional humor could result, taking you off-message in the reader's mind?

Malapropisms

Malapropisms refer to the misuse of words that have been put in the wrong context, often resulting in unintentional humor. Clearly, you might "hear" a word that is then written the wrong way—in one of its alternate spellings incorrect for the context. Here are three examples with the correct word in parentheses:

At the meeting, he told a humorous antidote (anecdote) about using a new prescription plan.

A thong (throng) of people attended the swimwear fashion event.

He was vivid (livid) when he saw the incorrect projections in the annual report.

Obviously, in any of these cases, confusion can result and, worse, your reader can become instantly distracted from your intended message.

To avoid malapropisms, be sure that you know all the terms you're using. Also, follow stringent proofreading rules (examined in Chapter 6), such as reading your correspondence out loud. The following are some common word pairs that often prompt malapropisms: adverse, averse; affluence, influence; allude, elude; conservation, consumption; deprecate, depreciate; desperate, disparate; elicit, illicit; eligible, legible; emanate, eminent; empathy, sympathy; initiate, intimate; jibe, jive; malady, melody; moral, morale; precede, proceed; predecessor, successor; pundit, pungent; secede, succeed; travel, travail; tunnel, channel.

A Devil in the Details

A high-profile and very manners-oriented celebrity was embarking on a tour to publicize a fitness product. Her promotional materials had been produced on a tight schedule, resulting in a most unfortunate malapropism making its way into the materials. Worse, the malapropism had been cut and pasted into several documents, so it showed up repeatedly. The phrase "exercise equipment" had been written as "exorcise equipment," and the spell checker passed over the word as correctly spelled (though it was completely wrong for the context). The phrase was on practically every page of the materials, and had the potential to turn her new product from a fitness regimen staple to a cult ritual staple. As an unwitting team was rapidly assembling packages to send to newspapers, radio stations, and network morning shows nationwide, someone noticed the error. Fortunately, the mistake was caught before the materials had been distributed, although they had already been created and printed at great cost.

Needless to say, the materials were scrapped. This person's reputation may have hinged on a misconstrued malapropism that might have cost her credibility and steered attention away from her product. On the second venture, despite the time crunch, every word was scrupulously pored over, and less-impressive but perfect flyers were mass-produced to make the tour's deadline.

Cast Out the Clichés

While clichés do afford your reader the commonality of an expression, they also drag down your writing with trite meaning. In most cases, you can probably find a more apt group of words to do the work. Your writing will be so much more effective and enjoyable without the overused expressions that all of us are so familiar with that they have lost any unique meaning.

Further, clichés often take up valuable real estate in your sentences. Shorter sentences are more direct.

The best way to avoid using clichés is to recognize them and then create shorter, fresher replacements. When you spot a cliché, first ask yourself if you know a single word that could work as an equivalent. If not, substitute your own phrase of two or three words.

Clichés and Possible Replacements

Take a look at the following clichés and some possible alternatives:

Agree to disagree . . . . Disagree
All over the map. . . . . Unfocused
At the end of the day . . . . Finally
Can't see the forest through the trees. . . . . Lacks vision
Dead as a doornail. Dead; over
Easier said than done . . . . Easier
Increase by leaps and bounds . . . . Rise exponentially
It goes without saying. . . . . Obviously
It stands to reason . . . . Evidently
Last but not least . . . . Last
Nip in the bud . . . . Finish
Out of the box . . . . Unconventional
Play it by ear . . . . Spontaneous
Push the envelope . . . . Innovate; pioneer
Rears its ugly head . . . . Endangers
There's no time like the present . . . . Now; immediately
Turn on a dime . . . . Change quickly
Up in the air. . . . . Unsure

Removing Clichés from the Beginning, Middle, and End

Sometimes, clichés serve as a poor setup, transition, or conclusion as overused descriptive expressions.

"If you build it . . ." Because *Field of Dreams* had many fans, this expression often has people remembering a baseball diamond (or trying to remember where they've heard this phrase before), rather than paying attention to the content you're trying to put in front of them.

"Welcome to the world of . . ." has become so overused as an introduction that it can immediately make your idea seem old and tired. Instead, burnish your writing with the energetic beginning it deserves.

"Fast forward . . . " often skips important intermittent details in providing a segue from old information to new. Next time this phrase feels comfortable, try to enhance your transition with more details.

"The rest is history . . ." always presents an uninteresting and unsatisfying conclusion to your writing project, begging the question "What is 'the rest'?"

"The rest of the story . . ." Similar to "the rest is history," this phrase poses the possibility that you left out a huge chunk of information, painting an incomplete picture or skipping details.

▶▶ Test Drive

You'll learn more about writing for Web sites in Chapters 13 and 14, but for now, let's look at how a writing style can be conveyed. Look at the homepage of a favorite Web site of yours (perhaps one that you've bookmarked), and survey the writing. Answer these questions:

- ⮑ What wording has drawn you into this Web site?
- ⮑ Are there fresh and original word choices?
- ⮑ Are there phrases that might have been a cliché, but the writer gave it a twist or different wording?

Now, take a look at a Web site that you have visited sporadically (or maybe only once) because it doesn't hold your interest.

- ⮑ What about the writing doesn't draw you in?
- ⮑ Right off, do you notice clichés?
- ⮑ What about sloppiness, misspellings, or poor word choices?
- ⮑ What would you change about the Web site's copy to prompt a better response from you?

Make Clarity Your Goal

In business communication, your first priority should be that your writing can be understood. You can't achieve the goal of your writing—be it to inform, to persuade, or to request—if ambiguity lingers. Clarity helps get your point and your point of view across.

For your writing to be its best, you must approach it with a keen sense of organization. That venture extends into creating an outline from the beginning, eliminating wordiness and irrelevant details, and working to bring unity and coherence to your entire piece of communication (be it a memo or a Web site).

When you have clearly established what you need to write, the audience you're writing to, and the tone you'll take, and have employed the mechanics of grammar and your own style in the process, you'll have set yourself up to succeed.

Let's recap these areas, in the form of questions you should ask to ensure clarity before proceeding:

- ⮮ What's the purpose of this communication: to recommend, to persuade, to explain?
- ⮮ What action do you want taken as a result of this writing?
- ⮮ Who's your audience? What are their needs? What is their level of knowledge?
- ⮮ What tone will you take for the audience and the situation? Is the matter complicated or controversial?
- ⮮ How can you say what needs to be said effectively and appropriately? How can you make it more easily understood?

If you can clearly answer these questions, you'll have a greater chance of accomplishing your communication mission.

Organization Is Key

Organization in writing works on two levels: The methods you use to organize your thoughts for your writing project, and the actual format you use to present that communication. Both of these organization modes work in tandem to present your intended audience with clear information. Without organization, your readers would be lost and confused, and you would be frustrated because your work would yield few results (if any).

Qualities of Organization

With an organized communication, you can lead the reader through your train of thought and connect your points without losing him or her.

Determine up-front your most crucial piece of information and then fill in details that illustrate it. While you do this, stay on topic. Don't be drawn into other areas that might seem interesting, but aren't relevant. If necessary, double-check your sentences and paragraphs and ask yourself whether they all relate to the predetermined, defined topic. You can include specifics and details that support your topic, but don't dwell on minutiae.

Outlining: Your Road Map

Granted, sometimes getting started on a mission for clarity can seem daunting. It needn't be. At your service, you have a wonderful tool called outlining. Imagine going somewhere you've never been without a map to get there. That's how it would be to write without an outline. Employers and employees fall prey to anxiety about writing because they immediately think a document must be created out of thin air. That never has to be the case. Rest assured that the process is much easier when it begins with an outline—your road map to a piece of writing. Outlining prods you to establish a beginning, middle, and end; find the most direct route to get from the start (or introduction) through the meat of the matter, with specifics and detail; and move on to the finish (or conclusion).

How to Outline

While you have probably made outlines for reports in school, here's a refresher course. Outlines offer you an ordered overview of the information you want to disseminate. Longer communications—reports, proposals, and presentations—will demand a great deal of structure, and thus a fairly detailed outline. For shorter communications, such as e-mails or

| Inside Track | No Time for an Outline |

A company I occasionally consulted for was in a crunch to get a crucial piece of business. They had waited until the last minute to finish a new business proposal, and had asked if I might "put it all together" for them. When I asked if I could see the outline they were working from, the team leader said, "An outline? We haven't got any time for an outline." This refrain is familiar from some execs and entrepreneurs who think they only have time to fly by the seat of their pants. However, in assembling the new business proposal for this company and putting the finishing touches on it, I was saving time by working backward to create an outline that would lend organization, and ultimately success, to the proposal.

They didn't have an outline, but they did have notes, e-mails to each other, scratch pads from a brainstorming session, and Post-it Notes. After a single conversation with the team leader, I drew up an outline that all of their assorted work and writings neatly fit into.

When I handed it to the leader, he said, "You've worked a miracle. It's all here, and it all makes sense. We never could have gotten this done in time!" If they had started with the outline first—which really jelled after just a few minutes of speaking with the team leader—all of their work and thought processes would have flowed more logically, quickly, and probably creatively.

There's always time for an outline. In fact, you save time by starting out with an outline, rather than spending frantic energy, more time and possibly money on a consultant trying to create one later.

memos consisting of a few paragraphs, an entire outline might not be necessary. Instead, you can jot down central ideas you want to cover, and then order them according to importance.

First, as with all business communication, you'll determine what your content is, who your audience is, and the action you want the audience to take. Your assessment at this point will determine priorities in presenting the information.

Next, group your ideas together, and arrange the material into sections. Then, to indicate levels of significance within each idea, work from general to specific, or abstract to concrete. In an outline, you divide the ideas into major headings indicated by Roman numerals—I, II, and so on—and minor headings indicated by letters, beginning with A. The more general or abstract the term, the higher the rank it receives in the outline.

This method orders your material logically, and requires a clear articulation of the relationship between the component parts that will be used in your document or correspondence. For your document as a whole, subdivisions of each main heading should have relative significance.

Outlining: An Example

Look at how this example illustrates the help an outline can provide. The situation: You've decided to hire a salesperson about selling multiple lines of products in your appliance store, and a local recruiter will help you find someone. She's asked for your expectations for the salesperson. In that situation, you've determined your purpose, your audience, and your goal. Before you send a letter to her regarding the position, draft an outline to cogently form your thoughts.

I. Experience Required
 A. Retail Sales
  1. High-volume seller
  2. Solid techniques and approaches
 B. Customer Relations
  1. Keeping happy customers
  2. Handling complaints
 C. Employee management
  1. Scheduling employee shifts
  2. Setting goals

II. Responsibilities Expected
 A. Sales Floor
  1. Greeting customers
  2. Ringing up sales
 B. Inventory
  1. Taking stock at certain intervals
  2. Placing orders
 C. Knowing the Products
  1. Microwaves
   a. GE
   b. Sharp
  2. Ranges

      a. Viking

      b. Wolf

   3. Refrigerators

      a. Jenn-Air

      b. Amana

   4. Washers

      a. Maytag

      b. Whirlpool

   5. Dryers

      a. Maytag

      b. Whirlpool

Notice that each of the topics and subtopics are of equal significance. Topic I should be as important as topic II, and subtopics A and B should have less significance than those assigned Roman numerals. Similarly, sub-subtopics 1 and 2 should have less importance than those indicated by capital letters.

Organizational Tool: Mind Mapping

Stuck for words? Try mind mapping. A mind map is a tool that some who are more graphically inclined favor for organizing their thoughts. With a mind map, you use key words, symbols, and charts to organize ideas. Instead of outlines and sentences, you start with a center theme, word, or image and build out from that center to conjure up subthemes. Then you use color, arrows, icons, and other visual aids to link elements. Mind mapping works particularly well for those who think visually, or who have an aversion to writing outlines.

In organizing your information, realize that for every I, you have to have a II; for every A, there must be a B; and for every 1, there needs to be a 2. This outlining rule guarantees that you'll have enough detail to substantiate your ideas and form complete thoughts.

As this example illustrates, you should be consistent in your outlining. Use topics or sentences for your headings, but don't mix them. In business writing, topics tend to be preferred over sentences because they offer quick, punchy headlines that force you to call attention to the main points. They're also faster to write than a sentence outline.

Ferreting Out Unnecessary Elements

Before you embark on the task of editing, which is discussed in Chapter 5, you can employ a few techniques to weed out words that clutter your sentences. These techniques foster conciseness, while instilling more strength and order.

One of the best ways to eliminate wordiness is to turn passive verbs and phrases into active ones. Check Chapter 3 to get more information about this space-saving device. You already know that using active voice can bring more vigor to your writing; it also jettisons unneeded words.

> **Wordy:** It was decided to contact the graphic designer about creating a new Web site.

> **Better:** I decided to contact the graphic designer about creating a new Web site.

Avoid "which," "who," and "that" clauses. Clauses beginning with these words can sometimes be reduced to a single adverb or adjective.

> **Wordy:** The loan officer, who was resourceful, offered multiple options.

> **Better:** The resourceful loan officer offered multiple options.

Take out "weasel words"—unnecessary words that weaken your sentences with obvious references.

> **Wordy:** Place the manual by your computer on your desk in your office.

> **Better:** Place the manual by your computer.

Look for key subject and verb combinations, and then evaluate your word choice.

> **Wordy:** How-to sessions are a part of getting customers interested in coming to our store.

Better: How-to sessions draw customers into our store.

Eliminate redundancies, which are special types of weasel words that repeat the meaning another word has already expressed. Check out the weasel words in italics in the following list:

3 P.M. *in the afternoon* . . . . 3 P.M.
At *a price of* $7.20 . . . . At $7.20
Blue *in color* . . . . Blue
Bridge *across* . . . . Bridge
Circle *around* . . . . Circle
Completely new . . . . New
Connected *together* . . . . Connected
During *the year* 2009 . . . . During 2009
Each and every . . . . Every
Early beginnings . . . . Beginnings
Exactly identical . . . . Identical
Few *in number* . . . . Few
Mutual cooperation . . . . Cooperation
My *personal* opinion . . . . My opinion
Positive benefits . . . . Benefits
Prove *conclusively* . . . . Prove
Round *in shape* . . . . Round
Small *in size* . . . . Small
Transfer *onto* . . . . Transfer
True facts . . . . Facts

Extreme Wordiness

When phrases such as the following appear in your writing, they inevitably swamp your sentences with extra words. Despite their clunkiness, they often turn up in business writing. Become familiar with them so that you can readily substitute a pithy replacement.

A considerable amount of. . . . . MUCH
A majority of . . . . MOST
A number of . . . . MANY; SEVERAL
A decreased number of . . . . FEWER
As a matter of fact . . . . ACTUALLY
At this point in time. . . . . NOW
Be of the opinion that . . . . THINK; BELIEVE
Bring to a conclusion . . . . CONCLUDE
Due to the fact that . . . . BECAUSE
For the purpose of. . . . . FOR
In all likelihood . . . . LIKELY
In the course of . . . . DURING
In the direction of . . . . TOWARD
In the near future. . . . . SOON
In the eventuality that . . . . IF
In view of the fact that. . . . . SINCE; BECAUSE
It is possible that . . . . MAYBE
In all probability . . . . LIKELY
It is probable that. . . . . PROBABLY
It would appear that. . . . . APPARENTLY

Policing Nouns

Sometimes nouns unintentionally become the focal point of the action, when an action verb will do the trick. Do you draw out your verbs into nouns or noun phrases? Take a look at these phrases, all of which can translate into a single action verb.

Conduct a discussion of . . . . DISCUSS
Create a reduction in . . . . REDUCE
Engage in the preparation of . . . . PREPARE
Give consideration to . . . . CONSIDER
Make a discovery of. . . . . DISCOVER
Make an assumption of . . . . ASSUME
Perform an analysis of . . . . ANALYZE
Reach a conclusion about. . . . . CONCLUDE
Take action on. . . . . ACT

Staying on Topic

As you work to achieve unity and coherence in your writing, always consider the sentences you're contributing to your topic. Are they relevant? Are they helpful? Are they necessary? Should anything be omitted that doesn't contribute to your "cause?" In answering these questions, you can determine whether particular sentences should be eliminated immediately or given further review.

What Are You Trying to Say?

Occasionally, I'll get a call from a colleague saying, "I keep looking at what I'm writing here, and it just doesn't make sense." The complaint usually includes the adjective "unclear." When that's the case, I typically respond with, "What are you trying to say—not on paper, but in your own words, no frills or thrills attached?" Boiled down to his or her own take, the result usually brims with clarity, and resonates with the writer. If it's clear but sounds uninteresting, we work together to spice it up with more descriptive words, some details, or an illustrative example.

Achieving Unity and Coherence

Unity and coherence are important aspects of paragraph structure. Delving into those concepts further, you'll find that—with a few organizational tools—they become a guiding force in clarity.

Coherence Defined

Coherence is having all of your sentences relate to one another, creating a smooth flow in your writing. A paragraph is coherent when it streams in a clear direction and when all the sentences are logically arranged. A document is coherent when it streams in a clear direction and all the paragraphs are logically arranged. So, the first order of business for achieving coherence is creating a logical order for your approach. This concept presents the perfect opportunity to tap into your outline again; with that, you've already orchestrated an ordered overview.

Transitional Words and Phrases

To make your paragraphs flow seamlessly from sentence to sentence, you can rely on several transitional words and phrases for segues. Transitional words and phrases cue readers to relationships between sentences, joining the sentences together, helping the reader follow along, and keeping ideas tied together. This list gives you the right words for specific contexts. You'll find that a paragraph without these devices comes off as ragged and disjointed.

Addition: Also, and, another, as well as, besides, further, in addition, moreover, too

Comparison: Analogous to, in like fashion, in like manner, in the same manner, in the same way, likewise, similarly

Concession: Although, at any rate, at least, even though, granted that, obviously, of course, while it may be true

Contrast: But, despite, even so, however, in contrast, nevertheless, on the other hand, simultaneously, still, yet

Details: Especially, including, namely, particularly, specifically, such as

Emphasis: Above all, certainly, indeed, in fact, of importance, really, surely

Example/Illustration: For example, for instance, ideally, in other words, in particular, namely, particularly, specifically, to illustrate

Result or Consequence: Accordingly, as a result, because, consequently, due to, for this reason, in other words, since, then, therefore, thus

Sequence : First, second, third; finally, next

Space: Above, across, adjacent to, along the edge, at the bottom, at the left, at the right, at the top, below, beneath, beyond, here, in the center, in the distance, nearby, next to, on the side, opposite, there, under, within

Suggestion: For this purpose, to this end, with this in mind

Summary: Finally, in brief, in conclusion, in summary, therefore

Time: After, afterward, before, concurrently, eventually, for starters, immediately, in the past, later, meanwhile, now, since then, subsequently, to begin with

More Tools for Coherence

Transitions aren't the only way to guide the reader. If necessary, you can repeat a key term or phrase so that the readers' comprehension isn't strained and their focus remains intact. If possible, instead of repeating a word, try substituting a synonym. These help enhance your word choice variety, while keeping the reader's concentration on the topic. Pronouns (it, they, he) are also useful in helping the reader refer back to a previously mentioned noun. However, be mindful that your clarity will suffer if you use an indirect pronoun reference, which causes a reader to be confused about whom or what the pronoun is referring to.

Coherence for Unity

Now that you've got a handle on making your paragraphs flow, make sure your paragraph lives up to its potential as a topical idea with backup subtopics that give it substance. Many devices can firm up your paragraph and make for compelling reading. The next time you write a document, determine whether your paragraphs are as complete as they can be. Does each paragraph contain a single idea that has been well fleshed out, but not overdone? If a paragraph seems skimpy, is there an idea that just needs beefing up? If that's the case, consider these "completion tools": using examples and illustrations, citing data such as facts and statistics, comparing and contrasting situations, examining effects and consequences, defining terms, evaluating causes and reasons, or offering a chronology. Again, turn to your outline to determine whether you've brainstormed, researched, or detailed enough information to give your paragraphs the substance they need.

> ### The Business Section
>
> The business section in your local daily newspaper or *The Wall Street Journal* gives you a chance to read—and learn from—coherent, unified writing pertaining to companies. Notice how an article's headline flows into a lead paragraph, which highlights the crucial information, and how the article then fills in the details as subsequent paragraphs flow from there. You might also pick up a few pointers on using transitional words and phrases, rewording clichés, and following parallel structure.

An Organization Checklist

Finally, take a moment to review this checklist after you've finished your communication, and before editing (which is discussed in Chapter 6):

- Is the intent of your communication clear? Did you establish and clearly define your purpose in writing, whether for information or to make a request? For example, if you are asking the reader to do something, will the reader understand what he or she is being asked to do?
- Do the opening words of a sentence contain the major point or general idea of the sentence?
- Does the opening sentence of each paragraph contain the major point or idea of the paragraph?
- Does the opening paragraph of a section state the major point or general idea of the section?
- Does the opening section of a document contain the major points or general ideas in the document?
- Did you include transitions that show your reader the relationships between your sentences and paragraphs?
- Does each paragraph logically follow the preceding paragraph and lead into the one that follows?
- Have you pruned away unnecessary words, phrases, sentences, and irrelevant information?

▶▶ TEST DRIVE

Find a lengthy e-mail you've received in your business. (You'll learn more about specifics of writing e-mails in Chapter 11; for now the focus is on clarity). This exercise demonstrates how organization can work even for ordinary e-mail:

➲ First, take a look at the "Subject" line.

➲ Do all the paragraphs in the e-mail relate to the subject?

➲ What about the sentences in each paragraph? Do they relate to the subject?

➲ Could any information be eliminated that wouldn't effect the e-mail's message?

➲ Can you readily determine whether an outline (even a brief listing of main message points) was or wasn't used for writing the e-mail?

The Particulars of Editing

Some people have a misguided notion that others in the workforce can magically transform a piece of paper into a perfectly worded, easy-to-follow, well-written document in a single draft. While that kind of writing may happen for a few extremely talented people, most of us need to edit our writing.

Granted, some quick responses may need no revisions, but they at least deserve a once-over. And for the majority of business communications, revisions—and sometimes rather substantial ones—will be the norm.

The better a piece of writing reads, the higher the likelihood that it was revised. Strive to make the editing phase a productive part of your writing. Realize that through editing, you ensure that your messages have a greater chance of accomplishing your communication goals.

Shift Your Perspective

Revising requires that you shift your perspective to that of the reader's to ascertain that the content you're putting forth will be understood, and, if applicable, that the action you're requesting will be taken.

If possible, depending on the importance of the document, try to take a break from it after your initial draft. For instance, if you're writing a business plan to attract potential investors, building "distance time" into your writing timetable should be mandatory so that you can come to the document later from an objective viewpoint. Only then will you be able to gauge the effectiveness of the plan and whether it will hit its mark with your target audience. If you don't take this breather, you'll have only been involved with the document as the communicator who has put time and energy into it—and who might still be under its spell.

Editing: A Three-Step Process

In the first step of the editing process, you'll concentrate on the "big picture" of your writing project. The goal here is to ensure that you've tackled the subject matter that you wanted to, have addressed the purpose, have identified the right audience, and have taken the correct tone with that audience. In this step, you'll check your content against your outline, so that you'll be sure you filled in all of the gaps, and have enough information to service your mission.

In the next phase, you'll delve into the core competencies, which you've learned about in the previous chapters. You'll focus on concise, precise wording, cohesiveness, and unity. You also will make sure that sentences and paragraphs flow well, and will eliminate unnecessary wording.

Once your correspondence or document has passed muster in the first two phases, you'll embark on the final step: proofreading, which is discussed later in this chapter. You'll check for misspellings, missing punctuation, subject-verb agreement, and other problems. When you finish this step, you'll have a polished piece of work.

Get Ready to Begin

If possible, try to conduct your editing at a slow, concentrated tempo. Though your workplace may be a fast-paced environment, editing benefits from a non-rushed approach and complete focus.

When working in revision mode, you're better off printing your document and working from hard copy rather than trying to edit on screen. It's easier on your eyes, and easier to check how the document physically looks in its layout. This practice is particularly necessary with proposals, plans, and presentations that might not give you the "full view" on a computer screen, regarding spacing and the visual look. It's true that much of the editing can occur on your screen, and if that's the way you're accustomed to working, you may be more comfortable using editing commands and the revision mode in your word processing program. However, the more important the document, the more it warrants a printout so that you can fully assess your content, layout, cohesiveness, etc., ensuring that you're definitely hitting all of your marks.

Grab a pencil or a preferred writing instrument (red pens aren't necessary), and read your draft out loud. While this method may seem uncomfortable at first, you'll quickly notice that some passages may sound awkward, and some words may not sound right in the context.

As the process continues, work on your editing in phases, examining, analyzing, and correcting a separate group of core competencies with each pass. If you get stuck on a passage or section, highlight it with a marker and come back to it. Sometimes—even when you're under a deadline—you're far better off maintaining momentum, moving on, and then returning to problems.

The Core Competencies: What You're Looking for in Revising

Following are questions you should ask to critique your writing. Your answers here will determine the effectiveness of your communication.

Format: Does the communication look the way it should? For instance, are headings where they should be?

Complete, Targeted Content: Did you include all of the details? Do you need more to perk it up? Is there any place where you might have left the reader hanging?

Appropriateness: Have you taken the appropriate tone, stayed away from language that might be condescending to your reader, employed tact, and steered clear of biased language?

Unity: Look at each paragraph. Does each sentence in each one relate to the paragraph's topic? Now take each paragraph into account. Does each paragraph relate to the topic of the entire piece of communication?

Coherence: How does each paragraph flow into the next one? Does each one lead logically to the next? Did you employ transitions? Is parallel structure intact?

Conciseness: Do you have extra words you don't need? Are there awkward phrases or sentences? Does every sentence come off with the meaning you wanted for it? Further, are there unnecessary words, sentences, or even paragraphs that simply repeat what you've already written?

Grammar: Is your subject-verb agreement consistent? Did you use active voice when you could? Are there any sentence run-ons or fragments that need to be corrected? Are all of your participles appropriately referred to? Are modifiers in the right place, located as close as possible to the word or words they're describing?

Consistency: Is your verb tense consistent throughout?

Diction: How precise and descriptive are your word choices? Did you dig deeper, or use the first word that popped into your head when another one actually might have been better? Do you find clichés that could be reworded?

Accuracy: Have you checked your facts, documented sources if necessary, and attributed quotes? (You'll get more pointers on this area later in this chapter.)

Effectiveness: Finally, does this piece accomplish its mission?

Don't try to tackle every revision aspect in one pass. Give yourself a few passes to catch every angle.

As you finish your revision, you may consider asking a colleague you trust to read your final draft. A completely different set of eyes brings an entirely fresh perspective, and can confirm that you're on the right track, or bring to light problems you never realized existed.

Do You Know Someone Who Has a Penchant for Editing?

Chances are you know someone who has a knack for picking apart a document. Don't let his or her editing marks deflate your enthusiasm. Instead, use that person's vantage point and know-how to your advantage. If you trust this person with your business matters, enlist the editor's help in correcting documents. Using him or her regularly can help ensure that you maintain a consistent style, appropriate tone, and on-target content in documents you send out. Further, he or she may help you recognize and stop making the same mistakes repeatedly.

A Revision Example

Using the editing techniques described—as well as writing strategies detailed in previous chapters—take a look at this paragraph and determine changes that you might make if you were revising it. Then, look at the italicized elements to see if you agree with the changes suggested. A complete revised paragraph follows.

SAMPLE PARAGRAPH, PRE-REVISION

The great American grills of the *1920's* were the landmark restaurants *of their day.* Using *home-cooked techniques,* they served *straight-forward food* purchased daily, soups and sauces slow simmered from homemade stock, and meats and fish prepared and served any way you *want.*

Reminiscent of these classic American grills, Cityside Canteen *holds its prestige and distinction* by serving "real" food consistently, year after year, in a clean, uncluttered and honest environment. City-side Canteen's menu includes standards inspired by *its* predecessors, like the *Brown Derby's "Cobb Salad," the "Traditional Beef Dip" from Philippe and meat loaf* from *time honored* recipes, in addition to its original creations *of steaks, chops and chicken dishes.*

Worthy of all great grills to have ever graced a city, Cityside Canteen is a restaurant you *would expect to frequent and we hope you do.*

Here are the notes on suggested changes.

- 1920's isn't possessive; use 1920s instead
- "of their day" is a cliché
- "home-cooked" seems an odd choice as an adjective for techniques; the writer meant to say "home cooking"
- as a word choice, "straight-forward" doesn't make food seem very appetizing; in addition, "straightforward" doesn't need a hyphen
- this verb tense causes unparallel structure
- "hold their prestige and distinction" is too passive
- "its" presents an indirect pronoun reference; does it refer to the restaurant or the menu?
- the menu items are not listed in parallel structure
- time honored needs a hyphen (time-honored)
- taking out "of" and "dishes" eliminates unnecessary words and makes the phrasing more parallel and active
- "Worthy" is a poor word choice, and makes the restaurant seem to be striving to be successful rather than accomplishing its mission

- this clause needs a more active take
- a case could be made for a run-on here; separating out the final independent clause puts a nice final point on the restaurant's description

THE REVISED PARAGRAPH:

The great American grills of the 1920s were the landmark restaurants of the era. Using home cooking techniques, the owners served honest-to-goodness food purchased daily, soups and sauces slowly simmered from homemade stock, and meats and fish prepared any way customers wanted.

Reminiscent of these classic American grills, Cityside Canteen proudly and distinctively serves "real" food consistently, year after year, in a clean, uncluttered, and honest environment. Cityside Canteen's menu includes standards inspired by the restaurant's famed predecessors, like the Brown Derby's Cobb Salad, Romanoff's Traditional Beef Dip, and Chasen's Meat Loaf, cooking time-honored recipes in addition to original steak, chop and chicken creations.

Evocative of all the great grills that have ever graced a city, Cityside Canteen is a restaurant you'll want to frequent often. We hope you do.

Notice that the editing didn't take away the writer's original intent. It only worked to strengthen and clarify the message the writer was trying to get across.

Oftentimes, Writing Is Rewriting

Don't think of revisions as some arduous chore. When you view your assignment as writing a series of drafts, you won't feel the need to be perfect on your first pass. Instead, realize that you'll be putting the document through an editing process immediately after your initial approach.

Plus, rewriting may feel vastly easier for you because you no longer feel encumbered, facing a blank screen.

If the process seems intimidating, try this approach: At first, just get all of your thoughts down on paper. Don't worry what others will think; no one will be reading this version. Follow your outline to get the words down in logically ordered sentences. Then, in subsequent revisions, concern yourself with crafting sentences that flow, employing necessary transitions, and tinkering with word choices.

If you're prone to sending out the first draft of your communication, beware: you're not serving your reader well. Think enough of your readers—and their time and commitment—to provide them with a well-prepared draft. You risk your reader being confused, and thinking less of your company, if you don't put your time and energy into careful revision. Careless, unrevised writing is almost always apparent.

Conducting Necessary Research and Fact-Checking

Whether you realize it or not, you often do at least a little research when you write. It may consist of simply looking up a phone number, reconfirming an order, or perusing past e-mails. Sometimes, substantial and extensive research becomes an integral part of your writing process. For a business proposal and PowerPoint presentation, you might have to gauge the competition's activities and/or products, market conditions, and possible promotional tools.

During the editing phase, you may realize that certain areas of your draft may be presenting information less than confidently, or your paragraphs may be sketchy, with points that need backup to really draw in the reader.

To beef up your material, you may consider adding facts, figures, personal anecdotes, news stories, or case studies that lend substance and credence. If your writing seems to be lacking in details, remember that you have a wealth of sources and resources to call upon that can enhance and enliven your document.

Once you have the information you need, use the editing process to verify it with the fact-checking methods described later in this chapter.

Writing, Rewriting, and Editing

Editing is important, no matter how many or few words are involved. Indigo Creative, a studio specializing in branding, print communication, and digital presentation, wanted to make sure that the copy for the firm's Web site homepage was as tight, powerful, and compelling as possible. Notice the subtle—but significant—differences in these "Before" and "After" paragraphs.

Before: Your company's brand is that distinguishing mark that makes it attractive enough to be noticed, intriguing enough to be sought after. When it is successful it leaves an imprint that is unforgettable.

In seven seconds or less, you could describe the most dynamic person you know and the effect on every life they touch. Can you do the same about your company?

Indigo. Your brand is our business.

After: Your company's brand distinguishes it from all others; makes you attractive and noticed, intriguing; set to be sought after. A successful brand leaves an unforgettable imprint.

In seven seconds or less, you could describe the most dynamic person you know and the effect they have on every life they touch. Can you do the same about your company? Indigo can. Your brand is our business.

Sources

Readers will perk up to your writing with the specifics and details that everyone craves. Those are fundamentals that allow your audience to understand an idea or concept better, or to digest a point being made. The good news: information is *everywhere*. A plethora of sources are readily available to you, such as the billions of pages search engines offer; the thousands of books in your local bookstore, and library, or on Amazon.com; the hundreds of magazines on a newsstand on any given day; the trade journals you can have mailed to your office; and the newspaper that can be delivered to your door each morning.

However, it is imperative that you do your best to rely on credible sources, ones that aren't doling out misconceptions or errant information. You don't want the research you include to cost you personal credibility and render your communication useless.

In addition to print media, consider visual venues that are jam-packed with information, such as national news programs and documentaries.

You can also look to other sources that fall outside traditional research avenues, such as attending a chamber of commerce meeting, a convention hall expo, or a business seminar at a local hotel, or interviewing a person who used to run a business like yours. Finally, never underestimate the research value of personal experience. That allows an undisputable first-person account that can add heft to an array of communications.

As you conduct your research, remember that recent is better. Look for telltale signs of professional reporting, with sources that are accountable, contain objective analysis, and provide excellent backup and details.

Dogpile.com

Consider using a shortcut for your research on the Web: *www.dogpile.com*, a search engine that canvasses the high-ranking hits on Google, Yahoo, MSN, and Jeeves to produce "all the best search engines piled into one." As with all the searches you conduct, be as specific as possible with words and phrases for optimum listings to peruse. If your search is yielding few relevant results, then go broader, with more general terms.

Verifying the Information

The rules you use to call upon sources extend to the care you'll take in fact-checking and confirming the information you've found.

Consider the source: Your best bet for reliable information is those outlets and venues that publish or broadcast regularly, which keeps their content fresh. To ensure that their information is correct, they often rely on fact-checkers. Their fact-checkers' work obviously benefits you too!

Use common sense: If a fact seems too good to be true, or a figure seems off, reconfirm the finding with another source.

Web sites can be challenging for confirming information, so be mindful of these elements, which give some assurance of accuracy: a credible reference to the source; a date stamp to show that the information was recently updated; links on the site to other credible sources; credited information; and a professional look.

Be a Strategic Researcher, Not Just a Good One

In conducting both written and verbal research, ask great questions. Sometimes, just by asking more questions, you can make sure you're getting more exact and precise details for your communication.

"Garbage In, Garbage Out" (GIGO) is a term used to describe how an unspecific question begets an ambiguous answer. So, for instance, instead of asking, "Do you sell hanging lamps?" try, "Do you sell the white, frosted-glass, schoolhouse-style pendant lamp made by Merko, product number 32579?" Instead of, "Can your company set up an office e-mail system for my business?" try, "Can you provide e-mail software for the three G5 Apple iMacs to network in our printing company?"

Attribution

Finally, during the editing phase, take care to attribute the information to the correct source. That gives your material authenticity, and shows that you have thought enough of your reader to provide a thoroughly researched, well-thought-out communication.

Facts and figures should have a source listed, including the date the information was published. Direct quotes from experts should be set off with quotation marks, followed by the expert's name and title.

Proofreading

Nothing takes your credibility down a few notches like a document brimming with misspellings, errant spaces, unnecessary punctuation, and wrong page numbers. Proofreading is your final phase in wrapping up your communication. This process includes zeroing in further on grammar, spelling, and appropriate punctuation.

That Troublesome Twosome: Punctuation and Spelling

This pair is most likely to throw a document into the danger zone. These two categories are the most basic, and thus the easiest to spot if incorrect.

Beginning with punctuation, move through your correspondence or document line by line.

Check that:

⮑ Periods are where they should be, and that there are no double periods.

⮑ Commas are where they should be, and not breaking up a sentence in the wrong place.

⮑ Semicolons, if used, are separating standalone clauses that relate to one another.

⮑ Colons, if used, announce what follows. If a complete sentence follows a colon, the sentence is capitalized.

⮑ Apostrophes and quotations are in place and headed in the right direction.

⮑ Any word that has been "red-flagged" by the word processing spell checker has been corrected or double-checked to ensure its accuracy.

⮑ Any word you're not sure of has been looked up in a dictionary to confirm its spelling.

⮑ Proper names have been spelled correctly.

Fact Accuracies and Unintentional Omissions

To ensure that your facts are straight, that extraneous items aren't hanging around, and that you haven't left anything out, check that:

⮑ If applicable, the address is the same on the letter and envelope.

⮑ All figures are accurate: numbers aren't transposed, totals are correct, and decimal points are aligned.

⮑ Web site names are spelled correctly; URLs are correct.

⮑ Dates are accurate and match the correct days of the week.

⮑ Phone numbers are accurate, and always include area codes.

⮑ Unneeded spaces between words haven't been added.

⮑ No characters are transposed, no words or letters omitted.

Grammar and Formatting

For language-usage and formatting, check that:

- ⮌ Nouns and verbs agree.
- ⮌ No participles are dangling and no modifiers are misplaced.
- ⮌ Titles, headings, section heads, and so on are consistent throughout.
- ⮌ Paragraphs are consistent in being indented or not.
- ⮌ Page numbers appear in the same place on each page and are in order.

Particularly Proof Materials for the Press

Any pitch letter, press release, or other material that you distribute to media outlets should be proofread with particular care. Don't make the mistake of putting your company's reputation on the line with writing that could be deemed unprofessional. You don't want to take the chance that a reporter may use that carelessness against your business, or may draw unwarranted conclusions about how you do business. The worst part: The reporter could share the mistake in a media outlet that could reach a sizable audience—all of whom might draw the same conclusion.

Editing Marks

Following is a table that highlights marks used in proofreading. Using these on your printed draft versions will cue you immediately to corrections to incorporate for a finished document.

An Invaluable Tool

For all grammar and style issues refer to a style guide such as *The Elements of Style Illustrated* by William Strunk Jr. and E.B. White. Maira Kalman's illustrations bring a fresh perspective to this classic guide.

COMMON PROOFREADER'S MARKS

SYMBOL	MEANS	EXAMPLE
⸜	Delete	Atlanta's⸜ Buckhead district is a shopping mecca.
∧	Insert	Atlanta's Buckhead district a shopping mecca.
stet	Keep as is	Atlanta's Buckhead district is a shopping mecca.
⌐	Separate	Atlanta's⌐Buckhead district is a shopping mecca.
#	Insert space	Atlanta's⌐Buckhead district is a shopping mecca.
∼	Transpose	Atlanta's Buckhead distrcit is a shopping mecca.
sp	Spelling	Atlanta's Buckhead district is a shopping mecka.
⌢	Close space	Atlanta's Buck head district is a shopping mecca.
cap. ≡	Capitalize	Atlanta's buckhead district is a shopping mecca.
lc /	Lowercase	ATLanta's Buckhead district is a shopping mecca.
bf	Bold	Atlanta's Buckhead district is a shopping mecca.
ul	Underline	Atlanta's Buckhead district is a shopping mecca.
ital.	Italicize	Atlanta's Buckhead district is a shopping mecca.
⊙	Insert period	Atlanta's Buckhead district is a shopping mecca
⊐⊏	Center	Atlanta's Buckhead
¶	Start paragraph	¶For downtime during the convention, Atlanta's Buckhead
⊙ ∧	Insert colon	Atlanta's Buckhead Shopping Mecca.
⸝ ∧	Insert comma	Atlanta's Ga.
⸝ ∧	Insert apostrophe	Atlantas Buckhead district is a shopping mecca.

▶▶ TEST DRIVE

Take a piece of communication that you've recently written that you consider important—a letter, press release, or memo, for example—and boost it with editing. Ask yourself these questions:

- ➲ Did you fully take the perspective of your reader into account?
- ➲ What about your assessment and execution of the core competencies? Did you address them well in your document?
- ➲ Were there additional, pertinent details you could have provided through research?
- ➲ Did you initially take a reprieve after writing the document before editing it? Did you have a colleague look it over?
- ➲ Did you proofread it? Even if you did, have you caught additional errors now?

Finally, if the communication didn't meet your needs at the time, determine whether the piece—with the aid of fresh editing—is more effective now.

Putting Words to Work

PART 2

It All Starts Here

For your business to be successful, you need a road map to lay out its direction, chart its path, and track its progress. A business plan precisely defines your business, identifies your goals, and serves as your company's resume. With it, you are more likely to allocate resources well, handle unforeseen complications, and make sound business decisions.

You may need a business plan in the short term to secure a loan or attract investors. However, it most certainly also will be a source you repeatedly turn to, plucking sections and sentences for communications that inform sales personnel, suppliers, and others about your operations and goals.

Despite the obvious and critical importance of a business plan, many entrepreneurs and small business owners are reticent to craft one, suggesting that the marketplace changes too fast, or they don't have enough time.

However, consider that those who plan, do better. In the book *What They Still Don't Teach You at Harvard Business School* (Bantam, 1989), author Mark H. McCormack discusses a Harvard study conducted between 1979 and 1989. In '79, MBA graduates were asked if they had set written goals and plans for accomplishing them—only 3 percent had. In '89, researchers found that the 3 percent who had clear, written goals and plans were earning ten times as much as the other 97 percent of the graduates combined.

Study Sample Business Plans

Don't ever believe that your business plan must follow a stringent format and formula. While plans share many components, they are all written differently. In fact, you could say there are as many different business plans as there are companies. Remember: one of the best ways to learn about and get ideas for a business plan you're working on for your company is to study the plans of established businesses in your industry. Several Web sites provide samples. One of the best places to start is the United States Small Business Administration Web site at *www.sba.gov*. You can also check out *www.businessplans.org* and *www.allbusiness.com*. Each of these sites has a comprehensive library that provides samples of plans from a variety of industries.

In the discussion here, you should be concerned with learning about finding the right words and messages to present a strategic business plan that will serve you well. This chapter will prompt you to examine areas that will effectively inform your business plan writing.

The Overall Structure

In writing a business plan, you must take into account where you're headed—not only in the sense of your business, but also in the scheme of your plan. Your plan will be much more informative, direct, and ultimately successful if you're aware of the components that constitute it.

Although there is no single, catchall formula for developing a business plan, some elements are fairly common:

Executive Summary: This element will be one of the most important you write, and you may wait to complete it until you've worked on all the other sections. It toplines—with flair—your goals, objectives, and mission for your company; what sets you apart; and what makes you attractive to customers, vendors, and investors.

Company Description: This section presents pithy information regarding ownership, history, products, location, services, and key strengths. This section will most likely include your all-important mission statement.

Target Audience Description: Your in-tune profile delivers the goods on your likely—and desired—customers.

Competitive Analysis: This section provides an overview of the industry in which you're competing, including descriptions and research regarding trends, target customers, and competitors.

Operations and Objectives: This information shows how you'll implement the plan and achieve your objectives, complete with timetables.

Marketing: This strategy component describes how you'll differentiate your company from competitors through advertising, promotion, publicity, and other measures.

Management/Organization Layout: This section provides biographical information on your key management team and advisers, and offers descriptions of positions.

Financials: Monthly cost breakdowns, salary specifics, and forecasts for your assets and liabilities make up this section.

Drafting Your Mission Statement

Many companies decide that a mission statement is simply a company's philosophy and just fluffy commentary that hardly needs to be addressed or put into words. However, a good mission statement expresses the core values of your company and provides the motive behind the company's direction. For many, the mission statement is difficult to write, but a good one says much about your business, influences your employees' actions, and—in guiding your company's attitude, values, and beliefs—leaves your customers with a favorable impression.

A mission statement should always be a part of your business plan. In a sense, by conveying the company's actions and ideals, it becomes both the orientation and direction for the reader and should be a harbinger for all that follows.

Snappy, Simple, Short

Your company's mission statement won't be too hard to put into words, once you answer a few questions and consider a few factors. Think of a mission statement as a 30-second snapshot of your company story and ideas. According to Inc.com, the best ones tend to be three to four sentences long, but many are shorter. The finest take into account all of your audiences: employees, customers, vendors, and investors.

First, list some words that you think best describe your company and the products or services you provide. From there, ask yourself the "5 Ws and an H" about your company: who your company is, what it does, why it does it, how it does it differently from other companies, and—perhaps less important, depending on your business—when and where it conducts business. As you ask yourself those questions, delve deeply: What is significant about who your company is and what it does? What distinguishing characteristics set it apart? In answering those questions, stay away from "we're the greatest," "we're the best" statements. Make your statement as unique as your company.

You might also think about how your company started to begin with. What was the passion that drove you to launch it? What do you want to instill or inspire in others who do business with your company?

While you may get some great ideas looking at other companies' mission statements and how they were articulated, remember that each company has to have its own statement. Copying another company's mission statement makes yours similar to them, not distinguished from them.

Finally, make sure you believe what you write. If you don't buy it, neither will any audience you're putting it in front of.

Mission Statement Examples

These mission statements from well-known companies will give you an idea of how well-worded sentences can define a company's priorities, create a culture, elicit emotions, and set up actionable goals. These statements are often studied in business courses because each so succinctly and quickly captures its company's essence and motives.

> **Courtyard by Marriott:** To provide economy and quality minded travelers with a premier, moderate priced lodging facility which is consistently perceived as clean, comfortable, well maintained, and staffed by friendly, attentive and efficient people.

> **Wal-Mart:** To offer all of the fine customers in our territories all of their household needs in a manner in which they continue to think of us fondly.

> **Otis Elevators:** To provide any customer a means of moving people and things up, down and sideways over short distances with higher reliability than any similar enterprise in the world.

　　　　Facing the Competition on Message

When a large chain supermarket opened in a seaside town, the one-store grocer, Delmonico's, initially suffered a severe sales dropoff. Initially, Mr. Delmonico considered slashing prices and adding lines of new items to compete, but that strategy would have drained considerable resources, and brought lower profit margins, too. Mr. Delmonico had never crafted a mission statement for his store and realized that if he wanted to stay in business, now was the time. Taking a look at what he could offer in his smaller-square-foot setting led his charge to redirect his resources and slightly alter his course. He articulated his mission as being "to provide home-towners and vacationers with fresh and desirable delicacies and convenience with class."

This strategy meant he kept some of the products he always offered—necessities such as milk, some fruits and vegetables, and so on that customers might run in and out to purchase—but also stocked items that would be considered gourmet or luxe, and thus have a higher profit margin. In the "delicacy" arena, he installed an espresso coffee bar, a wine "cellar," gift basket station, florist post, and a small fresh bakery counter. He also differentiated his store with service hallmarks. For instance, employees carried groceries to shoppers' cars, personally escorted shoppers to find items they were looking for, and made gift deliveries at no extra charge. After a year, the store not only increased traffic substantially, but more than doubled its average customer receipt.

Clearly, when he put the store's mission into words, he created an atmosphere in which ideas translated into actions.

Outlining Your Business Goals

Your mission statement should help you crystallize the goals you want to establish for your company. So, before writing the plan, focus on what you see as the goal and future direction of your business, and what your goal is for writing the business plan.

By identifying where you want the business to go in the next one, three, and five years, you can write a plan that adequately reflects your goals. Your personal skills, needs, knowledge, resources, acceptable level of risk, and the nature of your business will factor into the equation when you identify your personal business goals.

Before You Begin

Seattle Times reporter Helen Jung once described a business plan as a cross between a research paper and an advertisement. That being the case, it allows you a great deal of opportunity to elucidate and elaborate. As in other communications you prepare, you must answer some key questions before you begin writing your business plan. In a sense, these questions address the content of and audience for your business.

1. What service or product does your business provide?
2. What needs does it fill for the marketplace?
3. Who are your potential customers?
4. What makes your business stand out as the place to purchase the specific product?
5. How will you attract customers? What outreach will you provide?
6. What funding will you need?
7. Who will provide that capital?

Your Company Description

The answers to those questions furnish you many of the specifics you need to write a cogent description of your company, the basis for its daily operations, and its overall strategy in conducting a successful business. You also should include information regarding the company's staff: its principal owners, their backgrounds, and the expertise, passion, and experience they bring to the company.

Plan for Your Goals

For your plan to be the most effective, you should take into account many of the communication principles discussed in previous chapters. Your plan should be easy to understand and specific; include actionable, concrete elements; and map out objectives that can be measured.

At this point, you should also be certain of exactly what you're using this plan for. While a single plan can serve an array of purposes—define your business, support a loan application, evaluate a new product line— you must be aware of the purposes you're serving with yours. Before starting, make a list for yourself of the missions you would like your business plan to accomplish. Those goals for your plan will direct and enhance your writing of it.

Determine Your Priorities

To address the goals of your plan, decide which of these you're trying to accomplish. Are you trying to:

Attract Investors? If so, your plan should offer plenty specifics about how the business will operate and how their investment will be spent.

Delineate the Areas of Your Business? If so, your plan should provide an overview of all your business' aspects: the "5 Ws and an H" about each of your daily business operations.

Learn About Your Chief Competition? If so, you should concentrate on analyzing the marketplace, your target customers, and your competitors. This research allows you a prime opportunity to distinguish your company's products and services.

Determine Your Financial Needs? If so, you need to amass as much financial information as possible to lay out your entire financial picture.

Attract Top-Level Personnel? If so, mapping out your company's business allows you to offer a comprehensive look to those you might like to have involved.

Track Progress? If so, the plan should include your objectives and goals, and the timetable for them, to allow monitoring, thus keeping the company on schedule and alerting you to problems that might arise.

Fleshing Out Your Concept

As you work toward developing your plan—having now defined your audience and established your goals—take the necessary steps to put the plan in motion. For starters, draft a table of contents so you'll know exactly which sections you definitely need to include. Once the sections are listed, identify areas that need research and supporting data.

Then, make a list of the specific data you need to research. For example, you'll need statistics on your demographic audience, your competition, and the market; you'll also need to gather financials. (You'll receive more information about both of these areas later in this chapter).

Get Started

Don't put off writing the business plan, or wait until the bank or a prime investor asks for one. Sure, you're busy, but your time will be spent more efficiently when you make time to determine where you're going and how you plan to get there—crucial, strategic information a business plan can effectively provide. You'll find that the plan will have immediate, far-reaching, and positive ramifications that will infiltrate every aspect of your company: financial goals, employee actions, marketing objectives. When a well-thought-out plan is written, your chances will skyrocket for clear-cut direction in all areas to soon follow.

Answer these questions to make your plan as complete as possible:

1. What is your vision for the firm?

2. What does your company look like in one, three, and five years?

3. At those time junctures, how many employees do you have? What are your revenues? Where are you located?

4. Whom do you see as your clients? Will they change at one-, three-, and five-year intervals?

5. If you have existing clients, how can you better serve them?

6. How can you attract new clients? Are there marketing or community service initiatives that immediately come to mind? What about trade shows, publicity, guerrilla marketing techniques, and direct mail?

7. Define your company's "name-maker" characteristics. In other words, what sets your company apart from the pack?

8. What obstacles do you foresee in trying to attain these accomplishments?

Answering these should help you fully determine the substance and stance of your plan's components. As you determine more of your plan's contents, survey other companies' plans to make sure you're including all the information and sections you need. Read select plans thoroughly to study the tack they've taken. If possible, find out if the plan was successful in its goal of securing funds, attracting investors, or setting company timelines.

Primed for Financial Terms

In a business plan's financial section, you want to convince the reader that your company is worth investing in or loaning money to. Consider hiring an accountant or financial consultant to prepare your plan's financial section. Further, to communicate effectively in the business plan and to ensure that your company's financials are properly articulated, you should be on top of financial terms, including these: income statements, net and gross sales, gross profit, net income and profits, depreciation, the cost of goods, cash flow, interest income, loan proceeds, balance sheet, current and fixed assets, net worth, current and long-term liabilities, working capital, capital expenditures, and equity financing. By being familiar with these terms, you can discern whether your plan will make an impact.

Articulating Financial Needs

In a business plan's financial section, you want to convince the reader that your company is worth investing in or giving a loan to. With that, a realistic set of financial projections must be included. If the company has no history yet, this section details financial projections. If you've got a record intact, include financial data and statements for the past three years.

The Basics You'll Need

Whether your company has a history or not, you need to include the next year's financial projections by month and quarter; a five-year forecast; and a breakeven analysis, which is an overview of whether or not your business will bring in enough money to meet its costs. You also need to include your sources of funding, and give a description of expenses divided into categories, such as real estate, equipment, manufacturing, administrative costs, and advertising. After breaking down your monthly costs, you have to project how much product you'll have to sell to cover expenses. You also need a profit-and-loss forecast, which refines the sales and expense estimates of your break-even analysis into a month-by-month projection of your business's profit. Finally, a cash-flow projection tells whether you'll have enough cash month-to-month to cover expenses and buy more inventory.

In this section, you'll serve your company best by slightly understating projected revenues and slightly overstating expected costs.

Additional Considerations

If you're in a position of trying to convince investors to put money into your business, you may want to include some additional documentation, such as contracts or purchase orders with notable clients, biograhies of impressive advisers, favorable press, or outstanding product reviews. All of these supporting materials will point to a worthy investment in your firm.

Describing the Market and Competition

To prepare worthy competitive analysis, you should start by identifying all of your competitors: those nearby, in the next city, and on the Internet. Gather as much information as you can about them, such as the markets they serve, their revenues, and their customer creeds. Visit their Web sites, and do a Google search to find any relevant media reports about them. You may also find valuable research information on *www.hoovers.com* and *www.allbusiness.com*.

If possible, talk to customers and vendors you may come in contact with. As you learn more about your competitors, you'll begin to find areas they've overlooked that provide you with an angle, advantage, or edge.

Devote the initial information in this section of your business plan to the overall climate of your industry, your chief competitors, their market share, and their general milieu. Detail not only how they have sustained business—confirming that the area is a wise venture—but how their commerce provides a prime opportunity as well.

Then, spend the bulk of this section detailing your advantage over them, how you will compete against them, and why you will succeed. Your key concern here is why you present a viable, fresh alternative to your competitors. Focus on what makes you different, and profitably so. Still, be honest about marketplace challenges. Doing so presents you as a realist, and gives you the chance to lucidly and convincingly describe how you will address those challenges.

The Final Plan

Don't face your plan as a banal chore. It's your company, so use the opportunity of writing to plan to also show your enjoyment of the business. Nobody wants to read dense academia with indecipherable jargon or an oversaturation of market statistics, particularly if your business is snow cones or party planning.

Make It Yours

Incorporate your own style into the plan. While some terms and sections are consistent—such as the executive summary and breakeven analysis—you can add components that are unique to your industry or your company in particular (though they should also be relevant to your overall plan).

For instance, a trendy new boutique opening in suburban St. Louis played off its edge of bringing Hollywood fashion to the Midwest. The storeowner took an entertaining tone in her plan, with an overview that included the subhead "What's the Big Idea?" and a company description that included the subhead "Location! Location! Location! Hollywood and . . . Clayton?"

Get Others' Opinions

Have trusted colleagues read the plan when you have finished it. Perhaps consider a referral to someone who has excelled in your particular business and could give you applicable, appropriate pointers in making your plan even sharper.

Keep the Plan Going

As you write and assemble the particulars of your final plan, develop a corollary action plan for the entire year. As each quarter closes, assess the plan and update it. If the plan isn't working, and your company isn't meeting goals and timelines that you had prescribed for it, carefully review the document. Rework sections that are proving problematic.

Once you finish the plan, treat it as a living document that changes and grows with your company. That way, you'll always have the blueprint you need to keep your activities and goals on track and ever escalating.

▶▶ Test Drive

As you gear up to write a business plan, think about your planning for it:

- ⤺ Why do you need one for your company?
- ⤺ What is your primary goal for the plan?
- ⤺ What are your secondary goals for it?
- ⤺ Who is your audience for each of the goals?
- ⤺ What sections will you definitely include?
- ⤺ How can you make a distinct impression with your plan?

Are Memos Even Around Anymore?

With the seeming omnipresence of e-mail, many in the workplace wonder if there is even a need anymore for the memo (short for memorandum). It might even conjure up a quaint image of a secretary seated in front of a boss's desk, holding a stenographer's pad, ready for dictation.

Haven't Written a Memo Lately?

Memos are still around, and still have their place in the electronic age. Memos are actually the most official method of intra-office correspondence. As such, they can be vastly more appropriate—and more productive—than e-mail. (More differences between the two formats are discussed later in this chapter). While you may consider that there can be such a format as an "e-mail memo" at your company, realize that a memo—in its purest, most effective form—is distributed only as a hard copy.

Entrepreneurial ventures or small business operations often convey a laid-back approach; traditional memos may come across as fussy or formal. However, specific situations do warrant memos and, for certain occasions, you can't afford not to write one. Despite e-mail's speed and pervasiveness—or maybe even because of it—memos need to be, and remain, a fixture in your communications arsenal. Because of that, employers should know the best times to use them, and employees should understand that better results might be reaped from them.

Memo Attributes

Usually unceremonious in style, memos represent an official vehicle used to inform or ask in a short, to-the-point, and direct style. Forgoing the salutation, formal opening, and complimentary closing of a business letter, the memo still can create a permanent record of plans, decisions, and actions in a completely nonthreatening manner. Incidentally, composing great memos will also undoubtedly help you in crafting more efficient e-mails (which will be discussed in greater detail in Chapter 11).

Different Types of Memos

In deciding whether you should write a memo, ascertain what type of memo you would be crafting, and determine whether it's the best format for your purpose.

Generally speaking, memos work to provide information to the recipient, and then work on a further level to prompt that person to perform or complete an action, or to understand a situation. The outcome may be for the recipient to allocate funds, meet a deadline, offer feedback, or give a go-ahead.

The Memo's Purpose: Your Audience, Your Approach

This common form of business correspondence can serve vastly different purposes. Obviously, you need to determine why you're writing a memo. First, identify your audience. To whom will you be writing? What do you need to say to them? What is the context of the situation—serious and problematic, or purely informational—in which you're writing to them?

At this juncture, to make sure you've got a memo with purpose, treat your subject as you might a news story: Identify the "5 Ws and an H"—the who, what, when, where, why, and how—that you'll be addressing in the memo. Then resolve to make sure that you cover them all.

When to Use a Memo

Internally, memos may inform their recipients of:

- ⤷ Announcements for such diverse happenings as hirings or holidays
- ⤷ Changes in such aspects as policies, procedures, and prices
- ⤷ Confirmations of verbal discussions, decisions, and even meeting times
- ⤷ Documents to follow, such as reports, gathered research, and survey results
- ⤷ Recommendations for actions

⊃ Requests for information, further research, or reports

⊃ Solicitation for opinions

Different Ways for Different Types

Typically, your memo will follow one of these three patterns:

⊃ In the direct-approach memo, your most important points are relayed, followed by supporting details. This approach is the best avenue for distributing routine information.

⊃ In an indirect approach, you're attempting to gather support or momentum for an idea or initiative. You begin the memo with evidence that backs up your stance, then segue to a conclusion based on those facts. Ideally, you pique your readers' interest, then encourage them to take a specific action.

⊃ For a balanced approach, you utilize aspects of both the direct and indirect tacks, combining straightforward information with some persuasion. You would use this tactic, for example, when giving bad news.

Memos versus E-Mails

If the thought of someone forwarding a certain e-mail makes you cringe, you should consider using a memo instead.

As a rule, the more significant the subject matter, the more likely you need to opt for a memo rather than an e-mail. In addition, in many circumstances a letter is even more appropriate than either; you'll delve into that format in Chapter 8. The ease and breeziness of e-mail has no doubt made sticking to any sort of communication regimen challenging.

It's important to remember that corporate e-mails are not considered private. Even deleted e-mail can be found by industrious (or lawsuit-seeking) individuals. You've no doubt heard that simply deleting an e-mail doesn't erase it from your disk drive, and could even be subpoenaed!

As iVillage.com's Ms. Demeanor (Mary Mitchell) points out, "employees are very much influenced by symbols. A sheet of formal company letterhead commands respect and adds a dimension of ceremony."

Further, many times, memos offer a format that's just better suited to your message. If you've got an e-mail that's exceeding a few paragraphs, consider redeveloping it as a memo.

If you've got information that would be more effectively relayed with tables, charts, or graphs, don't try to create that information in an e-mail. Place it in a memo format instead.

Sensitive information such as Social Security numbers, private addresses, and health conditions have no place in cyberspace. If you're handling employee information that should be kept confidential, put it to paper rather than onto the Internet. While there is no guarantee that paper won't fall into nefarious hands, you have more control over its whereabouts.

Financial information, whether regarding salary, confidential pricing information, or such coveted information as wholesale discounts or upcoming sale promotions, should also stay in memo format. E-mail is simply too easy to forward, and though you certainly trust your intended recipient, it could still mistakenly get sent to the wrong place.

Perhaps you simply deem the information you're conveying to be just too important. That's perfectly fine. It's your call. Never be embarrassed to send a memo rather than an e-mail. If anything, you'll get points for professionalism.

The Memo Format

Memos typically have a one-inch margin on each of the page's four sides. The top line states the word "Memo" or "Memorandum," and is usually centered below the company's logo. Below "Memo" is the header grouping, which is discussed later in this section. A long solid line typically separates the header from the body of the memo (details pertaining to the memo's body are also explained later in this section). Finally, if appropriate, you include "cc:"—which actually stands for "carbon copy"—a notation that refers to those you wish to copy on the memo. In a memo, this abbreviation always appears in lowercase.

| Inside Track | A Case for Memos |

In today's exceedingly fast-paced environment, memos often get short shrift as an increasingly distant cousin of the seemingly more immediate e-mail. But every business is different, and some work situations—yours included—may have a number of occasions and situations that make embracing memos a wiser option than sending e-mails.

In handling publicity for the syndicated newsmagazine *Entertainment Tonight*, I realized that sometimes e-mail just wasn't fast enough. That's right: e-mail was the snail here. With the show shooting every weekday, intended recipients were often in the throes of taping, providing voice-over, shooting broadcast pieces, and screening video, often either onstage or in the field. Therefore, I had a better shot at providing valuable written, detail-filled information to talent, producers, and directors if I or a production assistant handed out memos. If I had relied on e-mail, information may have been received too late. The presence of a memo also persuaded people to ask questions or clarify issues sooner than later.

Survey your work situation: Are your intended recipients near a computer workstation or constantly manning a BlackBerry, or is their work away from the traditional office setting? How important or immediate is the information you're trying to disseminate? You may decide that memos are the best route for your communication, too.

Header

Below "Memo" is this lineup (or some close variation of it), known as the memo's header. These items are always single spaced, although you may elect to set off the subject line with double-spacing:

TO:

FROM:

DATE:

SUBJECT:

"To" refers to your readers' names. In the strictest formal sense, you'd also include their job titles. In small businesses, this measure may seem superfluous, but in a setting such as a doctor's office, you would use "Dr.

Jones" rather than referring to the doctor by his or her first name. In addition, you should never place someone's nickname on this line.

"From" would be your name. If you've included the job title in the "to" line, you should also list your job title after your name. After you finish writing the memo, you should add your initials or signature to the "from" line to let the recipient know you've signed off on the memo's contents.

"Date" is the complete and current date. If you worked on the memo over the course of a few days—though this normally isn't the case with memos—use the date of the last day you worked on the memo. In addition, be consistent with how you phrase the date. In writing your memos, stick with either a numeral format, such as 10/05/07, or spell it out, as in October 5, 2007. Either is correct.

The "Subject" line (which also sometimes just says "RE:") states your memo's topic and the reason the memo's being sent. (You'll learn about the best way to write a winning subject line later in this chapter.)

Paragraph Formatting

Underneath the header is your memo's body, or message area. The text here is single-spaced. The format can be in block or modified block format. In the block format, the paragraphs begin flush left, have ragged right margins, and include a double space between paragraphs. The modified block format indents each paragraph, keeps a ragged right margin, but forgoes space between the paragraphs. The choice is yours; just don't mix the two formats.

This is an example of block format:

> As you know, I will be taking a temporary leave beginning November 8. I have made sure that my responsibilities will be covered with the following measures.
>
> On Friday, October 1, I sent Annette Kinney, via messenger, all my folders and binders pertaining to the Essex Planter product launch. I have also been e-mailing her various documents pertaining to the trade show, i.e., the 2007 press kit, contact information, sample memos, status reports, clip reports, etc.

This is an example of modified block format:

> As you know, I will be taking a temporary leave beginning November 8. I have made sure that my responsibilities will be covered with the following measures.
>
> On Friday, October 1, I sent Annette Kinney, via messenger, all my folders and binders pertaining to the Essex Planter product launch. I have also been e-mailing her various documents pertaining to the trade show, i.e., the 2007 press kit, contact information, sample memos, status reports, clip reports, etc.

Regardless of the format, keep a ragged right margin. A justified right margin tends to create odd spacing in your sentences and also adds a formality not necessary for memos.

On CCs and BCCs

Your CC list should include anyone mentioned in the memo, as well as anyone who should be apprised of the information (such as a supervisor or investor). In addition to the CC list, you may decide to supply the information to other parties, without your CC list knowing about it. If that's the case, make sure you don't post your blind carbon copy (BCC) list on the memo; that would render the BCC useless. You'll have to keep track of that list off the memo page. However, you may want a certain recipient to know that others have received blind carbon copies. If that's the case, that recipient's memo can contain a BCC list on it.

Attachments

At the very end of the memo, you should notify your memo's recipients of any attachments you're including. This notification should be placed above the bottom margin, flush left, with the wording "Attachment:" followed by a brief description of the item (or items) attached.

Your Company, Your Format

Although your memos should include all of the elements described here, you can tailor the format to your company and your use. For instance, some companies put the CCs as part of the header underneath the subject and above the separation line. One agency eliminates the punctuation in its CCs, so that the names are TBrown or PGolins (rather than T. Brown or P. Golins).

Further, you may separate the memo heading with a line of dashes rather than a solid line.

Whatever your choices, use them consistently, and carry them over from memo to memo. That consistency will save setup time and also make it easy to reference previously written memos.

What If the Memo Needs to Be Revised?

If you've already sent a memo, and then realize that the information has been significantly updated or altered, reissue the memo with the new details as soon as possible. On the subject line, draw attention to the changes by adding ***REVISED*** at the end of the line. Keeping the body of your memo essentially intact, incorporate the new information that must be heeded. Of course, if the memo and its revised contents are especially time-sensitive, make sure to phone your recipients to let them know that new information is on its way.

The Writing Process

As in most writing, the most effective memos benefit from organization. You definitely should take the time to cogently set out a few points that you will include in your memo. You can do this with a brief outline, or simply by jotting down a few ideas.

While you organize the information, you also should give your memo a goal, and determine its ultimate suitability for your purpose. You can do this by asking yourself a few questions:

⮑ **What do I want this memo to accomplish?** For example, do you want it to inform, confirm, gather opinions, or achieve some other purpose?

⮑ **Is this memo really for the betterment of the company, or is it simply self-serving?** In answering this question, you want to make sure that you're writing and distributing this memo in order to contribute to the company's well-being and productivity, not your own. It's disconcerting to receive a memo that clearly ignores a mission or agenda, and comes off as a rant or a need for the sender to feel a sense of accomplishment.

⊃ **Have I ascertained the ideal next steps that this memo would prompt?** For instance, if you're writing the memo to confirm an interview, you want the recipient to conduct the interview. If it's a recommendation for someone to be hired, you want that hiring to occur.

⊃ **Is a memo the best format for this communication?** Is this message electronically sensitive? In other words, is it better suited to be communicated on paper than sent over the Web? Or, is this matter more appropriate for a phone call or a face-to-face discussion? (Parameters for those conversations are reviewed in Chapters 19 and 20).

Be Specific About Your Subject

For your subject line, you want to be specific without going overboard. Many times, your memo recipient will be instantly more focused on your memo and the memo will yield better results if you take the time to craft a complete, articulate subject line. In other words, instead of "Office Closed," your line could be more specifically worded "Office Closure Policy for Martin Luther King Jr. Day." Instead of stating "Vendor Input," strive for more attention (and probably input, too) with "Suggestions for Changing Overnight Courier."

When you select the memo format for your message, make sure you're tackling just one subject. The entire message can contain several related points, but every point should relate back to the memo's main topic.

Cute or Not?

Humor isn't always the best way—or the most appropriate—to write a subject line. While we all appreciate a sense of humor, a memo's subject line is rarely the place for it, as it can be misconstrued. You're better off simply and concisely stating the memo's purpose, rather than trying to be cute or making a pun. While humor may draw a reader in, it may also deflect and be incongruent with the true seriousness of the memo.

In the Opening

Some memos begin with a bottom-line statement, a lowdown on or summary statement of the memo's purpose that also notifies the reader of where the memo's heading. This statement should immediately mirror your memo's topic. Unless your memo delves into a sensitive issue or bears bad news, it will most likely benefit from this bottom-line-first approach.

In some cases, you also may need to provide context in your opening sentence or paragraph, some background to help the reader home in on the memo's purpose. In these instances, you'll also state the problem that prompted you to write the memo.

In any case, you want to give the readers an idea of what's in store in this memo, and let them know it's well worth the read.

The Meat of the Matter

Following the outline or notes you jotted down to initiate the memo, the opening should then always flow naturally into the paragraphs that round out the memo. This part of the memo offers solutions or recommendations to a problem, further information about a policy or plan, or details and descriptions pertaining to the memo's topic.

As you write and edit, include only the information that's needed in the specific context of the memo, steering clear of details that may be insignificant or off-topic. If your paragraphs seem convoluted, spend some time trying to rearticulate them. You may need to take a second look at your outline, and break it down further.

As you write your discussion segment, include all the details that support your ideas. In conveying your information, think of the way a news story is written: begin with the facts or statements that are most important, and then flesh those out with supporting elements. This flow may also entail your working from general to more specific information, and then segueing into further considerations and recommendations.

For easier reading, you may also consider listing your important points or details with numbers or bullets, rather than paragraphs. If you're including more than one list, be sure that they all follow the same style and format (in other words, that they're all complete sentences, or all begin with action verbs, for instance).

After you wrap up the memo's main points, try to read it from your recipient's perspective to verify that your messages are coming across clearly, and that your memo makes sense overall.

Divvy up the Details

Remember to help your reader follow your train of thought and the memo's purpose. If your memo contains several aspects to a situation but they're all related, break down the memo into sections that have different headings. For example, if you're giving an account of a meeting and suggested follow-up, break down the details into headings such as "Budget," "Marketing," and "Operations." If you're issuing an itinerary of travel or events, specify what will happen each day, where the events will take place, and the times. Stick with headings that are clear and brief.

If your memo exceeds a page—and if appropriate to your memo's topic—consider beginning the memo with a separate summary segment to briefly touch upon the key points or recommendations that follow.

Your Case in Closing

Too often, memos end with no definitive point. Take the time to make yours end in a way that will meet the goal you've set for it. End by kindly explaining the action you want your memo recipient to take, and include how you can make those actions easier (by being available for questions, for example).

One More Consideration

If you use memos to communicate short reports, the format takes on a different look. You may attach appendices, or break the memo's text into sections. If references arise in it, you need to include a list of those at the end. In this kind of memo format, sentences and paragraphs take on more of a report look and tend to be longer.

The following are examples of different types of memos:

O JOY COSMETICS

112 Seaside Complex, A-420

Laguna Beach, CA 92651

949/555-0205

www.ojoy.com

Memorandum

TO: Dierdre Ellington

FROM: Madison Humphrey

DATE: August 12, 2007

RE: Confirmation for COSMETICS QUARTERLY "Your Typical 9-to-5" Column on August 14

CC: M. Gonzales, T. Ringer, T. Thorington

We have confirmed that you will be speaking with Phoebe Hunter, West Coast editor of COSMETICS QUARTERLY, for a 20-minute phone interview for the November issue's "Your Typical 9-to-5" column.

<u>You will be calling Phoebe at 323/555-3550 on Wednesday, August 14 at 10:00 A.M.</u>

As we discussed, she will be asking you questions relevant to this column. For your answers, you can draw on a composite day. Your experiences may include:

- A particular challenge in the day
- An accomplishment you're particularly proud of
- How modeling has prepared you for being a cosmetics consultant
- A variety of assignments you have faced since joining OJOY
- How you strive to keep the work and your approach to it "fresh"

You can call me at 310/555-5333 if you have any questions.

I will phone you at 10:30 A.M. on Wednesday to get your feedback regarding the interview. Afterward, I will check in with Phoebe to conduct follow-up as well.

DeMANNING ACCOUNTING SERVICES

8909 Sunrise Boulevard, Suite 207

Des Moines, IA 50309

515/555-0111

Memorandum

TO: Fran DeManning

FROM: Daniel Dickens

DATE: August 20, 2007

RE: New Business Opportunities with Valejo Construction

CC: H. Windom

. . . .

Valejo Construction is interested in pursuing new opportunities with us in other services we can provide them, particularly as their upcoming construction project, Town Center at Harvest Fields, breaks ground on October 1.

At this point, they would—on the most basic level—want to discuss our company performing bookkeeping services for the new project. (I've attached a brochure for the new shopping center to give you an idea of the scope, budget, and timetable of the construction). However, our coming on board is a sensitive issue, as they would have to discontinue their current relationship with Tried-and-True Bookkeeping Services.

In our preliminary discussions, I mentioned our enthusiasm in helping them in any way possible. However, we would have to investigate legal ramifications of taking on this project. In addition, they are amenable to our expanding our services with them to include budgeting for projects they currently have on the drawing boards for 2007, 2008, and 2009.

I would be interested in your initial thoughts on proceeding. I've coordinated a meeting time with Bette, and she has set aside time for us to discuss this situation and the inherent possibilities after the staff meeting this Friday morning (8/22). I will reconfirm your schedule with her tomorrow.

Attachment: Town Center at Harvest Fields

The Rules for Effective Memos

Give your memo a thorough checkup with these rules for the most effective memos:

- ➲ Make sure you've identified the audience and the topic.
- ➲ Make sure your memo only has one subject.
- ➲ Keep the reader focused with your intention and bottom-line up front. Most memos, particularly those that make requests or announcements, are read quickly.
- ➲ Be coherent by limiting each paragraph to one idea. Keep sentence and paragraph lengths relatively short. Avoid complex sentence structure, technical jargon, and overly elaborate words.
- ➲ Use the first person, as in "I" and "we," and stick with active verbs. Also, though you should strike a conversational tone, don't become chatty.
- ➲ Be kind to your reader by using subject heads, bullets, or numbered lists to make important information stand out.
- ➲ Don't repeat yourself. Check your sentences, and check them again. Is there information that's simply a rewording of another sentence, passage, or paragraph?
- ➲ Try to keep the memo to less than a page.
- ➲ Let the reader know if there are attachments. If they receive the memo without them, they'll know to ask for them.
- ➲ Finally, of course, proofread.

Also, make sure that you're following procedure, protocol, and a strategy for your memos to get results:

- ➲ When determining your memo's audience, don't leapfrog. In other words, make sure that you're addressing those you need to, and haven't jumped the chain of command.
- ➲ Conclude with steps for action, be it to congratulate a new employee, attend a meeting, or find a new concrete supplier by this Friday. If you want a response by a certain day and time, include those specifics.

- If you state a problem, offer a solution, or at least a plan for further action.
- Don't use confrontational words like "insist" or "demand."
- Avoid biased language at all times, as well as inappropriate references to gender, age, disability, or ethnicity.

▶▶ **Test Drive**

Take a look at the e-mails you've sent over the past few days and ask yourself these questions:

- Which would have made more of an impression if it had been sent on company letterhead?
- Did I put the company or myself at risk by transmitting sensitive information that would have been better communicated in a memo?
- Was there an e-mail (or two) that would have been more effective had it contained tables, columns, or the like?

PART **2**

Putting Words to Work

Defining a Letter's Purpose

The business letter is the prime vehicle for sensitive or serious communication outside your workplace, especially for that pertaining to legal, financial, or personnel matters. Too often, once again, e-mail has become the preferred method of communication, though a letter is often more appropriate and provides a better format for getting a message across.

A letter is your most formal communication mode and—as such—may have the best chance of getting your recipient's attention. You should send a letter when approaching new outlets for business, collecting late payments, hiring someone, or extending goodwill to a long-term customer.

How Important Is the Letter You're Sending?

If you're sending a letter that requires legal proof of being received, consider options at the U.S. Post Office. Don't just assume your letter will be or has been received. Complaint letters sent to other companies or collection letters sent to customers, for example, should be sent by registered mail, so that you can obtain proof of receipt. Another benefit: Many times the recipient, on the sheer fact that there is a record of receipt, will realize the seriousness that the sender has literally attached to the letter and take care of business immediately.

Answering these questions will help you decide whether to send a letter:

- ➲ Are you dealing with sensitive information, or information that may have legal ramifications?
- ➲ Do you hope to create a good first impression, or a lasting one?
- ➲ Do you need to convey urgency or the importance of the matter at hand?
- ➲ Does the matter require you to keep an official record or preserve documentation?
- ➲ Do you need to ensure that the information is kept safe and protected?

If any of these situations apply, you should follow through on drafting a letter rather than writing an e-mail.

Kinds of Business Letters

Because business letters are generally brief, they can be judged on small but important aspects, such as proper wording, tone, grammar, punctuation, and—exceptionally important—openings and closings. In addition, don't use the opportunity to try new or inventive ways for getting a message across.

In business, several occasions arise that warrant good letter writing. No matter what kind of business letter you're drafting, the same rules of good writing—such as grammar, word choice, punctuation, and spelling—apply to each one. Following is a list of the most common types of letters that small businesses need to be aware of and learn how to compose. Later, this chapter delves into the structure and differences of each. The most common letters include:

- Introduction, in hopes of generating new business
- Adjustment, in appeasing a customer so that he or she will continue to do business with your company
- Cover, explaining a proposal, survey, or other document to follow
- Follow-up to a meeting
- Collection of payment
- Complaint regarding a situation or product
- Refusal of services
- Rejection of a job candidate

(In Chapter 16, you'll learn about how to write a sales letter, which is extremely helpful in direct marketing.)

Format

No matter the type of business letter, the basic guidelines for format and content remain the same.

For starters, make sure that you are sending your letter on company letterhead. For your business letter to be taken seriously, you have to be serious in your presentation of it. Letters can be very impressive tools for engendering goodwill for your company, creating new business opportunities, keeping customers, and explaining your company's stance on a matter. That being the case, your company benefits immeasurably from using legitimate letterhead, professionally printed, with all pertinent company information (such as address, phone number, and Web site) included. If a stopgap measure is needed, or in the case of an emergency situation, create a single sheet of letterhead using your Microsoft Word program. Once you have your company logo, a place to do business, and a Web site, creating company letterhead is a simple—and necessary—endeavor. Don't wait long to get yours in place.

Below your company's logo and information, each letter should include the first seven of these components, and may include the last two as well:

1. The date, two lines below the last line of the company's information, flush left margin

2. The address, four lines below the date, of the person the letter is being sent to: his or her name, title, and company (if appropriate); and his or her address, all at flush left margin

3. The salutation, two lines below the inside address, of the person being sent the letter, followed by a colon, as in "Dear Mr. Kensington:"; also at flush left margin

4. The body copy, beginning two lines below the salutation, in either block or modified block paragraph format, which addresses the purpose, information, and details of your letter

5. Complimentary closing, two lines below the last sentence, such as "Sincerely yours,"; also at flush left margin

6. Your signature, in blue or black ink

7. Your name and title, typed four lines below the complimentary closing, also at flush left margin

8. Another two lines down, the word "Enclosure" or "Attachment," if any item will accompany the letter
9. Two lines down, "cc:", followed by the names of people to whom you will send copies of this letter

The Business of Writing the Letter

No matter what type of letter you need to write, you first must establish your goal for the letter, decide who will receive it, and imbue it with the appropriate tone.

First off, delve into the three Ds:

Detect the letter's mission, purpose, or goal: Why do you need to write this letter? What situation has arisen? What needs to be fixed? What do you want this letter to accomplish?

Determine the letter's audience: Who are you trying to reach with this letter, and how will reaching that person change, fix, or solve the situation, or achieve any other specific outcome?

Decide the letter's tone: Once you've established the purpose and audience, how light or stern should your tone be? While business letters should always be professional and polite, how can yours strike a unique stance to prompt immediate attention and action?

Outline, Organize, Outreach

After you've set up your three Ds, take some time to prepare an outline for your letter, or at least write down some ideas down that will allow your letter to flow. Ask yourself:

- What is the main subject of this letter?
- What precipitated my writing this letter?
- How can I best bring my point across? (for example, a chronological listing of events, a summary of past experience, descriptions of key problems)

➲ What is the desired outcome of the letter? (for example, to receive a refund, to be hired, to rectify a business arrangement)

For Openers

Your opening paragraph should be friendly, but also make your letter's purpose immediately apparent to your intended audience. Don't bluntly word it or dance around it, but do get right to the point with specifics. For example, the following is a paragraph that needs improvement:

A litany of unpleasant experiences that we can't believe would have happened have arisen from our dealings with your company and we are extremely distraught after placing more than $2,500 in orders last Friday. At this point, we are completely unsatisfied with the service you have provided, and we will take action if you don't respond to this letter very soon.

Here is an example of a better opening paragraph:

While our company placed more than $2,500 in orders on Friday, August 5, we are concerned with the way our business has been handled, and need to discuss within the next two business days how the current situation can be rectified.

Getting It Down

In the paragraphs that follow the first one, you should continue to justify your letter's main purpose. Use background information, supporting details, and pertinent facts and figures to add heft and credence to your letter's quest. In closing, review the letter's purpose once more and, if appropriate, clearly state or request a course of action.

One Page, Please

Try to keep your letters to one page. If you deem it necessary to continue on to a second page, make sure to clearly label the following pages with a page number, followed by a succinct notation of the letter's topic, such as "Page 2/Petersen Proposal."

Avoid These in Letter Writing

Implementing certain key strategies will make your letter even more potent. For instance, don't begin a letter with "I." When you do, you cheat yourself of a stronger opening. Usually, when you substitute another sentence for one beginning with "I," you'll find that your letter leads off stronger and has more impact.

This opening sentence needs improvement:

I really enjoyed meeting you Tuesday at the teamwork seminar.

Here's an example of a better opening sentence:

The hospitality you extended on Tuesday proved to me once again your company's well-deserved reputation for embracing teamwork.

In addition, keep emotions out of the letter-writing picture. You'll have more success bringing your point across—and getting action—with facts, clearly stated, that are void of frustration or annoyance.

The Structure of Different Letters

While you shouldn't go with a one-size-fits-all approach, you can benefit from being aware of how to make the different types of letters their most effective.

Introduction Letter

You'll often use an introduction letter in hopes of generating new business. This type of letter serves as your calling card. It's your chance to introduce yourself to a prospective client, pointing out your attributes and the reasons why another company or an individual should do business with you. The letter should emphasize why your company would help the other one thrive; list key, pertinent accomplishments; and close with an action plan, as in "I will call you this week to determine if your needs and my company's abilities mesh."

For this type of letter, you may also want to include a brochure about your company, a recent article about it, or some other piece of credible propaganda. But don't bombard the recipient with materials he or she hasn't asked for.

Adjustment Letter

An adjustment letter strives to appease a customer or client or to make amends. In doing so, this type of letter recognizes a problem, acknowledges the time and energy the customer or client has spent trying to correct it, and offers a solution or some form of compensation (or both). The letter writer should be absolutely respectful in the approach.

Salutations and Closings

If you don't know the name of the person to whom you're writing, use "Dear Sir or Madam." If you do know the name, you can include Mr., Mrs., Miss, or Ms. When writing to a female, etiquette experts prefer business correspondence be directed to "Ms." unless you've been expressly asked to use "Mrs." or "Miss." Do be absolutely certain of a person's gender—particularly in the case of gender-neutral names such as Pat, Robin, and Tracy—before deciding to use the masculine or feminine. If you're tired of using "Sincerely" as your complimentary closing, a few others you can try include "Cordially," "Best regards," "Yours truly," "Best wishes," and "Respectfully yours." No matter how creative you may want to be, a letter is never the time to lapse into closings that are informal, such as "Cheers," "Ciao," or "So long for now."

In writing an adjustment letter, the first paragraph should focus on a clear understanding of the recipient's situation, segue into how much the company appreciates doing business with the recipient, detail a remedy, and conclude with gratitude for patience and allowance in fixing the problem.

Here's an example of an adjustment letter:

BABY BABY
217A Carriage Place
Tampa, FL 33606
813/555-BABY p. 813/555-2710 f.
www.babybaby.com

April 17, 2006

Mrs. Evelyn Everett
459 Bayshore Drive
Tampa, FL 33605

Dear Mrs. Everett:

We apologize for the frustration you've experienced in updating your registry. We know that your baby showers—and new arrival—are quickly approaching, and that you depend on our hallmarks of attentive service and easy shopping to help you in these months.

We value your patronage at Baby Baby, and appreciate that you chose us to register for the necessities and more that you'll need for your new baby. As the store manager, I have personally seen to it that items you registered for have been correctly added to your registry, and gifts that you have already received are reflected in the registry list as well. Further, the duplicate items that were erroneously added have also been taken off the registry. Please view the corrected list at www.babybaby.com/registrylist/everett to confirm that all the necessary revisions have been made to your satisfaction.

In my appreciation for your patience, please accept this $20 gift card to be used any way you like at our store. We look forward to furnishing your baby's life with all the essentials, and helping your shower guests in finding just the right gift for your baby-to-be. Thank you for taking the time to let me know about this problem, and giving me the opportunity to correct it.

Best regards,

Trudy Bedlow
Manager

Enclosure: Gift card

Cover Letter

Cover letters typically spend brief paragraphs explaining a report, proposal, or survey that will follow. These are the business world's equivalent of the letter that accompanies a resume. In it, you should open with enticing words that encourage the recipient to read the attachment, and summarize the main points of the contents that follow.

Collection Letter

Collection letters are written to garner delinquent monies owed. Even so, never take a vindictive tone, and realize that you may be sending letters for 30, 60, and 90 days past due before a collection agency is called in. Therefore, save your strongest words for later in the process. Remember that you most likely want to keep this customer, and that your bill may have been lost during a transition of staff or computer systems, or may remain unpaid because of a question. Whatever the situation, initially give your customer the benefit of the doubt. In each notice you send, take a professional tack, convey your appreciation of their past business up front, and close with your looking forward to doing future business with them. Also in your closing, offer different ways for the customer to respond to your letter, such as a phone number and an e-mail address, either to pay the bill or to set up a payment plan.

Follow-up Letter

A follow-up letter shows continued interest from you—usually pertaining to beginning a working relationship—after a phone call or meeting. A follow-up letter has too easily been shunned recently in favor of a simple e-mail, but you'll make a far more commanding and impressive impression with a letter. Take this opportunity to recap strengths and demonstrate enthusiasm. When you send a letter of this kind, you also benefit from having your company logo create a lasting image in the recipient's mind.

Complaint Letter

These letters, in which you're expressing your dissatisfaction with someone or a company's handling of a situation, policy, or product, also have the tendency to prompt harsh words—but resist the temptation.

Here again, taking the emotion out of the equation will make your letter stronger, and will more likely incite swift action. Begin the letter by letting the company know what prompted you to do business with it in the first place: good value, excellent reputation, stellar craftsmanship. Then, calmly and exactingly describe how doing business with the company has resulted in your current complaint. Offer details, but don't go overboard. Keep your sentences clear. In describing situations, you may feel the need to run down many aspects of the scenario, but this measure can be confusing for the reader and hard to follow. Offer an organized approach for your details. That approach may include an itemized list or chronology, and copies of receipts, statements, or agreements. In the letter, don't rush to angry judgment; give the company a chance to respond and fix the situation. In your conclusion, let your recipient know that you realize that your disappointment with the company will be short-lived, and that you expect to hear from them by a specified date. As in the collection letter scenario, use second and third approaches—if necessary—to escalate the seriousness of your tone, but again, never be disrespectful, sarcastic, or angry in your words.

Samples to Sort Through

Letters can take on a variety of personalities, so make sure you're using the format and approach that best suits your situation. At *www.insiderreports.com*, you can find literally hundreds of sample letters. While you wouldn't copy them verbatim, of course, you can find sample formats and a few ideas for getting started if you feel stumped. The array of letters will also give you a window into how companies take a professional tack in conducting business.

Refusal or Rejection Letter

These types of letters—which many try to avoid at all costs—share many attributes, with refusal pertaining to turning down an offer or service extended, and rejection referring to denying a job candidate employment. Never begin the letter blurting out the bad news. Again, you want to handle the situation professionally and tactfully, by explaining your sincere appreciation for being asked, for instance, to contribute goods for a philanthropic event, or your appreciation of the candidate's interest. In both cases, provide a context in the opening, or an arena for the news. Then list pertinent details that have prompted the decision. Close with good wishes. In the first scenario, that may entail good wishes for a successful event and the opportunity to be involved in the future. In the rejection letter, the last paragraph could describe the many skills that the job candidate will bring to another company soon. In the case of either refusal or rejection, handle the act of writing the letter swiftly; dragging out letting someone know bad news is unkind and disrespectful.

Bad News and Goodwill Messages

As described in the refusal and rejection letter scenarios, even when doling out bad news in a letter, don't endanger a future working relationship. When you're committed to stay in an industry and be a success in it, you undoubtedly will repeatedly come in contact and communication with some of the same executives, employees, vendors, and even media. Your correspondence can be a boon or a detriment to those relationships. Use your words to cultivate respect rather than incur wrath. Giving bad news is a part of doing business, but it doesn't have to be done insensitively, disrespectfully, or tactlessly. Many bad-news scenarios have eventually ended up paying dividends to the executives who handled the situations with dignity. When you use goodwill in your letters, bad news may someday lead to good news.

Evaluating a Letter's Content

Always in business communication, grammar and punctuation do count; letters aren't exempt from that rule. Don't lose credibility with a letter that hasn't been proofread properly. Companies—big and small—fall victim to letters that are rife with misspellings, misplaced words, incomplete sentences, and worse. If you've taken the time to write a letter, ensure that it leaves a favorable impression for you and your company by also taking the time to double-check it and possibly having someone else give it a once-over, too.

The Power of the Pen

During my career as a consultant, many employers have pointed out how much they appreciated receiving a letter I had written, and how much that made me stand out from the other prospective vendors. Sometimes, e-mail just won't make the impression that you're striving to create. Also, though you would never want to ramble on in a letter, it does serve as a more appropriate vehicle in which to spend a few more words to reinforce a message, your company's advantages, or your gratitude.

In many cases, the employer hired me as a vendor noting that, since I had taken the time to send him or her an articulate letter, I also—in the process—let that person know that I would be handling his or her business with the same precision, care, and thoughtfulness. Needless to say, those same jobs often resulted in referrals that led to other positions.

The next time you want someone to hire you or your company, consider sending a letter of introduction, or—if an introduction has already taken place—a follow-up letter. Make it sincere, conversational, and solid, and get it to its intended party promptly.

You'll be pleasantly surprised to find that, in many instances, a letter says more than the words on the page: it can leave a lasting, positive impact on your career and your company's success.

A Checklist

In giving your letter a final evaluation before sending it off, answer these questions:

- ⮑ Is your letter limited to one, and only one, subject?
- ⮑ Does your first paragraph set the scene in a pithy and respectful way?
- ⮑ Have you kept your subject matter as simple as possible?
- ⮑ Is related information grouped together?
- ⮑ Have you cut unnecessary or redundant words, information, and statements?
- ⮑ Is every statement in the letter accurate?
- ⮑ Have you employed a conversational style?

○ Have you used familiar words and eye-friendly formatting to make the letter as accessible as possible?

○ Have you included everything the reader needs to know?

Great Letters as a Guide

If you've written a letter that you feel serves your purpose extremely well, make sure to keep a copy of it, and use it as a guide for future, similar correspondence. While each situation is different, you may find that doing your homework the first time in a certain type of letter has prepared you for sending out another one that's in the same category, saving you time in the process.

▶▶ Test Drive

In analyzing other company's business letters, you often get a better feel for how you can make yours more effective. Look at today's mail pile, and take a business letter out of the stack. Determine:

○ Whether the writer followed business-letter writing rules
○ What category the letter fits in
○ The purpose of the letter
○ How clear the writer's approach to you was
○ What was done right in the writing
○ What you would recommend to improve the letter
○ Whether the letter was proofread
○ Whether the letter ultimately succeeds

Get the Business

Many people confuse business plans with business proposals. A business proposal is very different from a business plan: with a proposal, you're going after new business for your company, which you may—or may not—have been asked to do.

In some cases, to get this business, you may be responding to a Request for a Proposal (an RFP). This document, which could seem rather official and come from a government or corporate entity aiming to secure a vendor, succinctly lays out exactly the elements your business proposal should contain. You'll learn more about RFPs later in this chapter.

Aside from those instances, business proposals rarely follow a standard format. Instead, they take on many different formats, and may or may not contain pages and pages of descriptions and ideas. However, the bottom line is the same: to get new business for your company. Whether you're a drapery manufacturer, florist, bed-and-breakfast owner, car wash operator, coffee exporter, costume rental warehouse . . . whatever your business, you are likely to reach a point at which you have to figure out how to make it grow. To make that happen, or to keep from having "all your eggs in one basket," you will need to write new business proposals. Often, business proposals will also help you formulate "maintenance" proposals, or intermittent plans that keep your business going—or expanding into other services—with the same client.

In this chapter, you'll learn what to include in your proposal, and what not to include, and learn how to stick to a cohesive plan that will let your company shine.

Laying Out a Proposal's Prime Elements

With a proposal, you're trying to convince your audience that you're the best person or company for a specific job. Proposals rely on informative, persuasive writing in an attempt to educate the reader, and convince that reader to hire you. In assessing your mission from the outset, ask yourself:

➲ Who are you writing for?

➲ What is the problem your audience is trying to solve, or the success they are trying to achieve?

➲ Do they have any special needs or requirements in the timing or format of the proposal?

Your Audience

A consistent rule in business communication is that you must be absolutely sure that you know your audience. Your writing has to convince your audience that you know what they do, what they need, and how you best fit in with those needs. In that same vein, your writing should speak their language. Your words should show your familiarity with who they are and how they do business.

The Scope and Criteria of the Project or Relationship

Next, you want to ascertain what your working relationship will entail with offering this business proposal. For instance, what problem will your company solve for this audience? How will you make them successful in a certain venture? How will you make their life easier as a whole? In this realm, you need to describe your understanding of their needs in their terms. Only then will you be able to effectively put into words the reason why you're the one who deserves their business.

Research Involved

More than likely, your business proposal will require at least some research. Ideally, some of that will be accomplished in an initial meeting, phone call, or interview. If possible, find at least one contact at the company who can supply you with additional or follow-up information about the company's goals with respect to your business proposal. In addition, thoroughly investigate the company to glean as much information as possible. Some of your research should include:

➲ The company's Web site

➲ Trusted, approachable professionals who have previously worked with the company

- ⤴ Reference to articles about the company in trade journals and the consumer press
- ⤴ A Google search that leads to Web sites with relevant information
- ⤴ Information about competitors
- ⤴ Current knowledge, press, or information about the project itself that your proposal is addressing
- ⤴ Costs involved in performing the project

Responding to an RFP

As previously mentioned, sometimes you'll write a proposal in response to a solicited bid for your services. RFPs take on as many different forms as do business proposals themselves, but they offer exact guidelines for what the proposals should cover. That being the case, it is absolutely essential that you furnish exactly what is asked for to be considered a viable candidate for the job or project.

Further, if they've asked that you submit the proposal in a specific format, follow that as well. Often, those companies who don't take these aspects seriously are immediately eliminated from the proposal process.

Read the RFP carefully, ask questions about it to clarify points and show your interest, pay attention to deadlines and format instructions, and conduct research that will demonstrate your knowledge of the company's unique needs and overall industry which will help you devise an appropriate, substantial proposal.

Responding to an RFP is rewarding in other ways too: it can fuel ideas or help you formulate components you want to include in an unsolicited bid for business to another company or entity.

Generating Ideas for Proposals

Once you have your purpose, goal, and audience in mind, but before you begin actually writing the proposal, take some time to engage in a brainstorm session. Once you do, you'll realize that your proposal's prime components will flow much easier. Brainstorms aren't simply creative fodder.

When conducted correctly, they can supply you with fresh, innovative ideas, and elements that will truly make your company stand apart from others that may be submitting proposals. Brainstorms don't just belong in advertising agencies; they can benefit accounting firms, engineers, and lawyers, too.

Looking for RFPs?

If you're interested in learning what an RFP may demand in your particular business or industry, check out samples and examples online. For instance, the California Department of Health Services and the Pennsylvania Department of Corrections are just two government entities that devote part of their Web site to help potential bidders understand their RFP process. For instance, you can see a sample of a detailed accounting services RFP at *www.langancpa.com/client/SampleRFPS*. Type your industry's name and "RFP sample" into a search engine, and investigate what the search turns up.

While you may have a tendency to dive right into writing the proposal, you'll be much better off conducting at least one brainstorm session to cultivate ideas. The session will also help you identify gaps you might realize should be filled in delineating your experience and your approach.

For the session:

- ➲ Gather a few participants that you trust. These people can be colleagues in your company or—depending on your company's size—some trusted professionals from your field (who won't be competing with you for the business).
- ➲ Set a time limit of no more than an hour to conduct the session. If the proposal you're crafting is multilayered, with many complicated components, set up separate one-hour sessions (not back-to-back) to address each one.
- ➲ At the start of the session, offer a bottom-line summary of the proposal's goal and audience. Then, detail what you hope the session will provide: ideas that will enhance the proposal in its mission to garner the new business.

⮑   Also offer these rules at the start of the session: no one is allowed to be negative or put down others' ideas; ideas should not be restrained by cost, time or manpower; and every idea can be built upon.

⮑   Have someone record every idea—preferably on a flipchart—that is uttered during the session.

⮑   At the end of the hour, have every participant number the ideas from favorite to least favorite.

⮑   Finally, take all the ideas and determine which should be fleshed out and incorporated in the proposal.

The Proposal Parts

In the front matter of the proposal, you need to include a cover letter, title page, a table of contents, and the executive summary. Moving into the actual proposal portion, you'll write an introduction and detail the capabilities and attributes that make your company a perfect match for taking on this business. In the main section of the proposal, you'll set up your objectives, or the goals that the proposal sets up; the strategies behind achieving those goals; and the tactics to fulfill them.

At the end of the proposal, you should include mini-biographies of the personnel involved on your team; a budget that itemizes expenses and costs; details concerning materials, facilities, and equipment involved (if necessary); qualifications and accomplishments of your business; and, if appropriate, appendices and a bibliography of works cited.

A Summary to Begin It

As with a business plan, you'll most likely need an executive summary for your proposal. Also as with a business plan, you should wait until you've completed your entire proposal before writing it. The executive summary provides a concise description of your company, the purpose of the proposal, the essentials of the program and the services you'll provide for this specific job, the benefits that will result from hiring your company, the costs and expenses expected, and those who will be working to get the job done.

The Introduction and How Your Company Fits the Bill

As you begin the proposal, be mindful that you're trying to convince a company or entity that you understand exactly what it needs. In so doing, let the company know that you realize its obstacles, and know how to overcome them.

Sometimes It's Just a Bid

You might think your company wouldn't ever need to put together a proposal. If you fall into that mindset, consider any opportunity that comes your way to earn—or keep—business. It might not be called a proposal; you might get a call for an estimate of services or a request for a bid. In either of those cases, you still should treat the inquiry as a proposal. Put together a plan that covers the basics asked for—and maybe more. Don't pull in unnecessary information, but realize that while your proposal might not be pages and pages, it's still a chance to snag a new customer or client.

Unfortunately, many companies get so wrapped up in presenting the best proposal possible that, in their enthusiasm, they neglect to make a case for why they understand this prospective client's needs, how they can carry out their proposal well, and why they're the best company for the job. Remember, you or your company may not be the only one vying for the job. In a proposal, make sure that you include your company's credentials and specifically why those credentials make your company so ideally suited to handle the project or job in question.

In addition, offer work samples of previous jobs, particularly those that highlight your success in overcoming challenges that the potential client may face on this project. Depending on your business, work samples may be written materials, pictures, reports, or downloaded materials from your company Web site. However, in making a case for your company's value, concentrate on the services you provide that will benefit the client, not on tangential accomplishments or side areas that won't immediately impact this particular project.

Objectives: The "What"

This section sets up the overall purpose of the proposal, and how you would define the goals that the proposal should strive to accomplish. In so doing, the objectives refer to the "what" of the proposal: what the needs are, what the focus should be, and what the outcome should be. These should be considered specific, concrete, measurable, and achievable in a timetable that you provide later in the proposal.

The what also sets up the "what can I do to service the client with this proposal" mode of thinking. In other words, by stating the prospective client's goals, you're showcasing your knowledge and understanding of their business—an easy segue into how your company will uniquely provide benefits that will be detailed later in the proposal.

Often, you can help yourself in drafting this section by using action verbs to state the objectives. For instance, say a new cable network is launching and your marketing firm has been tapped to present a proposal to consult the network for the launch. Your objectives may be to attract advertisers to buy 50 percent of the airtime; to develop a publicity effort that drives sampling; to capture attention among teens 12 to 17. If you own a wallpaper company, and are soliciting the business of a boutique hotel that is coming to your town, your objectives may be to create a lavish atmosphere for the hotel guest; to provide patterns that are unique to rooms and suites but still match each room's décor; and to work seamlessly with the hotel's interior decorating team.

Keep on Topic

Your company may offer several products or services, or both, and you may feel the need to discuss all of the opportunities you can offer to a prospective client or entity. Resist that urge. Keep focused on the product or service that links directly to the problem that your proposal is specifically trying to solve. Don't confuse or water down that message by throwing in a host of other attributes, valid as they may be. Once you establish a relationship with a new customer, you'll undoubtedly have time to mention or introduce—organically—other capabilities that you and your company can bring to the business.

Making Your Company's Proposal Stand Out — Inside Track

In fulfilling RFPs, think about what you can bring or implement in your proposal that would make you stand out from the competition. Make sure your proposal is nice, neat, and crisply presented. If your industry warrants it, consider attractively packaging it in an eye-catching binder or folder. Chain office stores offer a multitude of ideas and products for presentations and packaging. Spend some time reviewing and choosing what could work for yours. If your proposal is being sent as an attachment to an e-mail, consider having your initial page contain simple line art or color. If you opt for color, make sure it's not a harsh or bold shade that would make words hard to read.

Your industry may also lend itself to parts of your proposal being "off the page." I've been involved with putting together several marketing proposals in which, instead of listing all the company's successes on a page, we produced a video that showcased clips from events or broadcast coverage. I've also helped caterers try to land business in which part of their proposal involved serving some of their specialties to give prospective clients a taste of what was in store.

In working on your proposal, devote part of a brainstorming session to the creative presentation your proposal could employ. Remember, however, to always keep it professional and don't go over the top. While you want to strike your audience as inventive and innovative, you don't want to convey an image of being outlandish or out of touch.

Again, your proposal's objectives should correlate directly and specifically to the prospective client's needs. If you're coming up with objectives that you find compelling but that hold little interest for the company you're trying to please, your proposal will be unsuccessful.

You may choose to use the action verbs you've selected to present the proposal's objectives in bullet points, or write these paragraphs in prose form.

Tactics: The How

Now, how will you fulfill the goals you've decided upon? You should look at the strategies you will use to implement the goals. This component helps differentiate how your company will bring its own unique slant to getting the job done.

In this area of the proposal, you need to explain the details of each tactic, the responsibilities involved, how each tactic relates to a specific objective outlined, and how the job will be done, broken down into separate tasks. You are providing definitive details on the methods and procedures you'll use to accomplish the goals you've set forth.

The Work, Budget, Personnel, and Timing

Your tactics—the main thrust of your proposal with the solution you're providing—will only seem authentic if you attach timetables for the work to be performed, a breakdown of monies associated with getting the work done, and descriptions of people who will do the work.

Each tactic should tie back in to each of these aspects. In formulating your tactics, make sure that you've answered these questions:

- Who will do the work?
- Who will manage the work?
- Who is the primary contact focused on the work?
- What are the deliverables?
- What is required to have each deliverable completed?
- What will each one cost?
- What is the project's entire budget?
- When will the job start?
- When will the job be finished?
- What milestones will keep the job on track?
- What is the payment schedule?
- How will the customer's satisfaction be guaranteed?

Tactical Alert

When it comes to laying out your tactics, be truthful. Don't offer pie-in-the-sky elements that you—and possibly they—know couldn't reasonably be completed. By all means, promise only what you can deliver in your tactics.

As you will see in the following example, proposals can take on many shapes and forms. This one presents a proposal's basic parts.

VERDE LANDSCAPE DESIGN
8270 Springville Boulevard, Suite E
Richmond, VA 23241

PROPOSAL PREPARED FOR:
Hilary and Rob Montano
827 St. Regis Way
Richmond, VA 23233

DATE: August 26, 2006

PROJECT: Landscaping front and back yards of the Montano family residence, located at 827 St. Regis Way, Richmond, VA 23233

SECTION A: WORK TO BE COMPLETED AND COSTS TO PERFORM

Description of Activity	Amount
1. Prep and grading of soil for planting	$1,200.00
2. Installation of various plant materials (Verde Landscape Design will meet with Clients to discuss plant palette for both front and back yards)	$3,100.00
3. Installation of two 24-inch box trees (Specimens for front yard to be determined with client direction)	$1,200.00
4. Seeding of lawn (Approximately 4,200 sq. ft. covering both front and back yards)	$2,850.00
5. Installation of bender board to separate plants and sod (In both front and back yards)	800.00
6. Demolition of all hardscape and existing plant material in both front and back yards	$2,100.00
7. Dumping and hauling of all debris (Includes dumpster rental)	$1,200.00
8. Relaying of irrigation system (In front yard)	$600.00

9. Installation of 5 automatic brass irrigation valves
   (Includes timer) $3,000.00
10. Trimming, clearing, and pruning of elms (In back yard) $1,150.00
11. Installation of flagstone walkway (In front yard) $600.00

GRAND TOTAL: **$17,800.00**

SECTION B: PERSONNEL AND WORK SCHEDULES

All work to be completed by a team of four Verde Landscape Design employees who will be on site from 8:00 A.M.–5:00 P.M., Monday through Friday. They will break from 10:15–10:30 A.M., 12:30–1:00 P.M. for lunch, and 3:30–3:45 P.M.

In addition, project manager Ian Leffer will be on the site at all times. Owners Nellie Roe and Tanner Dixon will visit the site three times per week to monitor progress.

Your project manager is your day-to-day contact. Ian can be reached by cell phone at 804/555-0964.

SECTION C: SCHEDULE OF WORK AND PAYMENTS

Work is to commence on September 7, 2007, and conclude on September 28, 2007.

Payment is to be made weekly on September 11, September 18, September 25, with the balance due on completion date, September 28.

SECTION D: PAYMENT CONSIDERATIONS AND DISCLAIMERS

We remove any debris generated from our work.

Due to undetermined conditions under soil, an extra cost may occur if excess rock or debris is encountered during excavation.

When any grading is performed, an additional charge may occur if excess rock or soil needs to be moved or removed.

We are not responsible for damage due to hidden conditions.

Prices subject to change if all work on this proposal is not done in its entirety.

Permits are not included in this quote. If any permits are required, an additional cost may occur.

We cannot guarantee transplants of existing plants.

SECTION E: UPON REVIEWING

The costs specified in this proposal, and other specifications laid out, are valid from one week of date issued.

After review, please sign and date below and fax back to Ian Leffer, project manager, at 804/555-2779.

....
Client Signature   Date

....
Project Manager Signature   Date

Copies will be distributed to client, project manager, and Verde Landscape Design owners.

The Conclusion: Your Final Impression, Evaluation, and Next Steps

In your conclusion, include salient selling points that explain why your company is the best for this client. In crafting those lines, consider these questions: Why should you be selected? Why have you chosen the approaches you have? In presenting your selling points, be careful to emphasize the benefits the potential client will realize from your solution.

Your conclusion should also point out that you've built in an evaluation component to monitor progress and results. When you point out that you care enough to track your performance and make sure it's meeting intended goals, you send a strong message that you mean business about achieving objectives you've outlined. Further, you're letting the company know that your success in this project is tied in to their own success.

Finally, clearly delineate the next steps for putting the proposal in action. Perhaps at the end of the proposal you can include a line for a signature with a fax number, or set a date and time that you will call to answer any questions the company may have. Take a proactive stance in moving your proposal to the next level: being hired for the job.

▶▶ Test Drive

Think about a piece of business you've been eager to get. Now, take a look at the proposal presented earlier in this chapter.

⮫ While your business may be different from landscape design, what are the basic components in that plan—such as actions to complete or costs to perform—that you would need to include, in some fashion, in yours?

What are other components that you know you would need to include in a proposal?

Factoring in Out-of-the-Ordinary Formats

In this chapter, you'll learn that more about several other written formats you need to master for complete business communication. Each one serves a unique and important function, but they aren't always thoughtfully considered. However, when you craft the right messages and words for them, they'll enhance your company's credibility and create a favorable impression, making them destined to increase your bottom line.

Thank-You Notes

The simple courtesy extended in a thank-you note can be beneficial for your company. When you take the time to express gratitude for a service performed in the business world, you have a unique opportunity to foster goodwill. Most people are familiar with sending a thank-you note as a follow-up to a job interview. But thank-you notes and letters enjoy far more uses for those in small business or entrepreneurial ventures. Consider these opportunities for writing a thank-you note:

- To reiterate your interest in a project or product
- To make or reinforce a good impression
- To promote opportunities for further collaboration
- To strengthen positive business relationships

You also should send a thank-you note for courtesies that may have been extended to you, including these:

- A referral or recommendation
- A reply or response
- Advice or a suggestion
- Help or support
- Assistance in your absence
- Hospitality provided
- Information supplied

↻ Media exposure gained

↻ A reference or recommendation written for you

Guidelines

Your primary goal in writing a thank-you letter should be to come off as genuine. The notes don't need to be lengthy; one or two paragraphs will usually be enough. Also, because the thank-you letters discussed here pertain to business, you should write them on company letterhead. Don't tack on a thank-you to another piece of business correspondence as an afterthought or side note; give it its own place.

Try to use wording that individualizes your thank-you. While you shouldn't be overly personal in the letter, you should strive to make it memorable. Of all occasions for correspondence, the thank-you letter is the one wherein you don't want to send a generically worded message that could be about any event and written from or to just anyone.

By all means, write the thank-you letter as soon as possible after the event or act of kindness. Having to explain tardiness for a thank-you letter can detract from the goodwill it hopes to engender.

A Reason to Write a Thank-You

Giving an appropriate thank-you in the business world will never go out of style, and could increase your chances in being hired for a job. A 2005 Careerbuilder.com survey found that nearly 15 percent of hiring managers would reject a job candidate who neglected to send a thank-you letter after the interview; 32 percent said they would still consider the candidate but would hold a diminished opinion of the prospect. Among other findings: nearly 20 percent said they expected both an e-mail thank-you and a follow-up letter by post.

Correspondence for Life Occasions

Although some people think that acknowledging events such as holidays and the birthdays and anniversaries of clients and customers may seem disingenuous, the small business—more than any other—can be truly genuine in extending these kinds of everyday courtesies. As a small

Inside Track	An Occasion to Remember

Small companies are often looking for a way to stand out, to be remembered by their clients, and to make a positive impression. Some of my favorite examples of this showcase the creative ways in which some businesses achieve those goals.

A celebrity gift-buying service, which counts A-list stars, studio heads, and network presidents as their clients, realizes—more than most, probably—how busy the holidays can be. Instead of sending a holiday message to current and prospective clients and risking it being lost amid the greetings, the company sends out a specially made New Year's greeting during the first week of January—after the seasonal madness and just in time for those getting back to work to experience a new round of cheer. That's a nice association for the gift-buying service to foster.

The owner of a real estate firm took special note of his clients' move-in dates when he sold them homes. Then, each year on that anniversary, he sent them a card or note wishing them another happy year in their home.

Instead of at the traditional times to remember to buy flowers, such as Valentine's Day or Mother's Day, a florist sends out cards each year for Arbor Day. Knowing that's not a typical day to commemorate with a floral delivery, she offers a classy, natural—and yet not self-serving—tie-in to keep her business' name in front of customers.

Think about an opportunity your business might have to make an impression with an unusual, relevant note or greeting that—regularly implemented—might create a tradition that drives business.

business owner, one of the advantages in your arsenal is the friendliness of a personal touch versus the facelessness of big business.

If you are referring to an anniversary a person is celebrating with a company, write the letter on your company letterhead. If the life occasion is a personal one, a handwritten note is more appropriate.

Your greeting needn't be lengthy, just a simple recognition of the occasion. For reference, consider how you correspond with business associates during the holiday season, with "Happy Holidays" and "Here's to Prosperity in the New Year," and a signature.

The card or note you write on doesn't need to be elaborate, either. The act itself is certain to leave a positive impact.

Newsletters

With the advent of e-mail, newsletters that enhance employee, customer, and colleague relations have become increasingly popular. (Newsletters serve other purposes, too. In Chapter 14, you'll explore the value of using some types of newsletters for Web site marketing and, in Chapter 16, as sales tools.)

In this section, you'll learn the ins and outs of writing a newsletter that has some degree of news value for your employees or customers.

While the expenses incurred in producing and distributing a newsletter to be mailed (versus e-mailed) can be substantial, the printed version does:

⮑ Offer an ongoing, physical representation of your company that maintains and raises your profile

⮑ Regularly highlight your company's missions and purposes, hallmarks, events, and milestones

⮑ Provide a "face" for your company and showcase company contacts

The Writing

In writing a newsletter, you can follow these step-by-step basics. In Chapters 14 and 16, these tips will be expounded upon for endeavors specific to the areas of marketing and Web sites.

1. In setting up your newsletter format, determine how long you want your newsletter to be, and how often you'd like to distribute it. This decision could be influenced by budget or simply the amount of news you have to distribute. Be realistic about the amount of content you can regularly provide.

2. With that in mind, determine who your audience is and what they would most likely be interested in reading in your newsletter. In that spirit, don't include articles that only matter to you, or to just a few people. Keep your entire audience in mind when selecting topics to cover.

3. Make sure the information you're including is news your reader can use; for instance, relevant information that pertains to upcoming conferences or events that can be marked on a calendar, or details about a current industry trend.

4. Newsletters aren't newspapers. Concentrate on a mix of a couple of longer articles with shorter items. All the articles, blurbs, and bits should be short and to the point, and not too long on details. For the pieces, strive for more of an overview than an in-depth analysis. Take advantage of bullets, short sentences, lists, and brief paragraphs in conveying your information. If you're including an article that runs long, break it up by shuffling some of the information into sidebars.

5. If you're eager to provide more information than space allows, refer readers to your company Web site, or offer a list of magazine articles or books that elaborate on the subject matter being discussed.

In writing your articles, remember that newsletters typically have a conversational tone. While you don't want it to sound chatty or dabble in slang, do lean toward an approach that's not stodgy or too formal.

The Layout

For a newsletter, include more than one article on a page. Tap into a layout that is inviting to the eye, offering snapshots of information that are interesting, but not overwhelming.

In addition to words, use artwork to capture the reader's attention. Digital photography has made gathering photos for products, events, and the like easy and inexpensive. If you don't have access to graphics or a large budget for including photography—and even if you do—consider the inexpensive alternatives of clip art, widely available and often free.

Surveys and Questionnaires

Surveys and questionnaires present fresh, singular opportunities for you to amass a great deal of information from—typically—current and prospective customers. When you use these formats, you'll be able to collect several aspects of related data that can help your business thrive in all kinds of ways. Both formats utilize questions to gather market research for a number of purposes—including, for example, to help launch a product, trigger sales for an existing one, improve customer experiences, beef up customer loyalty, or verify data such as demographics and preferences of targeted customers.

The Questions

Before you write a questionnaire, you should first ascertain the kind of information you want to collect. To get an idea of the vastness of your options, take a cue from big companies to generate ideas for yours. Marriott, Hallmark, and Martha Stewart all routinely dole out questionnaires that ask very specific questions about their products. In reviewing their questions, you can further determine and discover the kinds of information they're trying to collect from their customers, and maybe even glean how they intend to put that data—the facts, figures, statistics, and comments—to use.

Surveys and questionnaires also represent another area in which you must be aware of the GIGO (garbage in, garbage out) effect. Ask needless questions, and you may very well end up with loads of useless information.

With a very attainable goal of procuring useful information in mind, determine: What do you want to accomplish with this questionnaire or survey? What research are you trying to collect? What's the purpose for collecting it? Will the information gathered relate back to that purpose? What do you want to do with the research once you have it, and have made sense of it?

In answering all of those questions, give the questionnaire a specific goal, whether to increase sales of your new product line, learn about your customers' buying habits, determine your clients' satisfaction, or find out if there is interest in a service you have on the drawing boards. That goal will help inform the questions you want to include in the questionnaire. Your questions can include a mix of:

- ⮑ Open-ended questions, best described as essay questions, in which the respondent can fully describe an opinion about a product or service, give suggestions on its improvement, or offer examples of its use
- ⮑ Close-ended, such as "How many times a month do you shop here?" "Do you intend to use this service in the next fiscal quarter?"
- ⮑ Escalating scale responses, in which the respondent expresses an opinion about a statement made (as in strongly agree, agree, no opinion, disagree, strongly disagree), or question posed (excellent, good, fair, poor)
- ⮑ Numerical responses, in which the respondent gives a rating or score, such as on a scale of 1 to 5, with 5 being the best

In crafting your questions, state them simply and honestly. Be careful not to confuse the reader, or pose leading or lengthy questions. After you write down your questions, go back over them to improve their clarity, and to eliminate redundancy.

Once you edit and fine-tune the questions for maximum input, ask yourself whether each of the questions directly relates back to your stated goal.

Pick Your Audience Wisely

Choose an audience that will give you the most complete, accurate information. If you're trying to find out if there are buyers for your new industrial-strength postage stamp dispensers, it would be appropriate to survey office managers and mailroom supervisors, not maitre d's and carpet installers.

Structure It Logically

Start the questionnaire with a genial introduction that identifies who it's coming from, explains its purpose, and gives a deadline for returning it.

The questions should be ordered so the easy ones are first, to encourage the respondents to develop an interest and feel for the questionnaire. Then segue into more complex queries. However, and this can be a tricky proposition, in deciding their sequence, do make sure that they flow logically from one to the next.

If you've deemed it to be part of the information you want to collect, pose questions relevant to age and income bracket, gender, address, and interests toward the end of the survey.

Tap into the Trend

A trend has surfaced with large corporations including The Home Depot, Starbucks, Chili's, and Office Depot wherein customers can fill out an online survey, and, in so doing, have a chance to win $25,000. It's a smart move on the companies' part. For $25,000—a small sum for companies of their size—they're collecting information from thousands of people. These surveys often take fifteen minutes or more to complete, but if you have the opportunity to participate, it's worth your time just to view and analyze some of the questions they ask. You'll find more than a little value in seeing the questions they're asking, how they're phrased, and surmising what the company is trying to home in on to make its business better and—ultimately—more profitable.

Just before the close of the survey or questionnaire, offer the respondent a chance to offer any suggestions, improvements, or other comments. Doing so could tip you off to an unexpected appreciation of an attribute of your product or service—or a pending problem you didn't realize you had looming.

You may also want to ask if the respondent would be interested in answering further questions. In this case, leave space for the respondents' phone number or e-mail address.

Finally, make sure to express thanks for participation at the survey's conclusion. While a simple "Thank you" will do in most cases, consider offering a small incentive, such as a coupon or discount to be redeemed at your place of business.

Analysis

After you've put all the time and effort into devising and executing the questionnaire, put your work to good use. At the same time that you draw up your survey, decide how the questions will be analyzed. Careful analysis of the survey results will give you valuable information that you can use to enhance your customers' experience and, in turn, add to your bottom line.

You don't have to be a billion-dollar conglomerate to gather up precise, valuable information from your customers. For example, Fairytale Brownies, which was founded in 1993 and today ships three million brownies a year, has included highly commendable customer response cards with its orders from the very beginning. On the cards, you'll immediately notice the opinions the company is trying to collect as an incentive for returning the survey (a chance to win free brownies). Since these cards are routinely dispersed, there is no deadline, but they do encourage an action—a response in 30 days—to be entered in the drawing for free brownies. In addition—to constantly ensure product quality and customer satisfaction—if Fairytale Brownies receives any mark below "Excellent," the company contacts the customer via e-mail or phone for further feedback.

Forms

Filling out a form that doesn't make sense or appears to ask for unnecessary details can be frustrating and, worse, can cost you time and money in handling phone calls and e-mails from confused customers.

Before you create a form, you first must determine what kind of information you're trying to extract from the person filling it out: is she a client placing an order, an employee making a vacation request, a customer filing a complaint? What action will the form help you complete? Then decide what information you need to collect in order for you to complete the action successfully. Once you have determined that data, consider the form's integrity and value with this checklist.

RETURN THIS CARD WITHIN 30 DAYS FOR A CHANCE TO WIN
ONE DOZEN FAIRYTALE BROWNIES!
(Drawing held monthly)

Were these The Greatest Brownies in All of Fairyland?

Did you ___ order these brownies or ___ receive these brownies as a gift?

What was your overall impression? ___ Excellent ___ Good ___ Fair ___ Poor

What was the condition of the gift packaging? ___ Excellent ___ Good ___ Fair ___ Poor

How did the brownies look and taste? ___ Excellent ___ Good ___ Fair ___ Poor

How did you keep your brownies? ___ Refrigerator ___ Freezer ___ Left at room temperature

Comments / New Product Suggestions: _____

_____

Would you like Customer Service to contact you? ___ Yes ___ No

Telephone _____ Email _____

Provide your information to enter the monthly brownie drawing. Visit brownies.com/winners to view the results.

Name_____

Company_____

Address_____

City_____ State_____ Zip_____

WE APPRECIATE YOUR COMMENTS WHICH WILL HELP US MAINTAIN THE HIGHEST QUALITY.

A customer response card from Fairytale Brownies. With just five questions, the company can cull a wealth of information from customers. Further, the company provides an incentive (the chance to win a monthly drawing for free brownies) for those who fill out and return the survey. (Courtesy Fairytale Brownies, *www.brownies.com*)

1. Make it complete by asking for all of the information that you need to, but make sure you're not collecting extraneous information, too.
2. Keep the language on the form free of technical terms and jargon that can be misunderstood or misconstrued.
3. Leave enough space for filling out lengthy information such as addresses.
4. Keep related information together.
5. Use subheads and boxes to group the information in a sensible format.
6. Keep sentences short.
7. Have the type set at a reasonably easy-to-read size.
8. Make sure the respondent knows where to send the form once it's completed.

Perhaps your best course in ensuring your form's effectiveness, readability, and ease of completion is to test it with a sample of people and have them report on its perks or problems before you produce it for mass distribution.

Signage for Customers

Realize that every form of communication in your business gives you the opportunity to leave a good impression with your customers so that they want to give your company return business. Those communications can take the form of signage and postings you may not have considered to be important enough to matter—but they do.

If your business serves customers on site, you may occasionally find the need to post signage that directs customers or informs them of policies. "Please Wait to Be Seated" or "Line Begins Here" are common examples.

If the sign is a permanent one, have it professionally made in a manner that ensures it won't become worn and unsightly. If you have a temporary situation that warrants a sign, such as a freshly painted railing or a broken bathroom door, use your computer's word processing program to create a sign using an easy-to-read font in a large size. Print the sign on white paper that is heavy enough to be posted. Your place of business comes off as unprofessional if you scribble an illegible warning with a marker pen on a torn piece of cardboard.

Professional postings mean that customers will take all of your messages and your company more seriously.

Fax Cover Sheets

Attachments to e-mails are de rigueur for many workplaces, but many times faxes are the necessary and preferred modes for transmission, particularly for W-9s, letters of agreement, and other signed documents.

When you send a fax, include a cover sheet. The cover sheet announces the recipient and how many pages are to follow, so that the fax gets to the right person, and completely.

Designing a fax cover sheet is an easy proposition. You should use a piece of company letterhead, and include:

- A line for the date
- Separate lines for "TO:"—the recipient's name, phone, and fax number
- Separate lines for "FROM:"—your name, phone, and fax number
- A line for the number of pages that will follow the cover
- A contact number in case the fax is missing pages
- A message box for any comments that should precede the fax

It's always good form to contact the recipient to make sure that the fax was received and all pages are accounted for, and to answer any questions.

▶▶ Test Drive

In examining the formats for written communication discussed in this chapter, did you find any you haven't employed lately? Which of the ones explained here could benefit your business immediately? Consider the options and tackle one of these:

- Write a thank-you letter to a client
- Devise a plan for a newsletter by coming up with a list of topics for an inaugural issue
- Brainstorm some company goals that could benefit from the input a survey or questionnaire would provide
- Review your company's fax sheet to determine whether it contains all it should, or design a new one

Communication in the Technology Age

PART **3**

Types of E-Mails

In previous chapters, you learned the particulars about formal business communications, such as memos and letters. This chapter examines the most ubiquitous written communication mode in the workplace: e-mail.

A 2005 survey found that most people receive nearly 50 business related e-mails per workday. E-mail has become so omnipresent and commonplace that it is now the preferred mode of transmission for a host of communications that would benefit from another format, such as a memo, letter, or phone call. Because e-mail has become such a dumping ground for information and communication of all kinds, you may have a hard time discerning the truly important from the superfluous, the urgent from the unnecessary, and even—unfortunately—the business from the personal.

E-mail can be an incredibly useful timesaving communication device, but when you use it, you shouldn't forgo the rules of grammar and courtesy you'd use for memos and letters. Although the purposes of e-mails do cross over with those of memos and even letters, e-mails should concentrate on a single message, such as:

- To set a meeting or change the specifics of it (date, time, place)
- To confirm information, such as an order
- To offer all kinds of information, such as a password to access a Web site, or the benefits of selecting a particular vendor
- To gather opinions; for instance, about a proposal or the next steps to take in a project
- To provide a cover to transmit documents of all types, by attaching them to the e-mail

E-mail can be a boon for giving praise for work performance, exchanging ideas, and creating community by keeping people up to date. Before you decide to send an e-mail, however, take a moment to determine whether it's the best method for the information you're communicating. In some instances, that's easy to figure out: e-mail is fine if you're verifying someone's phone number, asking to set up lunch, or providing a quick summary of a few needs for a report, for instance.

Always remember that the more important your message, the more worthy it is for consideration of another means of communication. As discussed in the chapters regarding memos and letters, sometimes correspondence that is of great import contains lengthy analysis or details, or includes sensitive information that will achieve better results or be seen as more appropriate if it's sent in a more traditional format.

Still, though guidelines have been set forth in other chapters for a wealth of instances, every circumstance is different. Depending on the situation, you may occasionally find it necessary to submit a proposal via e-mail, to compile a substantial summary in the body of an e-mail, or to release financial figures in one. Just be on guard: e-mail is not secure. Hackers, criminals—even the FBI—can intercept it.

Mail Templates

If you find yourself composing the same e-mail messages over and over, consider using a mail template. With these templates, you create a guide—or even a fixed response—to questions or requests that you routinely receive, but find yourself repeatedly reinventing the response for. For instance, you can use templates for responses to customer service questions, follow-up messages on sales or with prospective clients, or to send out company announcements to different audiences. A mail template can just provide the basis; you can still customize it for the person or situation—and save time in the process. Most mail programs have a template tool; for instance, the steps for creating a sample template in Outlook can be found at *http://office.microsoft.com.*

A Decision to Make: E-Mail versus Phone

A 2003 META Group Inc. survey among businesspeople found that a whopping 74 percent responded that being without e-mail would pose a greater hardship than being without phone service.

So it's understandable that people routinely choose e-mail to communicate when they really should pick up the phone to get the job done. This is an escalating—and even troubling—problem in the workplace today. Everyone has a story about an e-mail message they received (or, unfortunately, sent) that should have, in hindsight, been a phone call.

The worst offense is using e-mail as an avoidance measure. Sending an e-mail in that case will most likely cause the problem to worsen, creating another layer that makes the situation you're trying to avoid become even more sticky.

Terse e-mails also can cause problems. Since the recipient can't see the writer's facial expression or body language, such messages can easily come across more harshly than intended. You can control the message—and the emotions on the other end—much better by delivering the news in person or over the phone.

Interpersonal communication aside, one of the most frustrating and common examples of e-mail offense can be in setting up a meeting. If you've sent e-mails back and forth more than twice trying to set up the right time for a meeting, you're into a wasting-time zone. Get on the phone and discuss a date that works.

Advantages of Each Mode

Consider e-mail's advantages over a phone call, and vice versa, in deciding your best method of communication.

The advantages of sending an e-mail include:

- ⮌ Allowing for a flexible response time
- ⮌ Creating a paper trail
- ⮌ Making global communications easier
- ⮌ Setting up a more targeted approach to a message
- ⮌ Minimizing socializing

The advantages of using the phone include:

- ⮌ Bringing an immediate response
- ⮌ Eliminating a paper trail
- ⮌ Responding more easily when traveling
- ⮌ Delivering a more personal approach
- ⮌ Creating a proper context

To illustrate the advantages of each method, consider these situations. In each pair, which merits an e-mail and which really deserves a phone call?

1. Communicating the time for an employee's evaluation meeting; advising an employee to show enthusiasm for a troubled project in an upcoming client meeting.

2. Sending a customer a delivery confirmation number; telling a customer that the order you've promised won't make its scheduled delivery, which means an event will be without a crucial component.

When Not to Send an E-Mail

Some subjects are too sensitive to discuss in e-mail primarily because the chances for misinterpretation could have serious consequences, either on employees, customers, vendors, or investors. If the topic can be classified in one of these categories, it shouldn't be put in an e-mail:

- ➲ Concerns or complaints about someone
- ➲ A sweeping change in a working relationship
- ➲ Disciplinary action
- ➲ A surprising, major development that brings bad news
- ➲ A conflict of a serious nature

By all means, if in the course of regular messages going back and forth in e-mail the dialogue escalates into a conflict, stop the e-mail thread by setting a time to talk or meet in person.

Making Your E-Mail Stand Out

When someone opens your e-mail among the dozens he or she gets each day, what can make yours convince the recipient it's worth reading? This context isn't referring to e-mails sent as a sales tool, but rather e-mails sent in the normal course of a business day.

Take the High Road

Once she received paperwork regarding a loan, a client of a small-but-successful mortgage brokerage firm e-mailed her broker with a plethora of questions. When she didn't get an immediate response, she e-mailed again. The broker than e-mailed her, apologizing for not getting right back, and tactfully indicating that he needed her to be patient as he was trying to gather information for her. Insulted, she fired back another e-mail about how inappropriate his most recent e-mail had been. He worsened the situation by sending her another e-mail that was apologetic in one sense but also stated that he "had shown the e-mail thread to colleagues here and none of them found anything remotely offensive." The client was furious that her broker had shared that information with his colleagues, and immediately withdrew her business from him.

Regardless of the fact that customers are always right, you can learn much from this situation. If you face a similar circumstance, don't ever feel that you have to keep engaging in the e-mail hijinks. In this instance, the broker should have realized that—while his client may have been demanding—she was expecting a prompt response. When she mistook his apology and fired off the third e-mail, he should have elected to calm down the situation, rather than look for support among office colleagues that, most of the time, will side with him and probably weren't very objective in their judgment. You always have the option of picking up the phone to rectify an e-mail "conversation" that has gotten off track. To keep a customer, you should take the ultimate responsibility—and the high road.

This bit of counsel may seem too logical and maybe even rudimentary—but the best way to make your e-mail stand out is to ensure that you've gone over it ruthlessly to make sure there are no misspellings, bad grammar, and the like. With frightening regularity, a staggering number of e-mails are sent out with errors, often under the misconception that shooting off e-mails with misspellings and omitted words is perfectly acceptable if you're really busy!

Stay consistently polished in your e-mail preparation and presentation. Doing so lets recipients know that an e-mail from you is worth reading. In sending out your professional-looking and professional-sounding e-mails, don't be afraid to add a little of your own personality. While that doesn't mean being jocular or opening up the e-mail with a canned joke, do inject some warmth and humanity into the e-mail.

Bear a Signature

Finally, have your e-mail bear a signature. Signatures are information you can provide at the bottom of your e-mail message that contains your title, company, phone number, and address, among other information. By using a signature, you provide contact information that your recipient can readily access, and that you don't have to repeat in your e-mail's body copy. When drawing up your signature, stick with the basics. Don't feel the need to include a "quote of the day" cute material. Research your mail program to determine how to create a signature for your e-mails.

How Does Your "From" Look?

When a message you send turns up in someone's e-mailbox, what does the "From" line say? You may be surprised at how often peoples' names are misspelled, or odd spacing has occurred when they type their name in their mail program's "Preferences" to set up their e-mail account. In addition, the address that you respond back to may have been input incorrectly, or contain an erroneous (or misspelled) ".com" or ".net" extension. Check your e-mail address right now: send an e-mail to yourself to see how it looks. Is your name spelled correctly in the "From" line? Is your e-mail address to respond back to correct? Even in the speedy world of e-mail, good, correct form—and "from"—still counts.

Examine This Example

In this real-life example, you can survey all that went wrong with this e-mail. If the sender had taken the time to review the message before it was sent, she certainly would have pinpointed spacing problems, grammatical errors, continuity and flow impediments, misspelled words and URLs, wrong dates, a general lack of cohesion, and the absence of a specific purpose for her request. Take note of changes in the corrected version to help make your e-mail stand out in a positive way.

TO: Len@PERFECTPR.com
FROM: Vivi.Tuxton@echo.net
SUBJECT: SAVE THE DATE

HI Len,
We have the following release screening coming up and it was suggested as per below that I contact you with regards to marketing PR help
we may need for the event and the weeks release!!!!Please call me at
310555=7707 THAKS VIVI TUXTON
www.kewlfilm.comwww.imdb.com.

SAVE THE DATE
Vivi Tuxton
in Assoc with
Avant Garde Films LLC
and Presenting Sponsers
REQUEST THAT YOU SAVE THE DATE for
***October 15 2006 between the hours of
8pm-ten*************************
for the Los Angeles
Screenings and small Premiere and After Party to be held in Beverly Hills,
Los Angeles
Screening of the film FERDINAND PARK (www.ferdinandparkthemovie.
com, shot ntirely on location
SAVE THE DATE
Invitations and GUEST LIST RSVP to follow prior to Oscars 2005.
Tieered sponsership packages and Naming Rights -,some positions still
available by calling 310-555/2311
www.ferdinandpark.com.

TO: Len@PERFECTPR.com
FROM: Vivi.Tuxton@echo.net
SUBJECT: PR OPPORTUNITY FOR INDEPENDENT FILM EVENT

Hi, Len:

As producer and star of the new independent film, "Ferdinand Park," I wanted to discuss your company handling the publicity and marketing for the movie's premiere event. Ava Montgomery, our mutual friend at Warner Bros., enthusiastically referred me to you.

I've included a "Save the Date" e-mail about the event that was distributed yesterday. Can you call me at your earliest convenience at 310/555-7707 to discuss your interest and availability? In the meantime, you can read up on the film at www.ferdinandparkthemovie.com and at www.imdb.com. I look forward to speaking with you.

Vivi Tuxton

***SAVE THE DATE – OCTOBER 15—
"FERDINAND PARK" FILM PREMIERE***

Vivi Tuxton
in Association with
Avant Garde Films LLC
and Presenting Sponsors

Gratefully Request that You
Save the Date for
"FERDINAND PARK"
Screening and After Party
Saturday, October 15, 2006
8:00 P.M.–10 P.M.
Los Angeles
For information regarding tiered sponsorship packages, please call
310-555/2311.
www.ferdinandparkthemovie.com

Subject Lines

Most people scan an e-mail's subject line to determine its priority in their day's activities. Mailboxes can become jammed with a flurry of new messages constantly popping up, but subject lines—descriptive, exact ones—have the best chance of leading the recipient to open and read an entire message, and be more in tune for precisely what's to follow.

Too often, unclear subject lines clog inboxes, offering no real insight into the e-mail's actual contents. That's a shame, because the subject line gives you the prime opening opportunity to have your reader truly focus on the message you want to deliver. Lines such as "General Note," "Meeting," "Problem," "An Idea…," "Follow Up"—or worse, no subject line at all—rob you of nabbing that concentrated focus.

In addition, lines that scream with "Immediately," "HOT Topic," "Important!" and "Must Know Now," have unfortunately become routine and, also unfortunately, are still not very descriptive. In each case, they're more likely to be considered a low priority as well.

If you can create attention-grabbing, clever but appropriate subject lines, so much the better. However, they only truly need to be well thought out and concise to do the trick. For example, instead of using "stockroom" as your subject line, immediately inform the recipient of the e-mail's content by using "Stockroom Fire Reported Last Night."

Guidelines for Body Copy

E-mails are often referred to and thought of as fast reads for fast times. With e-mails, you want to keep your message short, sweet, and generally not longer than one screen-full. Aim for no more than four or five paragraphs. With a longer message, you run the risk of your entire piece of mail not being read, or only having the first line or two responded to or acted upon. E-mails longer than a screenfull usually aren't read right away and—many times—deserve another format. This point brings up another reason for truly analyzing which format will be best. Your audience may be more apt to treat a memo or letter as a communication for which they sit down and read, rather than charging through it as they do with e-mail.

One message equals one e-mail. In most cases, two equals two e-mails. However, exceptions do occur. For instance, if you are laying the groundwork for a proposal yet to be written, or bringing up a few points after editing a document—in other words, if you have several messages that are brief and somehow related—you can bullet or number them in one e-mail. But if you've got much to discuss, don't feel obliged to jam-pack it all into a single e-mail. Sending one e-mail for each thought or message allows the recipient to delete, respond, file, or forward each item individually.

Attachments are covered in greater depth in the next section, but for the purposes here, it's enough to know that you must take time to announce an attachment that you're sending. Too often, the writer is focused on other points, and may forget to mention an attachment at all. Worse, the body copy may discuss one message, and then the writer includes an attachment, which hasn't been announced and that doesn't even relate to the topic at hand. This example reinforces the concept that if you have more than one message, send more than one e-mail.

If you're contacting someone cold, or e-mailing someone you haven't seen in a while, include your name, occupation, and other relevant information in the first few sentences to acclimate the recipient to the message you're about to articulate.

Overall, when writing e-mail body copy be organized in your approach, appropriate in message length, and considerate of other people's time.

Grammar Counts

In writing your e-mails, follow the rules of good writing discussed in Chapters 3, 4, and 5. Use active verbs, good grammar, appropriate punctuation, and sound word choices, and avoid fragments and run-ons. Run-ons seem to be a particular problem with writing e-mails, as senders opt for a conversational tone. While a less formal approach is perfectly acceptable, take care that you don't do what would also be unacceptable in a conversation: ramble or babble. Give your reader chances to breathe with crisp, clear sentences.

Be nice to your reader by using short paragraphs, with spaces between them. Don't be afraid of using white space to make your message easier on the recipient's eyes. Often, senders will blurt out an entire paragraph when, on second look, they should have broken up the paragraph into two or three to make the information easier to distill.

When making points, giving directions, or outlining next steps, number or bullet your lines of copy. Not doing so will wreak havoc on the reader's ability to understand your message.

Try not to use capital letters in entire words or sentences. A sentence written in capitals actually signifies shouting in an e-mail. Further, our eyes aren't conditioned to read text that's composed in all capital letters, so your recipient will find that it's hard just to read your message, much less grasp the entire, intended meaning.

Format Considerations

Realize that because people use different e-mail programs, the formatting of your e-mail may change once it's delivered. To make sure your message is delivered clearly and effectively, use standard block paragraphs. You should also try to avoid colored fonts, as colors vary and your recipient may have a hard time reading your message. Steer clear of background wallpaper as well. While it may look fun and vibrant, it can also be distracting and alter your message format.

If you're forwarding an article or other Web content, consider including the link as well as pasting the article into the e-mail. Your paste-in may have gotten rumpled in delivery, so providing an option for your reader will be appreciated.

Avoid High-Tech Shorthand

Steer clear of abbreviations (such as BTW for by the way) and abbreviated expressions (such as <G> for grin). Your recipient might not know what these mean and they're generally not appropriate for business e-mails anyway. Follow that same guideline for smiley faces and other "emoticons." While you want most of your e-mails to take a friendly tone, peppering them with computer shorthand and text-message lingo usually detracts from their professionalism and, ultimately, your message.

Disclaimers

Depending on the nature of your business, consider adding disclaimers to your e-mails that protect you, your company, and the information that's in transit.

You can box in the disclaimer with a line of asterisks above and below it, and have it state, for example:

> This e-mail may contain confidential material. If you were not an intended recipient, please notify the sender and delete all copies. We may monitor e-mail to and from our network.

Proofread

Read your e-mail before you send it. Many people unfortunately regard e-mail as just a conversation that may contain some mistakes. Don't fall prey to that attitude. Double-check to make sure that there aren't any missing words, which could detract from your message or inadvertently communicate a message you didn't intend. In your final approach, try reading the e-mail from the viewpoint of your reader to make sure that statements or questions won't be taken as inappropriate or create misunderstanding.

Regarding Responding, Forwarding, and Attachments

Unlike memos and letters, e-mail brings a unique set of circumstances in that responses can be instantly generated, and the entire text of a message can be immediately forwarded.

Responding

When you receive an e-mail that prompts a response from you, let people know what you're responding to. When you answer an e-mail, don't delete the message that was sent to you; it will help the recipient to recall the thread of "conversation." Some people receive so many e-mails that it's unfair to think that the contents of yours—though undoubtedly important to you—will be instantly remembered. If you're responding to an e-mail that contains many points, consider cutting and pasting each bulleted or numbered item separately, and then responding underneath your handiwork for each.

To appear professional and courteous, make yourself available to your online correspondents. Occasionally, that may entail letting them know you're on deadline, but will be available to them shortly.

If you'll be out for a few days, take advantage of your mail program's auto-reply feature to let senders know that you might not be able to respond immediately.

If the situation allows and is appropriate, consider responding to an e-mail with more information than was requested, by predicting what the next question might be. Perhaps a customer e-mails you asking which credit cards you accept. In responding back, include the credit card types, but then also politely give directions to your store, for instance, or provide a link for placing an order.

Forwarding

If you're choosing to forward an entire e-mail, or just a piece of one, review what has been written. In reviewing previous e-mails you've been sent, you may be amazed at some of the inappropriate, inaccurate, and even offensive information they include. If the e-mail has potentially damaging information, or if its contents might be misconstrued, don't send it as is. Either refashion the message, or, if possible, ask the sender to rephrase what's been sent. When you receive a message that you know is inappropriate or badly worded, don't forward it just to embarrass someone.

Finally, don't forward a message with a long e-mail thread unless you include an introduction regarding why that message is being forwarded. When you forward an entire e-mail thread, double-check it to determine, once again, whether it contains any potentially damaging or easily misunderstood communication or information.

Attachments

One of e-mail's best uses is that you can attach documents and files of all kinds, in some instances fulfilling a company mandate to create a paperless workplace.

If you send an attachment with your e-mail, make sure that you reference that it's there and then double-check to make sure you've attached the document or file that's referenced. In your body copy, provide a reason why the attachment is being sent. Don't just send an attachment without an introduction, particularly if the attachment hasn't been requested or the recipient doesn't know it's on its way.

E-Mail on Hold?

You may lose business if you don't reply to e-mails within a day. A 2003 survey by TargetX, an e-mail marketing firm, found that 13 percent of respondents would take their business elsewhere if they didn't receive a response to an e-mail within an hour. Another 15 percent said they were willing to wait up to three hours, while 8 percent said their wait time was six hours. But almost everyone—88 percent—expected a response within twenty-four hours.

If you've got an attachment that's only a few paragraphs, consider cutting and pasting it into the text of your message. While attachments are absolutely necessary sometimes, realize that they do take time to download, can carry viruses, and don't always translate correctly. As mentioned earlier, another possibility is presenting a link that the recipient can go to on the Web, to download or access materials at his or her convenience.

Standard Netiquette Practices

The number one rule in netiquette is don't "flame," which refers to writing an abusive personal attack. If you're writing with negative emotion, give yourself a break from the keyboard and weigh the consequences.

If you're responding to an e-mail that appears inflammatory, reference the line and add a neutral comment, indicating that you may not understand what's been written and need clarification.

Use the BCC (blind carbon copy) field instead of CC when sending sensitive information to large groups. The name of everyone in the CC list goes out with the message, but the names of people on the BCC list are hidden.

Before Pressing "Send"

Before you send your e-mail, you can answer these questions to determine whether your e-mail is as strong and appropriate as it should be:

- ⮑ Is the subject best handled in a verbal conversation?
- ⮑ Does the e-mail contain information of real value?
- ⮑ Does the message warrant more than one e-mail?
- ⮑ Is it clear and of a reasonable length?
- ⮑ If you took a five-minute breather before you sent the e-mail, would you still send it?
- ⮑ Have you made the e-mail's purpose clear?
- ⮑ Have you written a subject line that's descriptive and focused?
- ⮑ If you're responding to someone, have you referenced what you're responding to?
- ⮑ If your e-mail is forwarded, will its contents be embarrassing to you or harmful to others?
- ⮑ If you attached files, have you indicated that you did so?

E-mail should save time and make your job easier. When you don't follow simple protocol and procedures, however, the opposite can happen.

▶▶ Test Drive

Here is a tough one: review several e-mails you've sent during the past few days. Notice the purpose, objective, and tone. Now ask:

- ⮑ Having had a few days away from the wording, would you change the way the e-mail was written?
- ⮑ Was the e-mail successful in its mission? (Did what you set out for the e-mail to accomplish get done?)
- ⮑ If not, why do you think the e-mail was unsuccessful?
- ⮑ Was the e-mail truly an e-mail, or did it contain information that really should have been presented on the phone or in person?

The Basics of Web Site Writing

Many consider the Web site to be just an adjunct marketing tool for your business. However, no matter what your business, a Web site can be a vibrant and varied component of it, not just to offer details on your products or for selling your services, but also to communicate with customers, keep them apprised of key developments or the status of orders, and give them the basics, such as contact information.

This chapter gives the overall lay of the land of integrating a Web site into your business. In Chapter 14, you'll go further, gathering information on taking your Web site to the next level in communicating with your customers or clients, and selling to them.

Writing a Web site can be a daunting task. You may be consumed with questions regarding its presence: How big should it be? What should it do? What should it say? How many parts should be on its navigation bar—or does it just need to be a "placeholder" site, at least for now? (A placeholder site either simply announces your business with contact information, or provides limited information with a "Coming Soon" banner.)

Every site stands for something: your company, your entrepreneurial venture, your product. As you contemplate the site you'll be writing, think about this question: What can your Web site do to further your business?

Decide Your Web Site's Purpose

In creating your Web site, you first must decide what kind of Web site you want for your customers or clients. Keeping in mind that purposes can cross over, familiarize yourself with these three types of sites to determine exactly what you want yours to do.

1. **Promotional:** This type of site is geared toward marketing and publicity. In this incarnation, your Web site gives standard information about your company's services, products, location, contacts, and, perhaps, details on how to place an order over the phone or in person.

2. Informational: In this Web site—which strives to offer service and possibly build goodwill—you could offer customers valuable, free information. In a more advanced mode, the site could allow them to access information regarding their dealings with your company, such as to check inventory or to track shipping.

3. Transactional: This Web site focuses on selling via the Internet (e-commerce). Customers can shop on the site, viewing products or learning about services, and then place orders on the site. (Chapter 14 gives more details about writing for this site format.)

Once again, in learning about these types of Web sites, you may realize that the site you want to build or improve combines elements of all of them. While that's perfectly fine, you should apply the guidelines and tips set forth in this chapter and the next to each of the areas you plan to incorporate. Paying attention to each area will ensure that you're not shortchanging any of the intended goals for your site.

Web versus Paper: Different Worlds

Writing for the Web is much different than writing for print. In fact, some studies suggest that 79 percent of users scan a Web site page instead of reading word-by-word (as they might do with a memo or from a book); that reading from computer screens is 25 percent slower than reading from paper; and that Web content should have 50 percent of the word count of its paper counterpart.

Web writing, then, is geared toward a "scannable" audience. That is, the readers visiting your site take in your words in big chunks, searching for targeted information. They don't typically read every word, unless or until they find a topic or heading of prime interest.

In general, your Web site writing should use simple sentence structure, shorter sentences, and avoid cute or pun-filled headlines. In presenting information, Web sites usually make it easy on the reader by doing things such as limiting scrolling and using concise, straightforward, uncomplicated—though not dull or brainless—wording.

Become an Expert: What Sites Do You Like?

You should start your Web site writing process quite simply: find and study Web sites that you like. These could include other sites that may be competing with your business, as well as ones you admire for their substance and presentation. While you won't want to copy those sites, let them inspire and influence your approach, setup, and organization. As you visit a site you admire, respect, or want to emulate, ask:

- ⊃ What works on this site?
- ⊃ What doesn't?
- ⊃ What makes it appealing to you?
- ⊃ What would make it appealing to your target audience?
- ⊃ What would you change on it?
- ⊃ Does it include all the information you would expect it to?
- ⊃ If not, what's left out?

As you comb through myriad sites, you'll no doubt see sites you don't like. Perhaps they are confusing to navigate, unprofessional in their approach, jumbled in their layout, or poorly written. You can learn from these sites as well. Detect and pinpoint those Web sites' problems, so you can avoid them in writing your own.

A Small Investment

Some business owners are amazed at how little money it takes to start a Web site. Again, you can start out simply with a site that gives you a Web presence and at least offers the basics for your company, such as contact information. Find a reputable Web design firm either through referrals, or by following up with the firm behind a site you like. Many Web design firms can have you up and running with a polished, uncomplicated site for a few hundred dollars that will—at the very least—be a beginning.

Web Site Structure

As you get in the Web site writing mindset, you'll need to plot out your site's pages, parts, and navigation. At this point, you'll initially have to spend some time thinking about and considering the Web site you're ready to set up. Go back to your original purposes for it: is it for marketing, e-commerce, service, information, or a combination of those? Whatever purpose(s) you decide, writing for a site will require a strict sense of organization. You'll deny your site's maximum effectiveness if you don't dedicate yourself to that creed.

Steer Clear of the Junk

Too many Web sites instantly lose interest, credibility, or both with a look that bursts at the seams with headlines, subheads, content, and seemingly unrelated graphics and charts. Worse, you may scan down the homepage for an interminable amount of time before you realize what the site's all about. The side margin may have a lengthy list of links that overwhelm, confuse, and don't seem to relate to the site's purpose. Prevent any and all of these distractions from being a part of your site.

Focus, Focus, Focus

When you've allocated time, money, and resources toward building a Web site, you can easily get lost in the sheer potential of what your Web site can do, and the massive audience it can reach. But resist the urge to get too caught up in those possibilities. It's best to start out simply, if impressively, in crafting your site. Don't throw everything and the kitchen sink about your business into the site. Be judicious but creative in what you want to initially relate.

In figuring out what your initial focus should be, determine three goals you would like your Web site to accomplish. Review your business plan, financials, and business proposals to generate, fine tune, and confirm objectives you've been wanting your business to achieve.

Organization

Unless you're proficient with Web design, you will mostly likely contact a Web site designer who can walk you through the process of effectively organizing your site. After deciding the purpose or purposes you're fulfilling, you'll turn to organizing your site so that it makes sense on all levels—to the average person, not just to you. If you do that, you'll enjoy return visitors and repeat business. Make the information obviously easy to locate, with direct routes for visitors to get what they need without wading through links and information that don't interest them.

Brainstorming

Writing your Web site creates another opportunity for brainstorming. When you first set out to create your Web site, brainstorm a multitude of topics you want to include. If you have pages you know you want to include under those topics, write down those, too. You'll be best off using 3" × 5" index cards or Post-it Notes, which will allow you to start grouping the topics and pages together.

This process will actually be the genesis for a flow chart, which you'll most likely work on with your Web site designer. The flow chart brings order to your ideas, allows you to avoid repetition or redundancy, and frees you up to toss out subject areas that don't belong or aren't congruent with your Web site's purpose, message, or both.

Determine the five or six topics that your Web site will include. Then, under those five or six topics, consider the other pages that would beef up those sections, adding further details to each. Your flow chart should list all of these main headings, and then list the pages that each one contains.

For each page, make sure you have something to say. Don't include a page just because you think it should be there, or because it sounds good. Have the words to back up each section and page you include.

Your Navigation Bar

Each site contains a navigation bar, which is the row or column of buttons—representing the main topics from your flow chart—that readers click on to access pages on your Web site. Those buttons hyperlink (jump) directly to that page.

For instance, if you have an architecture firm, you'd have a "Services" section on your navigation bar, which would probably include relevant pages such as "Architectural Design," "Construction Administration," "Site Evaluation," "Interior Design," and "Cost Estimating." A "Media" section might include "Press Releases," "E-Press Kit," "Recent Articles," "Story Ideas," and "Request an Interview."

Consider Beginning with a Brochure

Know from the outset that—especially with the Web's ephemeral ways—what you commit to the screen now doesn't have to live there forever. While you don't want to risk your company's reputation with a slipshod site and copy that doesn't transmit your message well, you can start out with a homepage and a few pages to link to within the site. That's where the "brochure approach" comes in handy: brief but complete snapshots of your company's capabilities. However, the brochure approach is sometimes disdained for making a Web site just the online version of a company brochure, with little other application or use that could truly benefit the company online. If you go that route at the beginning, set deadlines for getting a more comprehensive site up and running. Don't waste the opportunity to make your company's Web site the valuable marketing tool that it should be.

Components and Content

Regardless of your Web site's purpose(s), it probably will include a few basics that every Web site has. They are:

Home, for your homepage, which is your reader's first impression of the site

About Us, the defining description of your company, and how it stands out from the competition in what it does

Service/Product pages, which highlight your company's offerings

Contact, for information pertaining to getting in touch with your company via phone, e-mail, and possibly in person

In Chapter 14, such common navigation bar features as "Shopping Cart" and "Newsletter" will also be discussed.

Fleshing Out the Navigation Bar

Navigation bar buttons also often include headings and topics such as "Media," "Upcoming Events," and "Frequently Asked Questions" (FAQ). Go back to your flow chart to ensure that you're being complete in your approach for the purposes your Web site is serving. Does every one of your page groupings have a topic? Does every topic relate back to your purposes?

Once you decide on the buttons of your navigation bar, be creative—if your industry allows—to spark your reader's interest further, and amp up your visitor's excitement in your site. Work to create a Web site experience, not just a series of pages.

For instance, on the site for GoodKarmal.com, which sells gift boxes of caramel, the buttons include "Karmal Raves," which actually refers to media that have covered the product. Once on that page, you can click on mastheads for such outlets as *Ladies' Home Journal*, MTV, and Oprah's O List, to link to coverage about Good Karmal. On a button called "Karmal Causes," site visitors can learn about philanthropies that receive some of the proceeds from Good Karmal purchases.

Standalone or a Series?

While each of the buttons on your site could hyperlink to a single page, many present an opportunity to offer other links that relate to each button.

In other words, though your homepage generally stands alone as the gate to the site's other pages, each of the other navigation bar buttons could spread into other valuable headings. Consider which of your buttons will benefit from additional pages to offer depth to your site.

For example, for your service or product pages, each of your company's offerings may deserve a page devoted to a description of that product or service, but other pages could highlight recent jobs, photos, and client testimonials related to each item, too.

The "About Us" button could be a company overview, but could also list bios of your company executives, with paragraph profiles on each one.

The Font Files

While you undoubtedly have an enormous selection of fonts for your site's language, choose one that is easy to read. Many fonts might draw your attention, seem an exquisite fit for your business, or express a fun or serious tone you're trying to impart. However, save those fonts for ad copy or marketing materials. You want your Web site to be easy to scan and read; frilly or unfamiliar fonts can detract the reader's attention or simply make it hard for the user to concentrate. Your best bets are Helvetica, Arial, or Georgia for a clean look in getting your message across. If you opt for another font, do stay away from those that use all capital letters, because most of the material we read on a daily basis isn't printed that way, making those fonts hard to read.

For your "Contact" button, you'll most likely want to include a phone number, company address, and an e-mail that hyperlinks so a customer or client can send a message.

Add to the Experience

As mentioned previously, many companies turn their Web sites into onscreen brochures. While this at least allows for a Web presence, some Web experts advise against it, regarding it as a wasteful use of the site.

For your site, try to get beyond the brochure mentality by offering other tidbits, articles, and advice that visitors will use. When you do this, readers are more likely to return to your site. Keeping a presence with them is likely to result in more sales, as well.

For example, if you own a frame company, use your site to provide articles about ways to frame cheap art to make it look expensive, or about the latest hot colors for frames. You could even list local art gallery showings. No matter your business, you can drum up relevant information to showcase on the site.

You can also tap into your own company news releases, suppliers' product information, and a listing of FAQs to get you started.

Attracting and Keeping an Audience with Words

When you take away the Web site's graphics, navigation bar, and photos, you're left with the words. The words you use determine the tone, grab the audience, and set all the other components in motion.

The first step to writing effective Web copy is the same as in other forms of business communication—know your audience. Consider how old they are, their income, their professions, their interests, and their reason(s) for visiting your site.

Your homepage should make two aspects about your company immediately apparent:

1. **Your unique selling position:** What makes your company or your product different from the rest? Take a look at your mission statement to guide you in crafting the most articulate statements for your homepage.
2. **The benefits you provide:** How will a visitor improve his business or life by using your product, service, or company? Give a clear, concise answer to that question.

Don't underestimate the importance of your homepage: it could be the first impression that your desired audience has of your company, and as such could be a make-or-break opportunity to entice new business. Make an immediately favorable impression with a clean look, simple but smart words, and easy viewing.

Writing Rules

In addition to the scannable attributes of Web site writing mentioned earlier, use these guidelines as you build your site.

Keep your most important information at the top to create an inverted pyramid type of format. This measure—putting information in order of priority, from most to least important—protects against those readers who aren't crazy about scrolling, and therefore would otherwise miss the news you most want them to have.

In that vein, always maintain a "news you can use" motto to help readers who have come to your site looking for something. Make finding information they're searching for friendly, easy, and quick.

Don't lapse into slang, but don't be afraid of a conversational, friendly tone that talks to your visitors, not at them.

Bulleted and numbered lists are favored in Web site writing to dole out information in an accessible way. You'll use these more frequently on your Web site than you would in straight business writing on paper.

Use active voice, rather than passive. In doing so, you'll make your Web site as engaging as possible.

Follow the Rules

Follow the same guidelines you would for other written materials. Edit, proof, take a breather, and come back to it. Repeat that process if necessary. Web site copy merits and demands the same professionalism as other business communications. Even though it's a fast-paced format, don't be too swift or cavalier in your approach.

Headlines

Lead off each page with a benefit-packed headline, giving your readers a reason to stay on that page. If necessary appeal to the visitor's self-interest.

Users may enter your site at any page, so use headlines to make sure that every page isn't dependent on another one, and to explain each one's purpose in relation to the site. Make headings clear so that the reader knows why this page is important. Also, make sure that the heading you're using clearly indicates the content of the information that follows. Finally, make headlines short and, of course, believable.

Your Credibility

In that respect, work to ensure that all the information you provide is credible. The Web definitely suffers from a reputation of being littered with unsubstantiated statements, outdated information, and overtly boastful claims. That's largely because the Web isn't monitored by a fact-checking authority, so legitimacy and truths aren't often questioned. You can stay above the fray by providing trustworthy words to your clients or customers.

Double-check and verify details you supply, be it for products you sell, industry trends you describe, or articles you provide. Also, hyperlink to sites that have supporting information to boost the credibility of your pages (hyperlinking is discussed a little later in this chapter).

Further, cite Web sites and sources that provide information and, if necessary, follow the proper procedure to get clearance to feature the site, link, statistics, or report. Most Web site owners would be flattered if you wanted to provide a link to their site; you just need to get their permission in writing (which may even be, in some cases, a quick e-mail).

Keywords and Hyperlinks

One of the keys to generating search engine traffic is getting your site into the top ten positions on the search engines for the keywords and keyphrases that pertain to your business. Because of that, keywords and hyperlinks are the lifeblood of your site.

Keywords are descriptive words in your site that are unique to your products and services, and serve as a kind of index to find your site via search engines, such as Google and Yahoo. In a sense, you want to think like your prospective client or potential customer: What words would they type into a search engine to expressly find your site? For instance, keywords on a site for a travel agency that specializes in booking family cruises to the Caribbean might include Caribbean, cruises, family, vacation, travel, Aruba, Barbados, Cayman Islands, St. Lucia, and schedules.

Make sure to incorporate targeted keywords in your copy that allow the search engines to find your site. You'll want to work with your designer to include these keywords in your meta tags, links, and file names as well. Good designers can also help you to determine and include the keywords that will work best for your site. Chapter 14 delves more into keywords and bringing more traffic and business to your Web site with them.

Your keywords may happen to be some of the links you use in your document. For instance, for that site regarding Caribbean family cruises, "Schedules" may be a button on the navigation bar, and also may be included in the copy on the homepage. If it's "lit up"—a link—you would click on that and then be instantly transported to another part of the site, in this case the "Schedules" page, wherein you could find out what cruises might be heading out during your family's planned vacation time.

When writing a document for the Web, be sure to use links to guide the reader through the document. Think of linking as the quickest means to get users to the most relevant information they're looking for.

Links embedded in a document are the primary links that you want a reader to see. Because readers use links as guideposts in scanning, you want to use them correctly and write in a way that takes best advantage of them. Make them organic to the copy. Writing links in this way keeps readers involved and engaged in your site for a longer period of time. However, only the most pertinent links should be part of the document. Don't let them become a distraction. According to David Beveridge, managing director of Web development firm Brook Group, "Use links to enhance, not scatter, the experience."

To that end, position less relevant but meaningful links in the Web page's margins or at the end of the document under a "See Also" label.

Inside Track   A Point of View and a Big-Picture Approach

I've been involved with the launch of many sites and have found that the best ones have obvious, recurring similarities. Those similarities may surprise you. They weren't all brimming with whiz-bang elements or showcasing already popular products. In each case, the business owner—from the outset—gave serious thought and ample consideration to answering key questions about the company's goals for the Web site: Would it be strictly promotional, informational, transactional, or some combination thereof? If it was a combination, what was the combination? Would it chiefly drive sales, connect with customers, or supply materials ancillary to the business? Outside of the belief that "every business should have a Web site up and running" was a core understanding of the company's goals, and a recognition of how the Web site could and would help achieve them.

When you first meet with a Web designer, you may think that you have to put up a Web site that's slick, with multiple layers, pages of product offerings, and Flash animation, but it really doesn't have to begin that way. While your site should be professionally presented and polished, just a few buttons on a navigation bar will get you going. Occasionally, I've advised clients against having me write pages and pages of Web copy for them as they realize that less can sometimes be more. In paring down the elements, your Web site actually became stronger.

The beauty of the Web's fluidity is that your site can always be expanded and upgraded. When you first start your Web site, create a big-picture plan. Draft a wish list of the components you'd like to include down the line. As your business grows and changes, add to (and, if necessary, delete from) that list so your site will remain congruent with your company's current strategies.

Keeping It Fresh

The Web is a fluid medium. Once you've got your Web site up and running, return to and update your material often. Don't let your business be considered staid or unattended. If you're not updating copy, switching out photos, or making relevant additions, your site can look like no one's minding the store. For instance, if your Web site is announcing an event you're sponsoring, include details or registration for it before the date. Afterward, post event pictures and a summary.

In particular, ensure that examples you cite, or any numbers, such as prices or statistics, are recent. In addition, make sure your Web site date-line changes daily.

There are a host of valuable Web sites that can help you find and verify information for your own site, and also can help spawn ideas, including:

> *www.refdesk.com,* which bills itself as "the single best source for facts"

> *www.ehow.com,* which offers "clear instructions on how to do (just about) everything"

> *www.dowjones.com,* which according to the site publishes "the world's most vital business and financial news and information"

> *www.questia.com,* which is the world's largest online library of books, and also contains hundreds of thousands of articles

People often visit sites repeatedly for updated information, but if the same information is there week in and week out, they'll probably stop returning. Use your Web site wisely to continue attracting them.

▶▶ Test Drive

Think hard about your business, your mission statement, and your business plan (if you've written them yet) as you answer these questions:

- ➲ What are five keywords or phrases that describe your business so well you could build an entire Web page for your company, using any of the words as inspiration?
- ➲ What are ten other keywords or phrases that you think are crucial to bringing traffic to your site?

If you already have a Web site:

- ➲ When you type your most important keywords into your favorite search engine, where does your Web site rank?
- ➲ When you type in the keywords, are you surprised at what comes up?
- ➲ Are your competitors listed? Where do they rank?
- ➲ What are more descriptive keywords and phrases that might improve your ranking?

Communication in the Technology Age

Making Your Web Site More Interactive and Communicative

After grasping Web site writing basics, you can take advantage of several methods and opportunities to strengthen your Web site's reach, to maximize your business, and to drive more messages home to your intended audience.

For starters, consider this recent research conducted by The Poynter Institute, Eyetools, and the Estlow Center for Journalism and New Media. Their study found some typical behaviors regarding the visual patterns of Web site users. The research, which is particularly useful to transactional sites (those with e-commerce involved), found that users conduct a fast scan of the entire visible screen with concentrated shots at headlines, the page logo, photo captions, subheads, links, and menu items. However, the most important area is actually the upper left corner of the screen, which is deemed a "hot spot"—the lower right of the screen is the least likely place to nab attention.

If you currently have a Web site, test it to learn which components draw visitors' eyes. If possible, poll colleagues and prospective customers who haven't previously viewed your site to find out what attracts their attention and what distracts it. That kind of market research can be your first step in taking your Web site to the next level: fine-tuning your writing and layout to be the most effective.

Web Words

When writing and planning elements of your Web site, you may often feel that you've stumbled onto a language that may sound familiar but doesn't make sense. Ever heard the terms VoIP, mash-up, spear phishing? You can stay apprised of Internet terms you hear at *www.webopedia.com*, regarded as "the only online dictionary and search engine you need for computer and Internet technology definitions." Particularly as your site pushes new boundaries, you may be stumped with some of the terms that come your way. When you are, turn to this trusted, innovative source.

Search Engine Optimization

In probing further into making keywords work for your business, you should know about search engine optimization (SEO). SEO refers to improving your Web site's ranking—and the ranking of its various pages—on the major search engines.

There are actually entire companies devoted to helping a company rank higher in search engines. But you can rely on several, simple basic optimizing techniques to increase your site's and its pages' rankings. For instance, page titles should contain your specified keywords—and then some. Most search engines give a high rating to page title text as a ranking factor. For instance, you wouldn't want a page that just said "Services"; that would be pretty vague. Create one that a search engine would value; turn "Services" into "Estate-Planning Services: Mr. Moneytip." By putting your company at the end of the page title, the keywords are actually absorbing more of the impact for the search engine.

For more valuable specifics, you could even add a location, such as "Estate Planning Services in Plano: Mr. Moneytip."

Don't underestimate the power of your Web content in search engine optimization either. Good content that provides solid information, contains links, and is well organized with subheads can also drive up your Web ranking. Employ tactics discussed in Chapter 13 in setting up pages that make sense, are user-friendly, and are well developed.

Finally, you should also work with your Web site developer for the words in heading tags, file names, and meta tags. These are other areas that can fine-tune your site's optimization further.

Linking Strategies

To rank high on Google and the like, you also need to work to get your Web site on other sites, preferably related ones. Inbound links from other sites can have a significant effect on your rankings. The text of the link is also important; for maximum effect, it should include keywords of the page being linked to. For instance, the behemoth Amazon.com also has all kinds of sites—of authors, book clubs, recipes, fan clubs, museums—that feed into it by providing a link to buy merchandise (a book, CD, kitchen gadgets). That keeps Amazon at the top of its game. For your

Web site, seek out other important, authoritative sites, and suggest a link exchange.

For instance, if you have an online fabric store, find reputable sites offering sewing machines for sale, sewing patterns, craft books, sewing classes, knitting group signups, and notions and thread as possible links to include on your site—and vice versa. Go to the site owners and ask if they are amenable to a link exchange.

In addition, investigate providing content to a site that will offer a route back to your own. Many Web sites are constantly in search of credible, well-written, and useful content. Whatever your business, there are related Web sites that could benefit from your knowledge and point of view. In turn, your site will benefit from you supplying your know-how to the other site. For example, if you operate a Web site that sells office products, you might offer articles to business sites, covering such things as new trends in ergonomic office furniture, new copy machine capabilities, shortcut ways to prepare presentations, or ten nametag options for the next company event. The article posted on the business site then contains a link back to your office products site.

Reach Everyone You Need to

To ensure that you're reaching all of your intended audiences, your Web site may need to utilize technology you might never have considered or even known about.

A new buzz phrase for some Web sites is "508 compliance," a phrase that refers to Section 508 of the U.S. Rehabilitation Act. Funtown Splashtown USA, a family-themed amusement park near Portland, Maine, had a company goal to accommodate special needs groups and to make the attraction inviting, easy, and accessible for everyone. Part of that mission involved making their Web site at *www.funtownusa.com*—which offers group sales and advance tickets for purchase—508 compliant. This is a feature that all government Web sites must have, but it's an option for others. Being 508 compliant means the site is a source for the blind or visually impaired. You may want to consider whether 508 compliance is a presentation mode your site should offer. It uses adaptive technology to gracefully "degrade" a high-impact graphic site to present a plain text site that can be easily accessed with text-based browsers, such as Lynx.

Linking Your Expertise

Thousands of Web sites are hungry for content that keeps their destinations looking fresh, updated, and worth returning to. Pitching your expertise to other sites—which then will provide a link back to yours—is easier than you might realize. You just need to commit to carving out some time to brainstorm article ideas that relate to your business, and then approach sites to run them. Though you may not receive monetary compensation from the site you're hooking up with, you'll certainly be compensated in increased traffic flow to your site.

Libby Gill, an executive coach whose Web site is at *www.libbygill.com*, has successfully parlayed her know-how about branding strategies, work/life balance, and charting a road map to success into several articles for numerous Web sites that deal with management, women's issues, and even astrology. In each case, her article not only gives them valuable information, but also drives traffic back to her site with a link. There, visitors can buy her books or DVD, set the process in motion to become a coaching client of hers, or investigate booking her for a speaking engagement.

Running a business in the industry you're in gives you knowledge you might not even realize others would considerably value. When I'm working with a client on Web site creation and writing, part of my services includes "pitch angles" to get their site seen on other sites by utilizing their skills to provide information and Web content. If you see a site that is relevant to yours, contains content from outside sources, and appeals to an audience that meshes with your target, you should come up with an idea for content, and then e-mail the site owner via that site's contact form. Remember, however, that a chief competitor—though you may serve the same audience—probably won't be keen on offering your business an opportunity like this one.

Copy Strategies for Valuable E-Commerce

If your Web site sells products or services and uses a shopping cart component, make sure that your shopper is coming to an atmosphere that is pleasant and conducive to buying. Your site is a direct reflection of your product. Will your shopper think you are a retail amateur, or a trained and seasoned professional?

Have you ever noticed that you'll pay more attention to someone speaking directly to you, rather than to a group? That carries over to the first rule in writing copy for e-commerce: know the audience you're trying to reach and speak to them individually, as if you're talking to only one person.

Do You Really Need Flash or Splash?

In a bid to seem more sophisticated, some Web sites employ opening splash pages to view before you enter the site, or showcase motion features within the site. While those introductory splash pages, for example, may look vibrant, colorful, or jazzy, they may actually put an obstacle between your prospective customer and your Web site. Because they take extra time to download, they may be time-wasting and annoying for some users. Determine whether a splash page or even motion features such as Flash animation truly contribute to your Web site or merely distract attention from your message. What would your Web site be missing without it? If you're committed to including them on your Web site, consider having them as an option for users to dive into if they have the time and inclination to do so.

Use the Right Words for the Right Reasons

When you take a look at the products you've got lined up to sell on your Web site, you should take the time to come up with the best words to describe them and to sell them. Start by making a list of the attributes of your product or service, and then pinpoint the benefits of each of those assets for your audience. In devising these lists of attributes and benefits, be as specific as possible in your words and terms. Don't rely on words like good, great, best ever, and life-changing. Be more exact. In coming up with terms, clearly differentiate and emphasize how your product differs from its competitors. Look at sites that have products you've bought, and analyze the copy. What made you buy the product online?

In crafting your products' or services' benefits into copy, use your own words. Your copy will definitely come off as more natural that way. Copywriting such as this is different from other Web site writing (and different from letter or memo or proposal writing). With copywriting, you're writing as you talk, so contractions will be more prevalent, word usage may be a tad informal, and grammar may not be as proper.

After getting down the words that you think truly reflect your goods, play and mess around with your copy. Try alternate words and different ways to say the same things. Move words around to check out what sounds better. Try different variations of the headlines. Read your copy aloud to determine whether it's pleasing to your ear. As you work out your copy, do make sure you're staking truthful claims and haven't fallen prey to hyperbole. As excited as you might be about your product, you always want to be trustworthy, so that your customers will keep returning.

Finally, incorporate these final tips into your copywriting:

- ➲ Be mindful that the Web in particular demands that your copy hold your reader's interest. In this ultra-fast-paced format, boring copy and lengthy descriptions force scanning eyes to flee.
- ➲ Similarly, avoid imposing blocks of copy, which can overwhelm your site visitors.
- ➲ While you don't want to be overly redundant, do find all the appropriate, effective places to use your keywords (which means you may have to be redundant to some extent).
- ➲ Finally, check out more advertising copywriting guidelines, ideas, and techniques in Chapter 18. These are also applicable to Web site copywriting.

Billing and Shipping Instructions and Fulfillment

Once your customer's shopping cart is full, he or she expects to easily check out of your site with an order placed and a timeframe for your fulfillment of the order. If your customers are frustrated by the checkout process, they could end up leaving your site empty-handed. Make sure that you have clear instructions on billing and shipping in the "Customer Service" or "Customer Care" button on your navigation bar. Use a commonsense approach in delivering the instructions and use short sentences that are step-by-step and logical.

You've probably been to a site where you were buying an item and had to resort to calling the Web site's customer service department for help. You may even have altogether abandoned the site. If you've had such an experience, think back to it and analyze it. If possible, find the site again and delve into the procedures. What was confusing, confounding, or frustrating? Be sure that your Web site does not incorporate similar elements.

Keep Your Customer Apprised

After an order is placed, your Web site should generate an e-mail confirming the order in specific, concise, and friendly terms. Thank the customer for his or her patronage and reverify the order, the shipping method, and the delivery date.

Daily Candy

Though it's an editorial Web site, Daily Candy (*www.dailycandy.com*) highlights products, services, and establishments Monday through Friday with pithy prose that always makes buying the featured item seem like a sound and smart investment. Written from a distinct point of view, the daily copy uses words that always give you a feel for the product, why you'd be inclined to use or try it, why it would benefit you, and where you can get it. Their catchy profiles include makeup and cosmetics, clothing, restaurants, gifts, jewelry, accessories, spa services, fitness equipment, lodging and accommodations, baby gear—you name it. In fact, the site's editorial is so convincing and enjoyable that it also has a separate advertising division, in which clients pay the company to write about them in the Daily Candy style.

If you encounter a delay in getting the shipment out, let the customer know. Your company will risk losing the customer and being seen as undependable if you decide to hide bad news about fulfillment. An e-mail that provides a new delivery date and a contact number for questions and includes an apology for any inconvenience is professional and appreciated. However, if the order is extraordinarily large or its delay will have a negative impact on a major event, take appropriate measures with a phone call and a readiness to offer solutions to anticipated problems because of the delay.

Ways to Reach Out Further to Your Target Audience

You may be surprised at a few options and opportunities you can call on to better communicate with your target audience. Some are obvious and some are subtle, but all are worth putting to use.

Be Diligent with a Survey

Call on trusted comrades to visit your site and use it. Consider conducting a survey whether by phone, mail, or e-mail, that asks succinct questions about your Web site, particularly regarding its ease of use and the words it uses to convey its messages and offerings. You can refer to Chapter 11 to learn how to set up a survey.

Questions for your survey could include these: Do you understand the product information, descriptions, and billing instructions? Is there anything that might deter you from placing an order? What words called out to you in a positive way? Did any words or phrases leave you with a negative impression?

Think who might be able to offer you exceptionally valuable insights into the Web experience your site provides:

- A contact who has a successful e-commerce site
- A graphic designer who specializes in Web design
- A person who conducts most of his or her shopping online ·
- An entire group you have access to, all of whom could be prospective customers (depending on your business), such as a book club, a parent organization, a Rotary committee, or a quilting class

In combing through their responses, give weight to similar comments that you receive multiple times. Don't fall in love with your words and your site too easily. Try to remain objective so that you can offer your customers the shopping experience they deserve, and one that keeps them loyal—and returning—to your site.

E-Mailings

On your site, work with your Web designer to capture and harvest e-mail addresses so that you can send customers or clients newsworthy or interesting messages about your business that will be of value to them. Obviously, you don't want to unnecessarily exploit having your customers' e-mail addresses, but you would like to give them offers and information they can use. In line with being respectful of having someone's e-mail address, always offer a way to easily unsubscribe to your list.

Make sure that any e-mail you send is substantive. For instance, you can craft one that lets your customers know about February specials, new merchandise arrivals, and one-time-only deals, or provides a coupon for a purchase made within a specified amount of time.

Selling aside, you can also send out news about recent accomplishments, or give analysis of a relevant current news story that may have an impact on your customers' business or personal lives. Whatever information or offer you provide, include a link to your Web site so that your customer can start shopping.

If putting together e-mails to send to your customers on a regular basis seems overwhelming, you can turn to one of several companies that provide this service. Constant Contact, for example, can help create an e-mail campaign, maintain and grow your list, and then analyze results to determine whether your communications are effective. If you decide that you'd like to add e-mailings to your communication arsenal, sort through e-mailings you may receive regularly from different places of business. Note whether the e-mailings are powered by an e-mail service you may wish to consider for your business.

Web Site Newsletters

Newsletters sent out from your Web site give you an intelligent way of staying connected with both prospective and current customers. In the best case, a regular newsletter allows you to provide them with an entertaining, informative diversion that keeps your company on their radar. If they're not interested in reading at the time, they can save it for later or delete it. Here again, as in e-mailings, you must provide the option of unsubscribing at any time.

Take a look at some online newsletters that you receive to trigger ideas for your own. The newsletters shouldn't be long. Some are formatted to just fill a screen. They should, however. contain fresh, appealing content that provides a service to the reader, and relates to your business on some level.

In writing your newsletter, don't use a hard-sell approach. Keep it light but informative. If you have some big company news—such as a new product that has been launched, or a major award won—by all means mention it, but don't send out newsletters that are rife with self-serving mentions. This presents your chance to keep awareness there, and focus on the goodwill factor. In addition, always provide a link to your site and contact information.

To keep content coming for future newsletters, jot down ideas as you get them. Look at other newsletters in your field—checking out the competition will no doubt help you generate ideas for your own company. Also, consider tackling a theme for each newsletter. That will bring cohesion to your approach for that edition, and help you stay focused to brainstorm for article ideas in a single, general area.

Opt-In for All

For visitors to subscribe to your newsletter on your Web site, use an "Opt-In" approach. With that method, potential subscribers enter their e-mail addresses in the "Opt-In" field on your site. Then, they receive an e-mail with a link in it to click on, to validate their e-mail address. This process prevents your list from receiving fake signups and assures you that you have readers who really want to receive the newsletter. Again, in the same vein, make it easy for readers to unsubscribe with a link in each e-mail newsletter you send out.

Consistency Matters

Once you start sending newsletters, be consistent. If you commit to sending out one a month, stick to that schedule. You and your company will suffer an unprofessional impression if the newsletters arrive scattershot. If necessary, backlog some evergreen pieces—articles or news that keep a current feel—for some breathing room.

In addition, be consistent with your format so that customers can readily identify which company the newsletter is coming from. Staying true to a format will also help in planning, storing ideas for, and writing the newsletters on a constant basis.

An Analysis Quiz: How Strong Are Your Web Site's Messages?

If your Web site is experiencing exploding growth and superior sales, you could probably surmise that you're connecting with your audience, employing easy-to-use navigation, and describing your products or services particularly well. So, with those goals in mind, consider your answers to these questions in taking your Web site to the next level:

The Text:

In writing the Web site, did you have your audience in mind at all times?

Is your text short and pithy? Have you chunked context into tight paragraphs?

Are your pages complete? If a page isn't ready, does it have a "Coming Soon" label? Do you have a deadline to have any "Coming Soon" elements finished?

Are you constantly updating your site?

The Navigation:

Are your menus meaningful, do they relate to the actual content provided, and do they make sense?

Can customers easily get to the information or products they're looking for?

Do your pages do a good job of standing alone, or are they too dependent on the other pages on your site?

Have you taken full advantage of links and keywords within your Web site?

The Products and Services Copy:

Does copy for services or products effectively and articulately point out unique attributes and exceptional benefits?

Will your customer experience speed, ease, and understanding, from picking out the product to receiving the contents of the shopping cart?

Do you have contact information readily available so customers can get in touch if they have a question about a product or service?

▶▶ **Test Drive**

Think of one way you could enhance your site's linkage to improve your search engine ranking, and implement it. You could:

➲ Review your site and look for new ways to insert valuable keywords into your site real estate.

➲ Create a site map for your site, or dissect the one you have, and make it more descriptive.

➲ Position yourself as an expert on your business, and offer content to a related Web site that will offer a link back to yours.

➲ Contact your Web site designer and set up a brainstorming session utilizing his or her expertise to create and implement new traffic-building initiatives.

Mapping Out Your Marketing Message

PART **4**

Getting Your Particular Message Out There

Among marketing professionals, there's a favorite saying that specifically relates to Web sites, but applies to marketing in general: Selling without a marketing plan is like having a billboard in the middle of a forest—you can't sell your product or service if you don't let people know about it.

After you spend so much time, energy, and money launching your business, you may feel that your tough work is completed, but that would be like running a race without completing the last lap. Your business can't succeed without a marketing plan to get your company's name, products, and services out there to the people who can make your business succeed or fail: paying customers or clients.

While your company, product, or service may be exemplary, revolutionary, life-changing, and top-quality, your business is doomed if it's not marketed. However, communicating your marketing messages effectively can guarantee your success.

Corralling Your Customers

A common rule of thumb suggests that most businesses will get 80 percent of their sales from 20 percent of their customers. Following that guideline, research becomes a vital part of the marketing plan, helping you to ascertain that prized target market by answering these questions: Who are they? Why do they need or want to pay for your product or service? When are their prime times for purchasing it? How can you attract them? All of those aspects feed into how you can reach that target market and turn them into paying customers.

The Power of Position

A marketing plan works to proclaim how you want your company, product, or service to be perceived by your customers. What's your unique selling position, that particular point of pride that makes your company stand out? Is it top-notch customer service, exclusive goods, bargain basement prices, worldwide experience? In this area, you must go for specificity; you can't select "all of the above" for your target audience. In homing in, you'll be able to take a more exact, and effective, approach in reaching your customers.

Brand and Your Big Picture

"Brand" has become an overused term in corporate-speak, as its meaning has stretched into a generic notion that sometimes confuses business owners. For instance, you may be encouraged to "take care of your brand," "make your brand have an impact," or be asked "what does that say about your brand?" These comments and questions don't make much sense if you haven't truly focused on what your brand is, or what it can do for your company.

Brand refers to the identity and personality of your company. It plays a particularly integral role in marketing. Your brand should be present in messages you want your company to convey, in images you hope to conjure up in clients or customers, and in feelings you expect to inspire in potential patrons. Understanding your brand and its place in your marketing becomes crucial because, to be effective, each piece of marketing material has to stay true to how you want your company to be perceived.

So, how are you perceived? Branding goes beyond the tagline or slogan at the bottom of an ad (which is discussed in Chapter 18), the direct mail piece you're sending out, or the news that fuels press releases this month and next. Advertising and publicity campaigns come and go, but your brand stays with your company always.

To articulate your brand, ask:

- What differentiates you from the competition?
- What are your company's core values?
- How would you verbalize the spirit of your company?
- If your company were a person, what would that person look like? How would he or she dress? Where would that person live? What would his or her favorites include?
- If you had to use five words or pithy phrases that describe your company, what would they be? Don't settle for general, obvious words like "good," "fast," or "cheap."
- What does your company offer its clients and customers in hard product or service terms?
- What does your company offer its customers in emotional terms?

⮑ Do your company's visual expressions (logo) and materials (letterhead, Web site pages) jibe with what you believe your company represents? Why or why not?

Clarifying the content and direction of your brand will make the task of creating and producing winning marketing materials much easier. Establishing clarity in what your brand represents allows you to present it more crisply to an audience. In turn, that audience will be more receptive to it because the brand's messages are targeted toward them, understandable, and effective in explaining what they will gain from buying into your product or service.

What Does Your Logo Say?

Often your logo is the first impression a customer or client sees. So what does yours say? Is it congruent with your company's philosophy and products or services? Does it fit the personality of your brand? While a logo can't possibly be all-inclusive in describing your company's personnel and activities, it should strongly suggest what your company stands for. In so doing, it must embody the enterprise's spirit, may that be seriously financial, entertainingly educational, or exotically fashionable.

Take a look at these logos. What does each one say about the company? Do you get an instant feel for what the company does, what it represents, and what it can do for you? Why or why not? (Logos courtesy of Indigo Creative, *www.indigocreativestudio.com*)

Letting Your Company's Image Do the Talking

Once you've successfully assessed your brand, and before learning more about putting it into company promotion, consider some corporations with strong brands, and the efforts they put forth to further them.

So often, people don't realize that their company's image and employees and the image they individually and collectively present can be the most valuable marketing tool. Think about the following five pairs of companies. Even though each pair could be considered part of the same category, they're remarkably different. In each pairing, what does each brand name conjure up to you? Is it positive, negative, or both? What background, experience, or information has formed your opinion?

- Apple versus IBM
- Coca-Cola versus Evian
- Mercedes versus Saturn
- Google versus Yahoo
- Neiman Marcus versus Kmart

You most likely have formed your opinion about the brand and image of each of these companies from several visual and experiential components that worked in tandem. You've seen commercials (advertising), or in-store or in-showroom signage, visited a Web site, heard or read news stories (publicity), or been on the receiving end of an offer or coupon (direct mail).

While you obviously want to get your company marketed to the right buying audience, you also want to make sure that in doing so you're projecting a constant, consistent, professional image.

As you create and produce materials, make sure that all of your marketing communications bear out and reflect those characteristics. While you may not have the budget of McDonald's or Target, you can still take a cue from their winning ways.

Before delving into higher-cost initiatives, first consider even the simplest means. Make sure to use every outgoing piece of paper—letterhead, faxes, even receipts—to promote your business. For instance, make sure your Web site, toll-free phone number, or both are on receipts, envelopes,

| Inside Track | Developing Five Key Messages |

Carrie Gerlach Cecil is CEO of Anachel Communications, Inc., a media firm specializing in sports, entertainment, and *Fortune* 500 companies, with offices in Nashville and Los Angeles. Anachel creates and implements branding strategies that work to impact corporate image and stimulate revenue growth.

Anachel advises that in developing your company's key messages, you identify the company's stance on five themes that showcase your company's value, its strength, its service, its tradition, and its relevance.

All of your company's employees must understand and embrace the key messages that develop. Following is a sample that Anachel might provide to a national sports league, such as the fictitious booming televised sport, the American Wrestleball League (AWL).

Value: AWL is a smart buy that delivers reach; an attractive, growing, and passionate audience; and thrilling and exciting programming.

Strength: AWL is a leading sports property with global, world-class media partners, and it is a property that helps build other media brands.

Service: AWL has a unique commitment to customer service and works diligently to help its partners be successful.

Tradition: AWL is a great American and family tradition.

Relevance: AWL is a culturally relevant and contemporary sport that is on the cutting edge of broadcast and new media technology.

The "smart buy" reference would be specific to the television arena, such as advertising sales and broadcasting rights and renewal—but for the sponsorship sales team, it could be tailored to fit their goals. For example "Value: AWL has 75 million adult fans, 60 percent male and 40 percent female, representing one-third of the U.S. population. AWL sponsors secured nearly $5 billion in total exposure last year."

and shipping boxes. Take advantage of every opportunity to have your name out there.

Use electronic documents similarly. For instance, you can easily change the signature (discussed in Chapter 11) on the bottom of your outgoing e-mail messages to mention the latest company promotion, offer a coupon, or include your tagline. Survey all possibilities. Never miss an opportunity to get your company's name, image, what it does, and whom it serves out there.

Telling the story about your brand could be one of the best ways to showcase its essence and value.

You can read more about the Post-it invention and how it became an American institution at *www.3m.com*.

Developing a Campaign

For some, developing a marketing campaign may seem to be an unwieldy task. If you break down a campaign into steps, however, you can see that you're essentially taking a three-pronged approach: you're trying to curry favor with your buying audience, encourage them to take an action that will reward your company, and leave a good impression of your company while you're at it.

While that task may seem arduous, simply arming your company with a mission statement, business plan, and the image you're trying to project puts you well on your way.

So, what is your particular message? What are you trying to project about your company, its goods, and its services? Once again, to begin, you must know your audience. Who are they? What do they look like? How do they spend their time? How much income do they earn? Are they single or married? Do they have kids?

If you're marketing your goods and services to another business, do you know all the specifics of that business?

A marketing campaign canvasses all the promotional aspects you may want to utilize for your company and its products or services. Typically, the campaign will employ several tactics to get your message out. Almost all of those tactics will fall into three categories or marketing vehicles:

Direct Marketing: This method draws on appealing to a potential customer through postal mail, e-mail, or flyers, often with a deadline attached to urge its audience to act quickly.

Public Relations: This category includes a company sending out news about itself to a variety of media organizations in the hope of obtaining positive coverage that, ideally, will translate into sales.

Advertising: Whether for print, radio, television, or the Web, a company pays for space or time on a media outlet that typically already attracts a large and, hopefully, extremely targeted audience.

Does Your Brand Have a Story?

Great brands tend to have great stories. For instance, the obstacles that 3M's Post-it Notes encountered in both manufacturing and marketing may cause you to wonder how the product ever launched—and then phenomenally succeeded—when it was almost killed on several occasions. In fact, its languishing would have slid the product into oblivion had it not been for the dedication of a new product development manager and his ally in sales. In a last-ditch effort, they made cold calls on the streets of Richmond, Virginia, to see if anyone would buy the product. Their success in sampling on that day parlayed Post-it Notes into one of 3M's most prominent and profitable assets.

Different Company, Different Campaign

Much as business plans differ greatly from company to company, each enterprise will also have a different marketing campaign. Some may rely mostly on direct marketing; others may try a pure publicity approach. You owe it to your company to determine which mix of methods will work best for your particular set of circumstances and objectives.

Goals

Begin writing the campaign with a section that outlines your goals. Strive to describe your goals as exactly, articulately, and specifically as possible. Don't rely on words and phrases that aim high but are vague. For instance, "We want to sell a lot" should be rephrased as, "We want to sell more of the surveillance equipment line to mid-size companies."

You should divide goals into two areas: those that can be measured and those that are more impressionistic. A measured goal would be: "Secure-All needs $75,000 in sales this month." An impressionistic goal would be: "Secure-All should be regarded as the low-cost system that brings high-price results."

In writing your marketing campaign, you need to consider each possible tactic and ask yourself these questions: How will this bring the company closer to this particular goal? Will the message in this vehicle augur well for sales? Will the message resonate with targeted customers?

Research

Research will prove to be incredibly valuable on multiple fronts as you assemble and craft a strategic, balanced marketing campaign. If your business plan is recent, you can consider the information you put in the marketing plan section of it to be instrumental.

If that market research needs updating, remember that doing so involves collecting and analyzing information about the customers you're most interested in reaching. The data may delve into buying habits, opinions, and attitudes of current or potential customers. As primary data, it can be gathered from surveys, questionnaires, or focus groups. Second to that information, you can also collect information from valuable ancillary resources, such as magazines, industry publications, government agencies, trade associations, and the like that can offer insights into sales trends, growth rates, demographic profiles, and regional business statistics.

Once furnished with these facts and figures, you can make informed, intelligent decisions that will drive your campaign.

Some pointers regarding research:

⮑ Be clear about the information you're trying to procure, and why.
⮑ Build on what you're already doing. You can use receipts and delivery addresses to find hotspots where your customers live or work. Of course, you can use sales info to gauge the popularity

of products, and the days, months, or seasons in which they are bought.

⮑ Take advantage of information already out there, such as statistics gathered by the U.S. Census Bureau or data that your local chamber of commerce has on hand.

⮑ Be vigilant in tracking the competition's advertising schedules, changes in their store layouts, and operating procedures.

⮑ Be precise. If you're using a questionnaire, ask pertinent, well-articulated questions, and be aggressive about gathering and evaluating responses. Don't have surveys at your place of business that are never handed out and, in time, become outdated and useless.

⮑ Don't rely on one information source, particularly the Internet. Make sure the information you're collecting is well sourced and easily backed up.

⮑ Don't throw away good research just because it doesn't support the tack you wanted to take, or the results you thought you'd see. Instead, heed the information and incorporate it into your efforts.

Brainstorm

Brainstorming is a premier strategy for generating ideas for your marketing campaign. With all vehicles—direct marketing, public relations, and advertising—firmly planted in mind, split up the session into three sections. For more information on each of those areas, investigate direct marketing in Chapter 15, public relations in Chapter 16, and advertising in Chapter 17. With each strategy featured in a starring role, have meeting attendees freely offer suggestions for different approaches that will appeal to your clients or customers. The guidelines, protocol, and stimuli for a productive brainstorming session are discussed more thoroughly in Chapter 20.

The brainstorm should produce a lengthy laundry list of ideas that you can then parlay and fine-tune into actual projects that you want to make part of your campaign.

Organizing the Campaign

Once you've got your ideas assembled, you need to put them in a cohesive format that can be easily followed and implemented.

In the opening section of the campaign, you should restate your goals, both measurable and impressionistic.

Then, divide up your plan into three sections: direct marketing, advertising, and public relations. Within each of those sections, list the main ideas you expect to implement, and the responsibilities and activities that will be pertinent to each.

For instance, in the advertising section, planning a thirty-second radio spot requires you to decide what the ad will feature or say, which stations you want to broadcast it (this is called the media buy), what the logline (a one-sentence description) for the ad's actual copy will be, and when the ad should run.

Budgeting

This aspect tends to weigh heaviest on a marketing campaign because most of your efforts need money to be completed. However, realize that some endeavors will take less money, and some might be practically free. Nevertheless, you must take the time to research the cost of running a thirty-second radio spot on the top radio station in your market, or a full-page ad in a national parenting magazine, or the fee for a targeted mailing list for a direct mail piece. Once you've done this homework, you may find that some efforts will have to be scrapped or refashioned because they're simply too expensive. Again, however, the best time to know this is in the development of the marketing campaign, not once it's already off and running.

Make sure that each "line item" or project in each of your sections has at least a rough estimate of costs attached.

The Timetable

All of your successful ideas—those that have made the cut for the campaign—and research for your marketing campaign will be unrewarded if you don't lay out a timetable for their implementation. Obviously, you need to attach a deadline to each activity. Although this timing is particularly pertinent to your campaign's initiatives, remember other scheduling that might factor in. For instance, you might want to get a promo card mailed before a trade show that you're attending, or you might want to place an ad for your hospital product in a medical journal before a doctors' conference convenes.

Once your schedule is in place, make sure that it becomes part of your company's overall calendar so that it smoothly flows along with and integrates into all of your business operations.

Realizing the Role of Direct Marketing

Direct marketing cuts a wide swath, but it basically boils down to pieces you write and develop that are delivered individually, either by e-mail or post. This category includes such pieces as a catalog, a sales post card, or an e-mail message. Because they run the gamut from simple pieces to extravagant mailings, direct marketing pieces can have widely divergent budgets. Your goal in any piece of direct marketing is for someone to take an action: to buy a product in your catalog, to come to your store for a special sale, or to jump to your Web site to make a purchase or to set up a meeting.

With direct marketing, there is no middle man: the company's message goes straight into the hands or to the eyes of the consumer, and pieces can be structured for reading when the audience has more time. Direct marketing also frequently takes advantage of specials, promotions, or coupons—often with a deadline attached—to urge its audience to act quickly.

Understanding the Purposes of Public Relations

While no marketing effort can be considered "free," public relations does afford the opportunity to try to secure coverage for your business by having the media transmit your message via news reporting, rather than paying for your message with an advertisement, such as a commercial.

However, while you work to deliver a tailored message, the media has its own agenda. It would be foolish to think or believe that you would have control over your message when the media is involved as the "mouthpiece." Remember that you're at the mercy of the media outlet, be it a newspaper article, magazine piece, nightly news report, radio interview, or Internet column.

Beyond Advertising

While advertising can be tremendously effective, it has lately been perceived as losing its grip amid the clutter that has seemingly ramped up on television and radio airwaves. As such, consumers have been paying not to see or hear commercials either with digital video recorders, such as TiVo, that allow viewers to skip over ads, or with satellite radio providers, such as Sirius or XM, that beam commercial-free music and programming.

With public relations efforts, the "news" could be linked to a special event, a product launch, or some important company milestone. With it, you hope that the media covers your company and that specific activity or product favorably, to engender a positive image and goodwill for the company that translates into higher sales.

Knowing the Elements of Advertising

With advertising, you control the message entirely, because you're paying for it—in newspaper or magazine pages, on billboards, on television interspersed in programming, in a movie theater before the previews begin, on the radio during music breaks, or on the Internet as a banner ad or image on a Web site. The choices for advertising your company are omnipresent.

However, advertising is much more than just selecting an outlet and deciding that you'll fork over money to get a commercial placed or your logo shown. You must vigorously research the audience the outlet reaches to make sure it's a match for your company's products or services. You must be committed to using the advertising to convey a focused message, whether that is to increase sales, to alert customers, or to raise awareness. You must consider the costs involved, which in advertising can be substantial.

So, while advertising can play a fruitful role in your marketing endeavors, you need to realize that the art of advertising encompasses the science of planning and analysis as well.

Therefore, communicators are busily and innovatively trying a host of other marketing methods to try to get their products seen and their messages heard.

SCORE

If you don't know where to turn first in trying to develop key messages for your company, consider contacting SCORE (Service Corps of Retired Executives). A resource partner with the Small Business Administration, SCORE—known as "Counselors to America's Small Business"—is a nonprofit association with nearly 400 chapters nationwide. More than 10,500 volunteer counselors provide individual counseling and business workshops for aspiring entrepreneurs and small business owners. These volunteers boast their own impressive backgrounds in business, so they can help business owners through such phases as generating and assessing ideas, preparing business plans, raising capital, and managing operations. SCORE volunteers can be exceptionally helpful in the areas of formulating a company's messages and marketing products and services. The organization has assisted more than 7.2 million people with online and face-to-face small-business counseling since it began in 1964. You can find a counselor in your area who can provide the expertise you need by visiting *www.score.org*.

Gauging Success

You'll do yourself and your company a tremendous disservice if you don't set up a plan to evaluate the marketing campaign you're implementing.

A few ways to assess the effectiveness of a campaign initiative include spikes in sales, new customers, store or Web site traffic, and click-through rates. Click-through rate refers to the percentage of Web site viewers who click on a banner ad of your company's that takes them to your site. Sites that sell ad space usually track those, and then provide you with performance reports. You also may set up a Web page specifically linked only to your banner ads, and monitor traffic on that particular page. You may already receive daily reports that record traffic patterns for your Web site, but if not, consider purchasing software that gives you those capabilities.

Other methods to monitor your success include offering a coupon with an expiration date on a direct mail card, or offering a free gift-with-purchase on an ad that the customer brings in with them.

While this point may seem obvious, remember to monitor all these components as a base line before you launch your marketing campaign. If you don't, you'll have no data to compare your results to, and judging the effectiveness of your campaign will be futile.

▶▶ Test Drive

Consider the marketing vehicles you already use. Now think about your competitors and the messages they send to customers or clients:

- ➲ Do they use similar marketing avenues, or different ones?
- ➲ Do you know how effective their marketing methods are?
- ➲ Using direct marketing, public relations, or advertising, or a combination of the three, how can you make your message stand out more from your competitors?
- ➲ Has there been a marketing category that you've been resistant to use for your business? Why? Is it now worth a second look?

Direct Marketing Pieces

Direct marketing covers a wide range of materials that can very effectively get the word out about your business, a particular product, a one-time promotion, or even your company philosophy in general.

In many ways, these varied pieces can promote a grassroots approach because you're putting information about your company straight into the hands—or in front of the eyes—of a potential customer or client without any middleman involvement. It's a shining opportunity to present a focused message appealing directly to an intended recipient, and it can yield highly profitable results.

Direct marketing materials include (but aren't limited to): ·

- ➲ Mail pieces
- ➲ Flyers
- ➲ Brochures
- ➲ Sell sheets
- ➲ E-mail messages
- ➲ Catalogs

Direct Mail

Most likely, one or more direct mail pieces sits in your mailbox today. At home, there may be a flyer from a neighborhood gardener, a postcard for a jewelry store's grand opening, or a brochure from a health-care provider. At the office, you may receive an order form for office supplies, a catalog for corporate gifts, or a press pack and rate card from a publication wanting you to advertise.

Each year, an estimated 50 billion pieces of direct mail are sent out, bringing in about $120 billion in sales. Organizations use them to raise funds, boost sales, sharpen an image, or generate leads.

In crafting a direct mail piece, you must first give it a goal by answering three questions: What's your message? Who's your audience? What do you want the piece to accomplish in reaching that audience? Be specific about the audience you want to reach. Although unexpected uses may arise for the piece, don't take a one-size-fits-all approach. Are you driving people to buy from your Web site? Are you encouraging an audience to purchase a new product you have on the market? Are you persuading people to try out a new service you offer?

With a direct mail piece, your goal is often to urge an immediate response from the recipients by promoting a benefit that speaks directly to them; this benefit enhancement is the crux of most direct mail pieces. The audience, in turn, should want to associate with or patronize your company to receive that benefit. To be the most successful in triggering a high response rate, your pieces must go specifically to the target audience that will care the most about getting that benefit, which means that getting your piece in front of the right people is critical. You can accomplish that by distributing the piece to a highly targeted mailing list.

Mailing Lists

Your best bet is a mailing list that includes previous and existing customers, as well as any acquaintances who could provide good referrals or leads. However, you can also purchase a list from list-rental companies; magazine publishers; and membership directories of trade, special interest, or local organizations. Additionally, you could pull names from public records and even the phone book. In any case, the list should be scrutinized, deleting nonessential and duplicate entries, adding others you deem possibilities, and checking for any errors, such as incomplete addresses or zip codes, or misspelled personal and company names. If you rent or buy a list, check the date the list was compiled to ensure you're not wasting money by sending your pieces to unintended recipients.

Form and Function

Your mail piece can take on many different formats. To keep costs in line, think in efficient but professional terms to create and produce your mailing. Pieces that are hand-stamped (rather than bulk-mailed) and addressed to personal names (rather than "Occupant" or "Valued Customer") carry more weight with the recipients. However, they also cost more. If you can fit your message on a post card, use that mode. Sending a post card also eliminates the barrier of an envelope, allowing your message to be immediately seen.

Have the paper or card stock you're using reflect your product. In other words, if you're promoting a high-end service or luxury good, opt for materials that would be suitably on-par.

Don't be afraid to inject a personal touch into your piece, which can make it seem even more targeted to the reader and more appealing for the recipient to open. For instance, there may be a postage stamp that the U.S. Postal Service sells that perfectly fits your company's brand. The Postal Service now even lets you custom-design and order stamps that bear your company logo. Also, while it may cost more, consider an envelope that might stand out from the crowd. Some envelope possibilities include vellum, colored stock with a raised pattern, or a style that sports an out-of-the-ordinary finish.

Finally, if you're using an envelope, use it wisely. Don't hesitate to put a message on the envelope's outside flap—there you have a captive audience for people opening the mail to get their first taste of what's inside.

Check into Post Cards

Post cards present a quick, inexpensive, and illustrative opportunity for sending a direct mail piece. You can find several vendors online—such as *www.4by6 .com*—that specialize in printing post cards for business mailings. Some even offer creative services that will take care of the design process for you. You can easily tailor a piece that looks representative of your company, and select a complementary finish, such as high-gloss, matte, or satin. Most of the printing companies have speedy turnaround times and attractive rates. Particularly if you're trying out a direct mail piece for the first time, consider this option for experimenting with the direct marketing process and return rate.

Your Message and a Call to Action

Don't waste the reader's time with ineffective copy. Start with your most important point, and flow from there with sound word choices, powerful adjectives, and compelling language. Be aware that readers will find hokey copy, screaming headlines, and over-the-top promises transparent. Opt for a conversational tone that speaks one-on-one to the reader and conveys immediate benefits.

PUT SOME HEART & SOUL INTO YOUR
HOUSE OF STYLE

Cushy, comfy baby blankets and super-sweet gift sets, tablecloths for your next supper or soiree, and pillows to make a room pop.

For baby, newlywed, new homeowner… or you, these vibrant vintage-inspired designs mix function with flair, glitz with substance.

All creations and designs are totally original and available only through **Practical Whimsy.com** and select retailers.

GROOVY GOODS. HIP TIPS. SNAPPY MENUS.
…ALL AT A DESKTOP NEAR YOU.

While browsing the on-line store, scoop up **Practical Whimsy's** tasty – and free! – recipes and ideas for both everyday eating and easy entertaining.

Founded by husband-and-wife Joe & Lori LoCicero, Practical Whimsy blends know-how from their extensive work in the creative arts for Hollywood studios and Fortune 500 companies with the charm and warmth of southern hospitality and wit.

Joe's from Atlanta; Lori's from the O.C. Together, they cook wicked-yet-healthy feasts, hip up the home, throw jammin' parties, and raise a **GQ**-boy and a little fashionista. Their sensibilities mesh to bring you chic goods that brighten your rooms… and menus and tips that warm your home.

Read the Practical Whimsy column in every issue of "Y'ALL: The Magazine of Southern People," on newsstands nationwide.

FREE SHIPPING ON YOUR NEXT ORDER!
Simply enter "Promo" as your shipping option during checkout.

PRACTICALWHIMSY.COM
Joe@PracticalWhimsy.com
Lori@PracticalWhimsy.com

SOUTHERN HOSPITALITY. HOLLYWOOD STYLE.

This direct mail piece, an initial promotion for the Practical Whimsy Web site launch, was highly, specifically targeted to current customers, handpicked entertainment industry contacts (such as network and studio executives, agents, producers, and celebrities), and select media outlets. (Courtesy Practical Whimsy, Inc., *www.practicalwhimsy.com*)

Make sure that your words can be easily read and aren't muddled by complicated graphics or overshadowed by neon colors. Use simple fonts. Also, while it's true that color will always attract more attention than simple black and white, don't bombard your piece with too much or too many. Often, one or two main colors with another one or two playing a supporting role will be eye-catching enough. One consideration worth noting: in a piece with just one or two colors, a metallic one can make a bold statement.

Craft your message such that you're serving your goal by clearly delineating the action you want the reader to take. By all means, give your reader a reason to act. Have a deadline for the offer you're making. You can entice that action with a promise of free shipping or delivery, a coupon, a free gift with purchase, or an extended warranty.

Look for Other Opportunities

Ever get a postcard about subscribing to *Vanity Fair* magazine in a mailed issue of *Bon Appétit?* Consider having a direct mail piece from your company put into the shipments of other businesses. Find out if a related but noncompeting organization is amenable to a reciprocal venture, or how much it might cost to have your printed piece included in its shipments.

Further, in your action line, remember that asking the recipient to place a call or visit a Web site requires less effort (and gets more action) than having them return a piece of mail to you. If your recipient is supposed to send information back to you, provide a postage-paid, pre-addressed envelope. Whatever your goal, make the action as easy as possible for the reader to take.

Learn from Your Mailings

Finally, code your mailings so that you can track responses and gauge success.

If you've never attempted direct mail before, start off with a small batch and make a test run. Work out the kinks. The call to action may be unclear, you may notice errors in the copy, or you may even find out that you haven't attached enough postage. It may be worthwhile to send one piece to yourself before you mail the others to see how it looks. Once you've got your bearings, you can expand your efforts and use your previous experience to make future mailings even more successful.

Brochures

A brochure gives you the opportunity to present your business in an extended format, for either sales or informational purposes. It presents a true chance to elaborate on your business, your products, and your services, and to showcase your strengths, lending credibility to even a newly formed company.

When taking on the creation of a brochure, be sure that you've assigned it an objective, know the audience you're trying to reach with it, and know how it will be distributed. If you're a real estate broker who's eager to add agents to his roster in a branch office of a national company, you could use a brochure to recruit those agents (your objective). With that objective, you could gear the brochure to potential recruits who are interested in an opportunity with a new company, who might be successful in another field but looking to make a career change, or who want to transfer from another company office to yours (these groups are your audience). The brochure could be distributed at career fairs, company conventions, business seminars, community forums, and housing expos (or other distribution points specific to your business).

Remember too that brochures can become their own direct mail pieces when sent to the right mailing list. For instance, the real estate broker's brochures could also be sent to a list of aspiring agents who just received their real estate license.

The Copy

Once you've assessed the brochure's mission, target audience, and points of distribution, assemble a rough outline of the categories and content you want it to point out. What would logical sections be?

Begin with a captivating headline that captures the spirit, tone, and content of the entire brochure, and draws in the reader. You may also consider a theme that pulls the entire piece together. For instance, in the case of the broker's brochure, the piece could be titled "Solve the Mystery to Your Future Success," with each section pulling up a "clue" to make that happen.

The clues for future success could be the financial benefits and advantages of joining the real estate agency; the familial office atmosphere; the office's growth rate since opening; other agents' success stories; and the booming real estate market in that particular area.

Write a headline for each clue, and then expound upon each area with short paragraphs or bullet points.

You may also want to include some other informative tips in the brochure that make the piece one that its audience will keep. For example, if you run a housekeeping service, you may include tips on treating stubborn stains, or keeping laundry smelling fresh.

For the content, do research that makes the best case for each section. That may include interviews with executives at headquarters, statistics compiled from your office's operations, and interviews with satisfied customers for quotes to be included.

The Illustrations and Layout

Make sure the outside of the brochure immediately resonates with the reader. Whether you're selling a product or launching a brand, use an image that strikes a chord, announces a benefit, or otherwise urges the reader to look inside. Don't take up the entire space with a company logo.

To complement the copy inside, determine what photography is available. You may also want to break up the copy with sidebars, trivia snippets, or a Q&A component.

Spend some time creating a sample design, roughly drawing in the layout, copy blocks, and illustrations to determine the feel and flow of the brochure.

Consider making your brochure in a shape outside the norm. While the typical brochure is an 8½" × 11" tri-fold, six-panel piece, you might consider the enlarged shape of a nail polish bottle if you run a salon, or a balloon shape if you run a party supply store. Of course, these versions will cost more than a standard format, but do consider a wide array of possibilities in trying to make your brochure produce the biggest return on investment.

Finally, while you should rely on your imagination in putting together a memorable brochure, don't forget to include the basics, such as your Web site address, a contact name and phone number, a company address, and other particulars that will remind and encourage the reader to take action.

Sell Sheets and Flyers

Sell sheets and flyers are often leave-behinds that companies distribute at people's homes, in offices, at conventions, and during trade shows. Because of their wide use and availability, you should plan to use them for several audiences.

With this format, there is usually no mailing list, and you may not know the intended recipient's name. The goal is to develop a multipurpose piece that you can use for a host of occasions, all in hopes of generating sales, increasing awareness, or both.

Sell Sheets

Sell sheets tend to be more expensively produced than are flyers. Often sell sheets are four-color, professionally printed, and contain sharp images, graphics, or photos to accompany the copy. The flashy visuals and lengthier (though pithy) copy bring attention to products and services.

Flyers

Flyers are usually simply copies that may (or may not) have been produced on colored paper, and may (or may not) contain a simple graphic.

In analyzing the following example of a flyer, which is a piece that was offered door-to-door in several neighborhoods, consider a number of the errors that you can learn from and apply to several direct marketing pieces.

SPARKLY CLEAN WINDOW CLEANING

Dear neighbors,
Our company is now offering special flat rates for outside window cleaning in this area:

> 1 story house................$89
> 2 story house................$149
> Interior windows +50%

Our window cleaners will be working in your neighborhood. If you wish to be scheduled, please call us now at 215-555-8773 (limited booking).

This particular flyer was printed on light blue paper. That backdrop and easy-to-read font are both good choices. However, the flyer offered little enticement for calling to book an appointment. In the first line, "special flat rates" should have detailed how much could be saved in this "special." How much in savings does the $89 rate translate into? The "Interior windows +50%" is unclear. Should the potential customer add on half of $89 to get interior windows cleaned as well? If that's the case, why not save the reader the trouble and use bullet points to specify prices to have interior windows done too?

Further, this piece would have benefited immeasurably from some graphic. Whatever artwork you use, it shouldn't be too plain or on-the-nose. Strive for an image that will pull the reader in with a clever bit of thinking. For instance, the art might be laced with simple humor or bring about a sense of relief in the recipient. Maybe this flyer could have included a line drawing of a worker on a piece of scaffolding shining a window at a home's exaggeratedly tall roofline. The reader might think, "Wow! They'll take care of my windows even way up there. It'd be great to have someone else do that!"

If you don't have ready access to a graphic designer, consider the options of clip art. Clip art books are widely available in local bookstores, and you can even download images online (for a fee). Literally millions of copyright-free images are available.

In the last section of the example, the flyer should include the actual dates that the cleaners will be in the area. When delivered, this flyer had the words "next week" scrawled in, but actual days and dates would have been more specific and directed a reader's mind to focus on when cleaners could actually come over. Finally, the phrase "limited booking" is unclear, although it probably means they have just a few spots available. If that's the case, say it. Or better yet, give a more specific deadline: "Call and book by tomorrow at noon, and receive an additional 5% off the service."

As with all direct marketing pieces, consider going a bit further with your flyer if your budget allows. In the case of this flyer, the business might have used a brad to affix a clear piece of transparent paper (similar to those used for overhead projectors) to give the effect of reading the flyer through a very (or sparkly) clean window.

Sales Letters

Sales letters are arguably the most common direct marketing device.

Think about your business, and write down some of the most pressing issues that face your clientele. Then, articulate the benefits that your product or service offers to remedy those issues.

With your letter, you want to immediately grab the attention of the reader with that provocative opportunity to make their life easier somehow. How can you let them know that your company has the answer to solve a problem of theirs? Or, how will your business offer a benefit or solution, but do the job better than a company they currently use?

As an example, look at a recent letter you've received to renew a magazine subscription. What's the lure they're tempting you with? Sales letters are often written in a persuasive tone that spurs the reader to feel that he or she is on the inside track, or receiving a special offer that is exclusive to only a few.

The sales letter is one format that touts the widely lauded AIDA approach, which means:

Attention: This component is your hook—the enticing call to read on. It suggests a matter or situation that would be a boon to resolve, or even fun to learn more about.

Interest: The letter goes on to expound upon the headline, offering more details that further whet the audience's appetite.

Desire: Here, the copy builds to elicit a "gotta-have-it" response, prompting and instilling a need, wish, or longing in the reader for the product or service.

Action: This final step works to command that the reader immediately take the next step and purchase the product, patronize the store, order the service, and so on.

AIDA is espoused by many marketing and advertising experts for several formats. You can apply it to brochure writing, direct mail packets, and advertisements (which is covered in Chapter 17).

In the case of a sales letter, consider this example from a company that offers a new, faster version of DSL for Internet service. The company knew that the key advantages of its product were speed and the resultant time-savings that the service provided. Also, the company's research verified that potential customers want more time to complete tasks. The sales letter headline may ask, "Wish you had more time at work to get things done?" We all want more time, so that would grab most people's attention. The copy could then segue into explaining this just-on-the-market DSL service, which cuts waiting time for downloading sites and images by 75 percent, saving hours of cumulative time monthly. Then, bringing up an attractive offer—a reduced rate to upgrade or a discount on signing up in the next seven days—would impel the reader to start saving more time now.

Finally, after the letter's signature, add a postscript. Research has shown that, second to the headline, the P.S. is the most widely read component of a sales letter. Don't waste that opportunity: use it to drive a point home or reiterate an important product benefit.

Multipurpose Marketing Pieces

While you never want to take a one-size-fits-all approach in your marketing materials, you should determine whether pieces you create and produce might fulfill more than one purpose. Particularly in this era of cost-cutting and downsizing, budgets matter. Ingeniously and resourcefully saving money for your company is always appreciated. For *Fortune* 500 companies and small businesses alike, I've written and designed pieces that could effortlessly, seamlessly pull double duty (or more), providing information about a company in several different venues.

For instance, I worked on a sell sheet for a nationally known speaker that, when it accompanied sales letters, became a successful pitching tool for bookings, was snapped up by customers at book signings, was used by his agent to fulfill inquiries, and was provided to the press before interviews.

A post card I worked on for a gift store chain to announce a new product was mailed to customers, provided in store, was part of a media packet, and even became an ad in a national magazine.

Take a look at the audiences you're trying to appeal to, and then consider how one piece may serve them. Is the tone of the piece universal or conversational enough to strike a chord with each audience? Will each audience benefit from the information included? Can it be useful in different venues? If the answers to those questions are all "yes," then you may be able to combine the resources from a few pieces, add to the budget of just one, and still save time and money.

Too often, a sales letter runs on for pages and, unfortunately, its details don't merit its length. If you find yourself creating a letter that's becoming too long, consider adding another component to the letter. For instance, staple the letter to a brochure or sell sheet that gives recipients more information, if they want it, but keeps your letter on track by bringing up the cogent point at hand.

Catalogs

Catalogs present an impressive direct marketing piece, though for some companies they can seem intimidating and costly to produce. However, this statistic bears considering: catalog recipients spend an average of

$39 on online retail Web sites, compared to $18 for those who don't receive catalogs.

That being the case, you may want to give some thought and allocate some budget to adding a catalog to your marketing plans.

More than likely, you will need to align yourself with a printing house that specializes in catalog production. You can find one through the designer you work with, or through a networking group you may belong to, such as Le Tip (*www.letip.com*) or your local chamber of commerce.

Even though you won't be physically printing the catalogs (unless your company is a printing house), you should be familiar with a few basics that apply to creating, designing, and publishing a catalog:

- Put a significant design element or bestselling, appealing product in the upper righthand corner of each spread—that's where reader's eyes typically go first.
- Be consistent with your layouts, but don't be afraid to shake the norm with a few page spreads that surprise the reader, and beckon them to study your products a bit longer.
- Don't confuse the reader (or your layout) with a mishmash of fonts. Stick with one or two that jibe with your brand, and make sure they are an easily readable size (no less than six points).
- For the copy, use simple, enticing language. Make sure that you clearly point out product benefits, using bold or italic type or headlines for key features.
- Stick with standard catalog formats, such as standard full-size (8½" × 11"), slim-jim (6⅛" × 11½"), or digest (5" × 7").
- Catalogs printed in sixteen pages or multiples of sixteen are the most cost-effective.
- Though it costs more, a four-color catalog will almost always attract more attention and interest, and therefore sell more items than will a catalog printed in one or two colors.
- Make sure to have your Web site information and toll-free number liberally sprinkled throughout the catalog in uniform places. In addition, have an order form so that even if customers call or go to your Web site rather than mail to buy the products, they have a place to organize their potential purchases.

Marketing Ideas via the Internet

While the direct marketing communications discussed so far in this chapter relate to printed pieces, you can also consider e-mail as a viable, inexpensive option. Check your e-mail inbox: right now it probably contains a few messages you've received from companies soliciting business in some manner.

Direct Marketing Resources

For more tips on how to plan and execute a direct mail campaign, check out the United States Postal Service (USPS) Web site. It offers tips, templates, and even signups for direct mail pieces that the USPS will send to you to facilitate your company's efforts. You can check out *www.usps.com/directmail* to review the information available to help your business.

If you're interested in more information regarding printing resources and terms that will make you more knowledgeable in creating and producing direct marketing pieces, check out a Web site such as *www.multichannelmerchant .com*. You can also become more knowledgeable about direct marketing as a whole by visiting the Direct Marketing Association's main Web site at *www .the-dma.org*.

For e-mail marketing, concentrate on crafting messages that people will want to receive, and make sure they have a way to sign up for them (and opt out, as well). Your message can offer coupons or discounts, but should also contain information that your recipient will find otherwise worthwhile. For instance, if your site sells party goods, you might give some tips for a super Super Bowl party. If you're a financial planner, you might include money-saving trends for the new year.

You should also follow these six basic guidelines:

1. Include an attention-grabbing headline, such as "Free priority shipping this week only."
2. Have copy that flows from there. Don't use a copy block simply to repeat what your headline just said.

3. List your easily recognizable company's name in the "From" box.

4. Provide hot links in your logo and the text so that the recipient can easily jump to your Web site to order or to get more information.

5. Supply a phone number or e-mail address to reach customer service (which is especially helpful if someone's having trouble viewing the e-mail).

6. Have instructions to the reader to ensure that messages from your company aren't considered spam or diverted to a Junk mailbox.

▶▶ Test Drive

In just this past week, you've undoubtedly been exposed to a stream of direct mail pieces. Ask yourself:

➲ Of the ones that went straight into the trash, what gave you an impulse to throw them away?

➲ Which ones did you hang on to and read?

➲ What made you read the ones you kept?

➲ Did you act upon any of them?

➲ If so, what prompted you to act?

➲ If not, what caused your hesitation in doing so?

What Is Public Relations Writing?

As companies doggedly pursue all marketing possibilities in a crowded marketplace, they're often enticed by the prospects of "good PR." Good PR—which strives to lure customers and increase sales—is driven by several factors, including people's perceptions of a company, how it treats its customers, and the value of its goods and services. The public relations writing necessary to foster good PR embraces different tactics to unleash positive information about a company.

Essentially, public relations writing draws on the tenets of news writing to present news, happenings, and information about your company, all geared toward bringing positive exposure. Presenting the information as a news story serves three main purposes:

- ⮒ The story is written in much the same way that news organizations would report a story, thereby making it the kind of piece a media outlet would be looking for to incorporate in its articles or broadcasts.
- ⮒ Staying moored to facts and eschewing outlandish claims or clever puns gives the information both credence and news value.
- ⮒ The information is released by the company in a clear, concise manner backed up by supporting details and presented as exceptionally interesting or newsworthy in the scope of a day's or city's events; extremely useful to its readers; new, novel, or never-done-before; or all of the above.

Strong public relations writing doesn't pander or contain puffery. While it should be well written, and can even be entertaining to read, it does not veer into or rely upon showmanship or sales tactics.

You may be surprised to know that many news outlets depend on news releases that companies prepare to fill their pages and broadcasts. While your company might not have routine offerings, events, or details that would suit the needs of *CNN Live Today* or *Entertainment Tonight*, you might have some information suitable for your hometown weekly newspaper or a local radio station. Once in a while, you may even have the goods that *NBC Nightly News* or *People* magazine would want.

It's Low(er) Cost

With publicity, unlike advertising, you don't pay for the media time that it takes to make the story part of the news. However, you also don't create or produce the news segment itself; you just supply the information for it. That being the case, you don't incur costs for a slick production, pay for the airtime or newspaper space it takes up, or put your story in a glossy format.

Because you don't pay for message placement, what the audience sees is a credible source verifying and passing on your information, thereby giving it status and cachet. That's the kind of standing you can't get with an ad or a direct marketing piece—no matter how much you pay for it.

The Formats

The public relations writing formats discussed in this chapter include press releases, media advisories, pitch letters, e-mail blasts, op-ed pieces, and entire press kits. Again, these formats can handily be adapted for all sorts of stories that spotlight your company. The key is timing. No one wants old news. Make sure that the information you distribute is fresh, current, relevant, and matters now.

Need Help with Media Distribution?

If distributing your news to the media seems like a daunting task, you have a choice of services that can come to your rescue. For instance, you can contract with PR Newswire, which is on the Web at *www.prnewswire.com*. This service specializes in distributing news for companies—in mass or pinpointed mailings— and provides guidance regarding the outlets the release should be sent to.

PR Newswire's delivery capabilities extend beyond releases to include distribution of video, audio, and photos to the media, as well as to financial audiences, and even directly to consumers.

This service even has a tool kit geared toward small business owners at *http://prntoolkit.prnewswire.com*.

The Outlets for Your News

Of course, you should make sure that if you're going through the trouble of writing any one of several public relations pieces, you've got an audience that will be interested in your story. Though you want current or prospective customers to be the eventual target, you'll furnish your information to the media, which will essentially be your mouthpiece in conveying that information. It must be noted that you will give up control of your message to the media, which will craft the piece or report on their own. They will do that without your direct participation (or your interference), though they might use the information you supply with the news release, and possibly also that from subsequent interviews and other company materials.

In deciding to give a story or release to the media, determine which outlets you'd most like to have the information. Are those the same ones that will be most interested in running your story? For instance, you'd like your company's new hair-care product—a shampoo with a recently developed sunscreen that brings enhanced protection—to be in the pages of *Vogue, Cosmopolitan, Elle,* and *Seventeen.* That seems to be a natural fit. Targeting food magazines, such as *Bon Appétit, Gourmet*, and *Cooking Light,* would be incongruent. However, many times, just twisting a news story and giving the same news another angle will make it popular with a whole other set of media outlets. For instance, the hair-care company may have an interesting story about how it decided to launch the new product which business magazines, such as *Inc.* or *Entrepreneur,* may be interested in.

Always keep in mind that when you go after national publications that have the potential to reach everyone across the country, the story needs to appeal to a broad audience so that a wide circulation would be interested in it.

It's also important to remember that you always have opportunities for local news, wherever your company is based. For instance, the hair-care company could hold an outdoor event in its hometown. For the event, salon chairs and hair stylists would be lined up in a city park to give out free haircuts and shampoos using the new product. That event would give your company a local angle that might appeal to the hometown newspapers and even the local newscasts.

A Contact for Good PR

Someone in your company—and it might be you—should be designated for fielding press inquiries and approaching the media for follow-up. When only one person from your company (or other comparably skilled person in a PR department) is talking with the press, you're guaranteed a uniformity of message and can prevent another employee or executive being caught unprepared and offguard (or worse, making ill-timed or inappropriate remarks about your company that end up in print).

To that end, you might even set up a separate e-mailbox for the designee to specifically handle press inquiries and distribute releases and photos.

Find a PR Professional

Let's face it: While you realize the value of public relations, you might have absolutely no interest in cultivating publicity, or you might find the idea of dealing with the media intimidating. Never fear. You can often find someone, at a reasonable fee, who can help you with anything from writing the occasional press release to being instrumental in launching a full-fledged campaign. Consider contacting your local chamber of commerce for recommendations it may have. Or, if you have a college or university in your area, check to see if professors in their communication departments might be able to recommend or refer you to local professionals.

Writing a Press Release

The most pervasive format in public relations writing is the press release. In setting up a press release, you're giving your media audience the 5 Ws and an H: the who, what, when, where, why, and how of a story.

Sometimes, business owners gravitate toward first creating a winning headline. A solid headline is important, but you're not writing an ad, so the headline really will have more to do with how a newspaper headline might read than how an ad headline would.

Before writing the release, take the time to devise an outline. This step will bring order and cohesion to the release, and allow you to see where your information may be lackluster or missing facts. Start with your most important news first—the core reason you're sending out a release—and then prioritize the other details in descending order of importance.

Try to include a few pertinent details or even rough sentences for each point in your outline. This elaboration just makes writing the final release easier.

As you move into the draft phase, start with the release's first paragraph, not the headline. Come back and write a headline after you've come up with all the cogent points you want the release to include. That way, you'll know you're truly reflecting what the body of the release contains. While journalists will glance at the headline, they're much more interested in what's in the first paragraph.

When you begin actually writing the release, make sure you include the who, what, when, where, why, and how in that first paragraph, which is also known as the lead paragraph. The information doesn't all have to be contained in one sentence, and it should absolutely give the reason why the news is important to release in the first place.

One of your best teachers in press release writing is your daily newspaper. Reading the articles contained therein will give you a full range of examples of how your press release should be set up. Articles begin with the most important news first, and then allow the reader to glean further supporting details—from most important to least important—as the paragraphs move along.

Other Release Components

After you've written the release, spend some time on an appropriate, relevant headline. Once again, resist the urge to indulge in humor or word play and stick with the straight facts. That doesn't mean your headlines should be boring, however. You can write interesting headlines with well-chosen words that announce the release's contents and encourage the reader to continue.

Granted, certain occasions and companies benefit from dollops of humor in release writing. If your company sells novelties, or you have quirky or wacky news that brings on a smile, your headline may benefit from an appropriately humorous tie-in. More often than not, though, you should stick to straight-faced headlines that include robust and descriptive words but don't make outrageous claims or trumpet inflated news.

Releases should generally not run longer than two pages. If one does, analyze the release and determine whether or not you actually have two stories contained in it. If all the information seems relevant to the topic at hand, consider breaking up the release copy with subheads that announce the release's different, but related, components.

At the release's conclusion, add a boilerplate paragraph, a couple of sentences that describe your company and what it's known for. For instance, "Based in Boise, Idaho, Eyelash Solutions offers a line of mascaras that allow consumers to select one appropriate for their eyelash width and length. The company, founded in 1989, has its products available at national beauty supply chains, and online at *www.eyelash solutions.com*." Always include a boilerplate paragraph; it gives you another chance to present information about your company and gives a press person a snapshot of your enterprise as well.

Finally, don't forget the contact information. You can include the company representative's name, phone number, and e-mail address at the beginning of the release (above the headline), or at the end of the release (after the boilerplate).

Don't make the mistake of thinking you just send out the release, and then you're done with it. To ensure placement or pickup, you need to follow up with your media list either by phone or by e-mail, and gauge their interest. Determining their receptivity to your news will also help you in forming and guiding future efforts. Once you learn more about the media's wants and needs, you can tailor your releases even more keenly to their specifications, and ensure even greater pickup.

The following sample press release announces the launch of a company's product line.

FOR IMMEDIATE RELEASE
Contact: Francie Ledbetter
Fashionable PR
850/555-9123
Francie@fashionablepr.com

HOT WATER LAUNCHES
THE DEBUT OF ITS SWIM LINE
AT SWIM SHOW IN MIAMI JULY 17–21, 2007

**Brand's Success Extends into Swim
with Edgy 2008 Styles that Echo
HOT WATER's Signature Beach and Street Wear**

SEAGROVE, FLA., July 7, 2007—HOT WATER, the fresh, daring surf-inspired lifestyle brand targeted to teen girls, will introduce its debut swim line at Swim Show in Miami during July 17–21, 2007.

"A swim line was a natural progression for us as strong sales and demand for our collections reinforced that we had tapped into the styles, look and beach-to-city cross-culture that this age group was after," said Evalina Truscille, vice president of **HOT WATER**.

Initially launched in 2005, **HOT WATER** enjoyed immediate success with a line that included T-shirts, casual dresses, Capri pants, shorts, and accessories such as trucker hats, knit caps, leather belts, and vinyl travel bags. The brand has become synonymous with twisting hot trends and incorporating a fierce independent streak, as consumers are encouraged to create their own look with the fashion forward separates that infuse beach chic with a city vibe.

For swimwear 2008, **HOT WATER**'s lineup incorporates some of the colors and themes found in its 2007 clothing line—such as pirate, '80s vice, and rockabilly—for its "Shoreline," "Surfagraph," "Crest Rider," "Skyglow Dawn," "Citrus," "Silhouette Strut," "Urban Wave" and "Punch Party" bikinis, one-pieces, and halter dresses.

HOT WATER Launches Swim Line/Page 2

Highlights of **HOT WATER**'s inaugural swim line:

- **"Shoreline"** incorporates orange, rose, lemon, and sapphire in microstripes.
- **"Surfagraph"** mixes bold lemon and rose solids in block patterns.
- **"Crest Rider"** uses cross-hatched denim, rootbeer- and rose-colored stripes, and subtle florals.
- For **"Skyglow Dawn,"** wide bands of orange, lemon, and kelly green blend together for a rainbow effect.
- Orange- and lemon-colored stripes against white backgrounds highlight the **"Citrus"** styles, which also play up palm trees and sunsets.
- The **"Silhouette Strut"** suits use outlines of the **HOT WATER** logo in black-and-white and white-and-turquoise color combinations.
- **"Urban Wave"** brings raspberry, turquoise, and black shades together with a "graffiti floral" look: a mod mix of scrawled hibiscuses and dots.
- **"Punch Party"** uses combinations of raspberry, apple, and black for one-two punches on bikinis and belted two-pieces.

During the Swim Show, **HOT WATER** is located at Booth #4917A. Based in Seagrove, Fla., **HOT WATER** is available at swim, surf, and skate shops nationwide. The brand is on the Web at www.shophot-water.com.

Releases Over the Internet

Although it's still acceptable to mail or fax press releases, it's more likely that you'll send yours via the Internet. Therefore, take the time to have your company artwork created in such a way that it can be cut and pasted into a document. When your release is opened, it will appear to be on official—albeit digital—letterhead.

Ideas for Press Releases

Think you don't have any news fit for a press release? Think again. Chances are you've got a wealth of stories ripe for distributing to the media and helping your marketing initiatives.

Several ideas may be obvious choices: a new product launch, new clients you've procured, a patent or trademark you've received, inventive uses of your product, awards your company has won, and stories about how your product or service significantly impacted a person or organization.

You might also consider events that may draw media attention: tie-ins with local philanthropies; celebration of a national holiday; a special event that benefits an entity—such as a school or library—or a charity; or speaking engagements that you secure.

If you can link your business to a story currently in the news—or provide appropriate commentary about a controversy in the news—you have a chance to get your company mentioned. Further, you can create your own news by sponsoring a study or conducting research that news organizations may also find of value.

Photographs to Accompany the Release

Photographs lend an immeasurable amount of support and impact to your press release. A good photo increases your chances of placement, offers a visual cue for your story, and increases the connection of the story with your media recipient.

In addition, with the ease and speed of digital photography, you can easily attach the photo with your release in an e-mail.

Make sure the photo you send has news value and a logical connection with the information you're sending in the release. Don't send images that are hokey, hard-to-discern, or too artsy.

Also, when framing the picture, try to capture a moment or element that will make the photo stand out. For instance, to accompany a release about the grand opening of a hardware store, a picture of the store's owner using a power saw to slice through a grand-opening ribbon made of "Construction Zone, Do Not Cross" tape would be more visually interesting than a picture in which the owner is using standard-fare scissors to cut standard-fare ribbon. If you're sending out a release about the state-of-the-art wood-burning oven your restaurant has just installed, take a picture of a chef loading it with pizza, rather than a shot of the appliance itself.

Media Advisories

In this format, you're presenting a fact-sheet version of an event your company is participating in or hosting. While it could draw its information from a press release you've written, a media advisory should definitely relay the immediacy of an impending event. It still contains the who, what, where, when, why, and how approach.

The following media advisory is provided courtesy of Leukemia & Lymphoma Society, *www.lls.org.*

For Immediate Release

Contact: Anna Kazon

310-555-4732; Cell 310-555-8821

kazona@lls.org

MELISSA FITZGERALD, *THE WEST WING*,

MARTHA MADISON, *DAYS OF OUR LIVES* & NESTLÉ FOODSERVICES

JOIN

THE LEUKEMIA & LYMPHOMA SOCIETY'S

7th ANNUAL LIGHT THE NIGHT® WALK CAMPAIGN

Los Angeles, CA—September 15, 2005—Actresses Melissa Fitzgerald (*The West Wing*) and *Martha* Madison (*Days of Our Lives*) are

---

joining Tim Connor, president of Nestlé FoodServices North America and the 2005 Corporate Walk Chair, for The Leukemia & Lymphoma's 7th Annual Light The Night® Walk, a two-mile walk at twilight where participants hold illuminated balloons—white for survivors and red for supporters—to commemorate lives touched by blood cancer. Both Fitzgerald and Madison are celebrity co-chairs.

DATE: Sunday, September 18, 2005
LOCATION: UCLA Campus, Wilson Plaza
TIMES: Festival begins: 5:00 P.M.
Opening ceremony: 6:30 P.M.
Walk begins: 7:00 P.M.
Closing ceremony: Immediately following the walk

GUEST CELEBRITIES:
Martha Madison *(Days of Our Lives)* – Co-Celebrity Chair
Melissa Fitzgerald *(The West Wing)* – Co-Celebrity Chair

HIGHLIGHTS:
Nestlé Food Zone, including free Nestlé food and refreshments; Kids Zone, including old fashion carnival games & face painting; live music; live dance; inspirational smiles and much more!

National Presenting Sponsor:
Bristol-Myers Squibb Company

Local Presenting Sponsor: Nestlé FoodServices
Platinum Sponsor: Griffin New Homes
Gold Sponsor: Ernst & Young TAS
Silver Sponsors: Kellogg & Andelson, Providence Health System, Westfield Topanga, W Los Angeles Westwood, Newhall Coffee Roasting Company

Pitch Letters

Instead of a release, you may find yourself mulling over the idea of a story that could veer off in many angles, all of which would be beneficial to your company. If that's the case, consider writing a pitch letter to your media targets. A pitch letter can include several ideas that you have for a story.

Even though you may have brainstormed several possibilities (or angles) for a story about your company, be organized in your approach in outlining them. A pitch letter shouldn't be a rambling discussion about all the newsworthy events, products, and services you're excited about in your company.

Once again, begin with an outline to break down the ideas you have into a logical format. Once you have that developed, start with an engaging paragraph. Herein, you don't have to be confined to the 5 Ws and an H of newswriting. Pitch letters, while they do contain aspects of the news story you're trying to secure, are more conversational, less formal endeavors that don't have to adhere to a press release's code of delivery. Be aware, though, that while you can be conversational, you should also be sincere. The media will definitely pick up on huckster-type pitches or false-sounding claims.

E-Mail Blasts

Sent to multiple recipients simultaneously, e-mail blasts are quick announcements that offer information about an upcoming event. Often, these are also used much like media advisories and serve as reminders that an event or launch is coming. In addition, e-mail blasts can provide great follow-up to an event, letting recipients know how much money was raised, for instance, or who attended.

While the blast itself is kept very brief—usually containing a headline and a paragraph or two at most—you should provide a link to your company's Web site for more information should it be needed or wanted. Further, make sure you include the name of a company contact who can be phoned or e-mailed to answer questions or provide additional information.

> ### Make One Article Lead to Another
>
> Good press tends to feed upon itself. If you receive favorable publicity for your company, its services, or one of its products, leverage that coverage to get more. Keep track of the publicity you secure. Make sure you have scans and color copies readily available, and then use them in pitching to other outlets. The publicity your company receives makes it more of a commodity and, once you break in, you can usually succeed in accruing more rather quickly. Further, maintain ties with your media contacts. Send notes of appreciation to a reporter or writer after a story about your company runs to keep a dialogue going. However, don't send expensive gifts; this approach is considered taboo, as it can seem that you're trying to "buy" stories.

E-mail blasts can also contain news items, little bits of interest that might be useful to columnists, in particular, who run brief news stories. The item wouldn't be enough to fill out an entire release, but it might be a positive piece of news for your business nonetheless. For example, many daily newspapers have people columns. If a celebrity was in your town and visited your place of business, you could let the paper's columnist know that you had a celebrity sighting. People who hadn't checked out your place of business before may then be encouraged to do so, since a celebrity thought it was worth patronizing.

Press Kits

A press kit is an appealing, complete package of information about your enterprise that you can supply to the media as a means of introduction or follow-up. Press kits should include the following:

- **A company fact sheet:** A one-page document that highlights the company's main facts and details, such as the company's main business, principals, location, number of employees, the year it began, and recent accomplishments.

- **A company overview:** A one or two-page document—written in prose form—that gives information about the company's core businesses, and also includes details about its philosophy.

A recent news release: A press release that provides details about a company happening or an upcoming event.

Biographies: Brief paragraphs about the company heads that include their current titles, responsibilities, and previous experience.

A company timeline of highlights and milestones: This document provides information about key events—such as product introductions and awards—for the company.

Prime media coverage: If possible and if available, include color copies of significant coverage the company has garnered.

Images: Headshots of the principals, and pictures or diagrams of products.

In addition, all of these materials should be available on your company's Web site for the press to access. While press kits are generally provided in hard-copy form enclosed in folders, they have increasingly taken on a paperless format. If you opt to provide them on disks, do have hard copies available as well.

While press kits should absolutely contain the essential elements, let yours stand out from others with fresh, valuable components. Always try to include at least one element or document that speaks to the company's individuality, unique selling position, or media worthiness. As long as you can create a link of relevance from the document to your company, don't be shy about being creative with an additional piece or two in the press kit.

Some of the value-added pieces you can include in press kits include: an explanation of lingo relevant to a company's business; entertaining ideas (such as party themes using featured products); housekeeping or home maintenance measures that utilize highlighted company goods (such as tips for natural pest control); and lists or calendars of various kinds (such as a schedule of out-of-the-ordinary holidays); the most frequently given gifts for different occasions; and the busiest or slowest days of the year for certain activities.

These pieces can definitely vary from the straight news-article format. For instance, depending on the subject, they can be bulleted or "Top 10" lists, be written as a glossary, or be a first-person testimonial.

While these pieces might not bring your company full articles in the press, they may lead to sidebars to larger articles, which would most likely mention your company as a resource and command attention from potential customers.

▶▶ Test Drive

Sometimes the best way to generate ideas for gaining publicity for your company is to study newspaper and magazine features and articles. As you do, ask yourself:

- ➲ What press releases might have been issued that jump-started the article?
- ➲ Are specific companies and products mentioned?
- ➲ Is the coverage favorable?
- ➲ What might that company's angle have been if they pitched the story to the reporter?
- ➲ What possibilities have you not considered for angles that could publicize your company?

Mapping Out Your Marketing Message

A Quick Course in Copywriting

Copywriting is crafting words that sell your business—its products or its services. Those vital, descriptive, vibrant, targeted, alluring words can be the key to raising awareness of a product or your company, selling a new item you're offering, detailing a special sales event, or announcing that your enterprise is open and ready for business.

More often than not, when people use the term copywriting, it's associated with advertising in all of its many forms.

So What's Involved?

For print formats, advertising usually takes the form of a snappy headline that is followed by a few tight but descriptive sentences or short, punchy paragraphs and may or may not be accompanied by photos or illustrations.

For radio, you rely on the spoken word to quickly draw in an audience and conjure up images that listeners can create in their own minds, or communicate feelings that they can resonate with.

For television, you only have moments to captivate viewers with a combination of striking moving images, crisp words, compelling sound effects, and, usually, a well-told story.

In each case, your goal is to make a connection with the audience, enticing, suggesting, and hopefully proving to them that they need to purchase your product or service for their lives to be easier or better.

Keep in mind that, particularly with print and radio ads, you want your words to create pictures. You may even decide, as some copywriters do, to think backward. In other words, dream up the visual images first, and then attach associative words to them that draws a bridge to the appealing pictures.

Advertising Tenets

With advertising, you want your message to be focused on the reader or audience, and the benefits that they'll receive from your product or service. Some advertisers make the mistake of putting the spotlight on the company. If you make your customer the priority instead, your ads will be more focused and effective. Outlining and organizing the benefits and selling points of your product or service is crucial. Commit to a detailed approach in preparing and setting up to write your copy.

Remember that presenting an ad should be similar to having a conversation. Use a "you, your" approach, and write the way you talk. Don't, however, lapse into slang, and always steer completely clear of biased language relative to sex, race, religion, or creed.

Let your headline be a natural, enticing, relevant setup to segue into your copy, and get to the point quickly. With the copy itself, go for simplicity. Don't try to write an essay or the great American novel. Be spare but not incomplete. Use short sections and sentences. Embrace white space.

In crafting the actual copy, use "words" instead of "verbiage." That is, don't try to impress with pompous or extravagant words, when a simpler word will be more easily understood and quicker to digest.

Still, in following the general rules of good writing, be concise and specific in your details. Don't say "good" when your product could be "time-saving." Don't say "colorful" when the style being offered could be "psychedelic."

Although you may be in a technical field or offering a product that has a slew of whiz-bang components, don't languish in techno-speak or dabble in jargon that will confuse your reader. When you use words that everyone knows, your message will have a much better shot at connecting with the reader.

Finally, realize that advertising does not always follow the rules of good grammar. Since you're taking a conversational approach, your ad may contain a sentence fragment. Your paragraphs may be very short. With ads, your main concern is connecting with your audience and ensuring that they're getting your message—it's not English class. Don't take advantage of that fact, however; you still should stick to subject-verb agreement, use proper punctuation, be choosy with your words, and spell correctly.

AIDA Coda in Advertising

You'll find that advertising draws on many components discussed in Chapter 16, which focused on direct mail pieces. In that vein, you'll follow the Attention-Interest-Desire-Action coda once again.

The "Attention" element relates directly to your headline. How will you first appeal to your audience? What will you say to them that makes them want to read on?

More than likely, you'll want to showcase a benefit that your product or service will immediately bring to the audience. That attention should translate directly into garnering "Interest," impelling the audience to become interested in what's being offered. That interest will probably have been prompted by your having made a connection with them. You've tapped into a concern they want resolved or a need they want fulfilled.

That takes the audience into the "Desire" element. You want to create a sense that your product or service is a must-have.

Finally, once they want your offering, make sure to let them know where they can take "Action" to find it, or how they can get it: at a local chain store, at your store location, on your Web site, or by calling a toll-free number.

Other Advertising Guidelines to Know

Advertising is a thrilling proposition for some companies, and granted, the results can be astounding. But every smart businessperson should take a few more of the weaknesses—and strengths—of advertising into account before shouldering the creativity and budget involved in an ad campaign.

Cut Through the Clutter

Particularly lately, advertising has gotten a bum rap. Because television is deluged with commercials and magazines packed with ads, conventional wisdom suggests that consumers are at a tipping point, and little is breaking through that they're interested in.

Critics surmise that if you don't have the budget to buy a commercial during the Super Bowl, a full-page, four-color ad in *USA Today*, or the back cover of *Vanity Fair,* you're wasting your time and money.

In fact, consumer psychologist David Lewis suggests that, "Copy is getting shorter, and a major factor behind this is that people these days suffer from acute shortages of both time and attention. Younger generations are extremely visually literate." He suggests that their entertainment diet of computer games and music videos has made them particularly underwhelmed by detailed, polished copy. It's just not part of the visual repertoire as it has been in past generations.

Those are sharp words to heed, particularly if you have a company that's reaching out to a younger demographic.

Yet advertising still has a plethora of benefits, beginning with the fact that you can completely control the message that you're disseminating. And several outlets, such as print and broadcast, boast a segmented audience that could include your perfect, prized target group.

Realize that just because the field is crowded doesn't mean it should be ignored. Companies still advertise for a reason. Good ads sell. Still, it should only be a part of your marketing efforts, used in tandem with other marketing vehicles. For the most success, use an integrated marketing approach that combines advertising with public relations, direct mail, special events, trade shows, newsletters, brochures, and other marketing materials.

Realize the Cumulative Effect

In advertising, the prevalent attitude that emerges—particularly for first-time advertisers—is an expectation of immediate results. But studies cited by *www.allbusiness.com* indicate that the average consumer needs nine exposures before recalling an ad. So to make a heady impact, your ad may need to run dozens of times—meaning that advertising requires patience. However, when its effectiveness does kick in, make sure you've planned for it; be ready with the appropriate staffing, inventory, and other resources.

Hiring Someone Else to Create Your Advertising

Copywriting is indeed a talent. Those who churn out words for ads, direct mail pieces, publicity materials, Web site content and other collateral possess a vital skill that can lure and intrigue targeted audiences—and impel them to act.

Often, though, people try their own hand at copywriting. Sometimes, that approach makes sense—you should know your product or service better than anyone else would, making you expressly, exquisitely qualified to write about it.

Remember, however, the value of an objective point of view offered by a third party who could uncover product aspects and attributes you didn't realize. Further, an enthusiastic third party can also be a prime source for demystifying your approach. Sometimes, you're too close to your company and, as such, can be putting out a message that—to you—speaks articulately and represents your product well, but to others could come off as incoherent and garbled.

Whether you go the solo route or hire someone, become a copywriting connoisseur. Study ads that you like and dislike in both print and broadcast formats. Check out the ones that prompt you to take action. Notice what makes some more persuasive than others. You then will be that much more aware of what makes good copywriting sing and sell.

Capturing the Best Words and Descriptions for Your Business

We're a country awash in words. It's estimated that the number of words in the English language is upward of three million—200,000 of which are in common use.

With that kind of volume, how can you possibly come up with the best, most succinct and descriptive ones to apply to your business?

Venues to Turn to

When some advertising professionals sit down for the first time with clients—from both start-up and established brands—they often ask them to come up with five words or phrases to describe their business. That exercise extends to new products they're launching or new services they're offering. Interestingly, that request often provokes telling responses. Many times, clients struggle to fulfill that seemingly simple request.

Could you? Apply the same exercise to your company or products.

If you're struggling, start with simple words or terms and then grab a thesaurus. If you select a word from the thesaurus to use, do look up the meaning to make sure it means what you want it to. Next, check out the Web sites of companies or products that you think market themselves well.

Then, speak with trusted friends and colleagues. What words or phrases do they use to describe your company? What feelings does your brand or logo or product routinely elicit when you ask people whose opinions you respect?

Also, enlist help from the slew of magazines in your local bookstore. Magazines often stay on the cutting edge of language as they introduce trends, products, and stories of the moment. Their descriptions can be specific, illustrative, and inviting. You could particularly look at fashion magazines, such as *Cosmopolitan* and *Elle;* home magazines, including *Dwell, Domino,* and *Inspired Home;* do-it-yourself magazine *Ready-Made;* lifestyle magazines *Real Simple* and *Weekend;* family magazine *Cookie;* and the woman's business magazine *Pink* to read how they write for today.

While you never want to use exactly the same terminology to describe your company, brand, or product that someone else uses, harvesting these words and phrases will allow you to compose (or direct someone else to write) more exciting, compelling ads.

Remember: keep adding to your arsenal of words. As you think of other words or are reminded of ones that may apply to your brand, jot them down. They'll no doubt come in handy in advertising down the line.

What's Your New Spin?

In your advertising endeavors, realize that people generally respond better to a concept that seems fresh and original, something they haven't seen or heard before, so it commands their attention. Therefore, advertising once again harks back to your business plan: What makes your product or service stand apart? What's your unique selling position? What makes your product different from the competition's?

Are you the exclusive carrier of an item? Did it just launch? Is it manufactured in a never-before-done way? Take this kind of positioning into account and emphasize your uniqueness to create advertising that will be the most effective for your company.

Print Ads

With newspapers, you have an inexpensive way to reach a mass audience, and you can typically get your ad in print pretty quickly. Newspaper ads are particularly useful for sales you're announcing, grand openings, and special price promotions. Despite newspapers' vast audience, there is a downside: many ads run in each edition, so yours may be hard to find.

Magazines offer a wide-yet-targeted circulation. Therefore, you can home in on an audience that meshes with your specific demographic and may signify huge potential. However, magazines do require a long lead time, and ads for them can have rather significant production costs.

Memorable Campaigns

"Where's the beef?" "When you care enough to send the very best." "99 and 44/100% Pure." AdAge.com's rundown of the Top 100 Advertising Campaigns, with an accompanying article by Bob Garfield—all at *www.adage .com*—delves into the principles behind memorable ads. In so doing, the site's pages also allow insights into how you can make your ads stand out and be seen and remembered, even if you don't have a multimillion-dollar budget. I wrote thousands of trivia questions for the game show "Supermarket Sweep," and during that time, I was reminded that product recognition and loyalty to companies are often the result of wit and wisdom that helps customers realize the benefits they'll receive from using a product. In other words, mere words often reap much more profit than do high-drama productions with space-age special effects.

The yellow pages may provide you with another viable alternative on a local scale. Studies show an astounding rate of return, because those who turn to the yellow pages are usually in the throes of making a decision fairly immediately. Remember, though, the ad will be there for the next year. If it contains a typo, or your services change, you're still stuck with the ad.

Clarity Sells in Print

For a print ad, be sure the headline is clearly distinguished, and use simple, straightforward fonts for the copy. Don't overlap fonts or images. Make the ad easy to read, easy to follow, and instantly inviting.

Choose a font such as Arial or Helvetica, in sizes that aren't too big or too small. For instance, 12 point is a good size. Type that's too small or too large is difficult to read, making your ad less likely to be read. Look at library books and the newspaper for guidance. While you want your ad to stand out, you also want to present it in a typeface that people are accustomed to.

Use the space wisely. Don't fall in love with an image that may look beguiling but is completely irrelevant to what you're advertising. Don't fill the space with a quote that doesn't make a logical connection to your product or service. Don't frame the ad with a stained-glass window pattern or have whirling dots skating through it.

For maximum readability, try using dark-colored words against light-colored backgrounds. If you opt for color, remember that while chartreuse and magenta may be attention-grabbing, they can also be hard to look at if you're trying to read copy placed on them.

Stay away from using all uppercase letters. Here again, that's not typically how people read an article or a letter. Taking that tack can burden the reader, who may quickly withdraw from the ad.

Be sure to position your headline where it can be seen the quickest. The eye naturally falls to about one-third to one-quarter of the way down the ad space, not at the very top.

Be smart about the images you use. While photographs reproduce well and are attractive in magazine ads, they can look distorted in a newspaper ad. Also, use images wisely and carefully to ensure that they convey your message. A team of real estate agents went to great lengths in their ad to tout the value of having two people working for you to sell your house. However, their photos were positioned at opposite ends of the ad, leaving the reader with an impression of separateness, which worked against—rather than for—the message.

Magazine Rate Cards and Demographics

You can thoroughly research magazines to see which are best suited for your needs by contacting each publication via its Web site (or by phone) and requesting a rate card. Often, those cards are available for downloading on a publication's Web site. That piece will spell out costs to place color and black-and-white ads. Further, most magazines also have conducted extensive research about their audience in order to share numbers and statistics about their readership demographics. In doing so, they've done your research for you, so take advantage of it. Find the magazines that will most likely appeal to your specific audience.

Broadcast Ads

As in other forms of advertising, whether you elect to use radio or television, you should have a predetermined purpose for your ad: Are you driving people to a grand opening, introducing a new product, or announcing a special sale?

With both of these broadcast formats, each of which will be discussed in greater detail in this section, you'll use a script to create the spot. You must be sure that your script fits into a preallocated time space. While your audience can take as long as they'd like to read a print ad, radio and television commercials have specific time periods—such as thirty or sixty seconds—that fit into a station's overall programming. Further, the listener or viewer can't usually rewind to pick up any detail that may have been missed.

For both television and radio, take advantage of verbal white space. Just as you wouldn't cram too much copy into a newspaper ad, you must prevent your broadcast audience from being overloaded as well. Take a conversational tack and make sure the ad is well paced so that the narrator or actors won't have to race through the copy to reach the end of the ad in time. For instance, a phone number may just be 1-877-555-1611 on paper but when it's pronounced, you have to consider the time it will take to say one-eight-seven-seven-five-five-five-sixteen-eleven.

The Particulars of Radio

Typically, radio spots provide a fairly economical alternative to some more costly forms of advertising, such as television commercials or high-end magazine ads.

Particularly with a radio ad, you have to be cognizant of keeping your message confined to one (or a few closely related) points. Again, organize your thoughts beforehand and be specific about your exact purpose for the ad: Are you telling shoppers about a one-day sale? A one-time holiday promotion? A discount good until the end of the month? That your dealership is open for business?

Also keep in mind that within the allotted timeframe, you need to repeat certain information, such as a location or a phone number, several times.

After you have the copy in hand, make sure to read the script out loud. Don't skip this step! As you read aloud, take note: Does the copy make sense or sound too formal? Are you having to move too fast through the copy to stay within the time limit? Do you get hung up on any words?

Research the stations in your area that will be the best demographic fit for your potential customer base. The age groups that listen to specific formats tend to be fairly uniform. For instance, those that tune in to news/talk stations aren't likely to also be listening to contemporary hit radio. And a classical station has a different fan base than does an alternative music station. Again, the radio stations can clue you in to the audiences they reach.

You can either furnish a radio station with a prerecorded spot, or you can have a radio personality do the voice-over for you. In terms of running the ad, the most favorable times are the morning and afternoon drive time, when listenership is at its peak.

Television Strategies

Television commercials often employ unique storytelling devices, clever scripts, and dramatic images to leave a lasting impression on viewers to buy a product. However, the television landscape is littered with commercials that are witty, urbane, or laugh-out-loud, but are more memorable for the actors, the humor, or the special effects than for the brand or product they're advertising.

While creating effective television commercials can be a tricky proposition, the benefits can be substantial because you have the opportunity to reach a huge demographic audience. In doing so, you can quickly create brand identity, launch a product, and gain tremendous exposure.

While you can have free creative rein in presenting a television spot, the downside involves the cost both to produce a professional-looking spot and to buy time to have it broadcast nationally, or in large and medium markets.

The process of creating a commercial starts with a script and a storyboard, which basically attaches pictures to the words. To navigate this area, many companies turn to ad agencies that routinely and successfully depend on the medium to distribute their clients' messages. If you decide that your company will benefit from advertising on television, make sure that your analysis of the product benefits is fine-tuned, and your goals for the ad firmly established. Besides the production end, an agency can also handle the science of where on a television schedule your product's commercial would make the greatest impact and draw the most viewers, which would translate into the most sales.

Internet Advertising

Advertising on the Web hews most closely to print advertising in that it usually offers a simple headline to read about a service or product. However, an Internet ad may also incorporate sound, visuals, or both.

On the Internet, you're likely to draw even more on using slogans and taglines (which are discussed in the next section) to catch the attention of the rapidly scanning Web user with a snapshot of copy.

However, the Web also employs some other, unique methods to advertise. For example, Google, with its vast search engine capabilities, offers companies several opportunities to increase traffic to a particular site through advertising means. One option allows your business to appear as a "Sponsored Link" on search engine results pages. When you set up this form of advertising, you choose search words that—if typed in by a user—prompt an ad for your business to pop up. For example, suppose you owned a surfboard shop in Malibu. If you chose the words "surfboard," "buy," and "Malibu," the ad for your business would appear on the results page whenever someone typed those words into the search engine. If the user then clicked through to your site, you would pay Google a predetermined amount. For more information about this process, check out Google's AdWords program at *www.google.com/ads*.

TV Commercials Classroom

If you're interested in creating a commercial yourself, or working with an agency to do it, conduct research by watching ads. The Internet serves as a veritable classroom for viewing classic and current ads and finding out what works in commercials—and what doesn't. For instance, at *www.tvcommercialsnow.com* you can see commercials in such categories as airlines, clothing, utilities, perfumes, deodorants, and even Super Bowl ads that have sparked attention and controversy. In watching several of them, you can ascertain what's enjoyable or annoying, whether the commercial succeeds in selling a product, and which visuals are the most effective in conveying a message and connecting with an audience.

Slogans and Taglines

This category can bring a company much grief, because these kinds of copy may very well end up on every piece of advertising that a company generates. The slogan or tagline also frequently appears on printed materials, such as letterhead, that can last a while. However, slogans and taglines are important because when used on all of your materials, they provide a cohesive message for your company. In the best sense, they can resonate with buyers, and provide constant, friendly reminders of the goods and services your company offers.

Slogans and taglines should possess ten characteristics. They should:

1. Be original
2. Invoke a positive emotion
3. Be instantly associated with your logo

4. Curry favor with your audience
5. Never be a cliché
6. Avoid unclear wording or geekspeak
7. Relate a specific rather than a generic "We're the best!"
8. Never beg a sarcastic response
9. Be easily repeatable and remembered
10. Be absolutely unique to your company

Think about taglines that you find particularly memorable. Here are a few to get you started: Macy's: It's Your Store; Maxwell House: Good to the Last Drop; You're in Good Hands with Allstate; Volvo. For Life.; Nike. Just Do It.

If you're interested in drumming up your own slogan or tagline, start by brainstorming the very best attributes of your company—especially those that differentiate you from the competition. Write down as many as you can. Here, quantity counts just as much as quality.

Then, group your outcomes. Do many relate to the same asset? What are themes or patterns that seem to be emerging? You should start noticing some.

Narrow down your list, and strike lines that seem repetitive. Then play with the words and phrases that are there. Have some fun with them. Can you think of other words or terms that might do well in a tagline but aren't on your sheet at present? Try to come up with complete phrases that describe your company's prime benefits or its unique selling proposition in an engaging, memorable, approachable way.

Once you've decided on a couple, test them out with associates, colleagues, and advisers. Get feedback. See if you're missing any prized component that could speak even more to your customers. Finally, make sure the slogan is easy to say and read and not too long. Many of the most famous and successful taglines were a mere four or five words in length.

A Look at the Copywriting Process

In my copywriting experience, I've had to write several taglines for television series. Here is a window into the process with several lines that were devised for The WB Television Network series *Maybe It's Me,* a half-hour comedy about an adolescent girl, Molly Stage, who feels that she is the sole normal person living in a family of zany outcasts. These lines are only a sampling of the dozens (maybe hundreds!) generated before one was decided upon.

- For any teenager who wishes she *was* the girl next door.
- If family ties could be cut, Molly Stage would own more scissors.
- There really is no place like *this* home.
- Is there a return department for families?
- Just when she blossomed, her family's making her wilt.
- In a family of misfits, Molly's desperately trying *not* to fit in.
- Molly really wants to belong . . . except when it comes to her family.

The final tagline: "There's *no* place like home . . . fortunately."

Take a survey of your business, its practices and promotions, and think about how advertising might serve it best:

- ⮂ What advertising medium would your company benefit most from on a continuing basis? Newspaper, television, the Web?
- ⮂ What's a headline you could give to one of your products or services?
- ⮂ Do you have a company slogan? If so, how has it served you so far? If not, why have you been reticent to create one?

Communications with Spoken Components

PART 5

Professional Phone Calls

With the proliferation of e-mails, maybe you don't use the phone as often as you did even a year or two ago. But don't let being e-mail literate make you lax with phone calls. Even though you may favor e-mails, current and potential customers may still be more comfortable using the phone. The phone is still—and will continue to be—an essential part of conducting business.

In fact, sometimes placing a professional phone call is savvier for business than is sending e-mail. Phone calls allow real-time opportunities to communicate; e-mail messages don't always provide that function. In addition, the phone allows a degree of warmth and a human touch that's not often possible with e-mail.

Sometimes, a phone conversation can bear as much weight as a face-to-face discussion (which will be discussed in Chapter 20). For that reason, you should take care to conduct yourself professionally when picking up the phone to make or receive a call.

AT&T developed toll-free numbers in 1967 so that companies could conveniently pay the cost of customers trying to reach them. In the beginning, 800 was the only prefix available. Today, toll-free numbers can also begin with 888, 877, and 866.

The Value of a Phone Number

Make sure that all company correspondence, collateral, and information avenues—including your Web site—includes a phone number to reach someone a customer or client can talk to. You might even want to investigate setting up a toll-free number if your company doesn't have one already. While not all businesses need one, toll-free numbers have several advantages: you don't need an additional phone line to have one; you can use the number to "advertise" your company or spell out a unique company trait; customers can easily recall them; your business can seem bigger than it is and reflect a national presence; and you can set one up through your current phone carrier.

Be Prepared When Placing the Call

In making a call, have an exact reason for why you're calling, or what you'll be requesting. If necessary, jot notes down beforehand so that you'll be organized and time-conscious in your approach. Don't jump on the line and be content to figure it out once you've got the person you're trying to reach. That tack breeds confusion, wastes time, and presents a poor image.

When making a business call, identify yourself and your company. If a receptionist or assistant answers the phone, be ready to give the name of the person you're trying to reach.

Also be prepared with a one- or two-sentence explanation for why you're calling. Then, when you're connected, relay your reason, and ask if you're calling at a convenient time. Unfortunately, many callers don't routinely offer this courtesy. When you do, however, you actually give yourself the advantage of reconnecting with the caller when he or she can more fully pay attention to your needs. On the issue of time, be honest: don't ask for a moment when you're expecting a ten-minute conversation. Also, make every moment count. If you need ten minutes of someone's time, have the professional, organized content to fill it.

When you reach someone for whom you've left a message, don't assume that the message you left has been communicated as you gave it. Repeat the reason you called. Then, use the time as you would in a face-to-face meeting. Understand that the person you're talking with may have a different agenda than you do. He or she may have just been given a monumental task, lost an important piece of business, or been in an afternoon-long meeting. If you sense that you've called at an inopportune time, ask if you can call back at a more convenient time.

Accepting a Call

When answering your line, identify yourself and, if you're answering the main line, include the company name as well.

If the person jumps right into a request or discussion that leaves you unclear or confused, don't become frustrated or impatient. Courteously ask to "pause" the conversation, then rephrase what they've just said to help focus the dialogue.

Be ready to take notes so that you can take action, forward a request, or keep track of the exchange.

In the event that a conversation becomes heated or otherwise difficult, keep calm and always maintain a professional demeanor. If necessary, reschedule the call for another time so that both parties can regroup. In some cases, having to postpone a call may also signal that the conversation should actually be conducted face-to-face (which is discussed later in this chapter as well as in Chapter 19).

Speakerphone Usage

If you plan on putting someone on speakerphone, ask him or her first. It's not rude to use the speakerphone, but it would be rude if you didn't get consent to do so. Oftentimes, it's easier to take notes if you're not trying to balance a receiver. However, if you're using the speakerphone to keep your hands free, then consider trying a headset instead, which won't include as much ambient noise for your listener.

When using the speakerphone, taking turns in the conversation is even more important than usual. Sometimes, a speakerphone can only pick up one voice at a time, losing important snippets of dialogue when conversation overlaps.

If more than one person is listening in on the speakerphone discussion and will also be chiming in with comments or questions, make sure that person is properly introduced.

Conference Calls

Conference calls are popular because they allow several people to be on the phone at the same time to discuss a matter at hand. However, when left unchecked, a conference call with many participants can be a jumbled mess.

To get the event started and to keep it running smoothly, the person who initiates the conference call must take the role of the host or head. That person should be in charge in maintaining an agenda for the call, calling on people at appropriate junctures, and making sure that no one is commandeering the call, cutting off people, or not allowing others to be heard.

As the host, you set the time for the call, and send out a reminder e-mail to ensure participation. Then, whether you're the one heading up the call or the one being contacted, be at your desk when the call is supposed to begin.

Of course, speakerphones are often a necessity in conference calls. Once again, when they are used, everyone should take a turn in talking so that no one gets squeezed out of the conversation or goes unheard.

All of the participants in a conference call should introduce themselves to the others at the beginning of the call. When more than two people are on the call, each person should also introduce himself or herself again at the beginning of each comment made. These introductions may seem overly formal, but they are extremely helpful in eliminating confusion and making points of view clear.

Don't ever treat your conference call as confidential. Many times, silent associates may be on the line to glean insights, or to give clandestine tips, ideas, details, or instructions. Be mindful that not everyone on the call may be actually announced.

When the call is finished, be certain you have hung up the phone from all parties, particularly if you're continuing an internal discussion. Do not continue a conversation that you want to keep among an internal team until you are certain the call has been completely disconnected from the other participants.

Phone Calls Using Your Computer?

A new technology generating buzz in some circles is the advent of Skype, a company that allows users to make free calls over the Internet using your PC, Mac, or PDA to anyone else who has Skype, anywhere in the world. You can also use software provided by the company to dial regular phone numbers (for a fee). With Skype, you can also have up to five people on board for a "conference call," and share files and photos. The software has won raves for its ease of use, its sound quality, and its secure encryption. You can find out more about its features and the technology behind it at *www.skype.com*.

Home-Based Businesses

Home-based businesses present challenging circumstances for phone use. If you truly want to come off as professional when you work from a home office, install a line dedicated just for business. Also, of course, have a voice mail feature on it such that if you're on the other line and the phone rings, the call will go directly into voice mail. For your business line, do not have a feature that blocks private calls. You don't want to turn off or frustrate a potential (or existing) customer or client that has to dial number prefixes to take the block off their number and provide access to your line.

Is It Too Detailed for a Phone Call?

Don't let a phone call confuse a client. An escrow officer was having some difficulty with insurance information for a customer's home equity loan. He called the customer, rattling off a slew of numbers and instructions for having the customer contact the insurance company to clarify the information that was needed. Rather than put that burden on a customer, the officer should have taken responsibility for the situation. It would be far more courteous to send the customer an e-mail (or a fax, depending on the information's sensitivity) that succinctly outlines the needs than to sound off with a list of actions to take—and more than likely invite mistakes in the process.

As it was, the customer, while seeming to understand, actually became confused about the instructions given over the phone and had to repeatedly call the escrow officer to straighten out the matter. The transaction caused everyone to lose time and patience, and even led to wariness and distrust on the part of the customer.

Keep the call-waiting feature off your business line as well. Not only does it signal to people that you're doing business from home, it also interrupts the call with an audible signal that comes across as unbusiness-like. If your business were in an office building, the phones there most likely wouldn't have call-waiting features.

Further, don't invest in an answering machine for your home-based business. Instead, contact your phone company about the voice-mail features it offers. Normally, such voice mail conveys a businesslike setting and professionalism, and is extremely easy to access from off-site locations.

Finally, don't use a cell phone as your main business number. While cell phones are convenient, pervasive, and mostly necessary, they still don't have the sparkling, crystal-clear presentation of a landline, and still aren't 100 percent dependable. While having a cell phone is recommended so that you can be available for clients, don't make it your primary business line.

Phone Manners

When you're on the phone with someone, you don't have the advantage of seeing that person face-to-face. Therefore, you have to be particularly sensitive to the other person's voice so that you can pick up on any misunderstandings or confusion.

While on the phone, help your cause by enunciating your words clearly, not eating or drinking, keeping background noise to a minimum, and not succumbing to distractions such as reading e-mail or sorting papers on your desk.

In that regard, give your full attention to the phone caller. Don't try to do two activities at once. While multitasking during a business call may seem enticing, you'll actually be more prone to make mistakes, be forced to ask that key phrases or sentences be repeated, or misunderstand the entire conversation.

If you're in the middle of a meeting and the phone rings, don't answer it; that would be rude to both the caller and the person who convened the meeting.

If transferring a call, let the person know to whom you would like to transfer the caller, and why, and ask permission to do so. Then stay on the line until you know the transfer has been completed. If possible, announce the call to the person receiving the transfer so that he or she knows that the caller has already been routed from one person at the company.

Finally, if a call is somehow dropped, the person who initiated the call is the one who places it again. However, if you've been dealing with a customer or client and the call is dropped (or a transfer went awry) but you're not the one who placed it, be respectful of your caller's time, and place the return call yourself. The caller will no doubt appreciate the courtesy and your attention to customer service.

Matters Particular to Cell Phones

No discussion about phone conversations would be complete without mentioning cell phones. For various reasons, some who use cell phones think that a different set of rules applies to their usage, which unfortunately often neglects simple manners.

Because cell phones can seem to beckon bad manners, try to take an even more courteous tack in using them for business matters.

For instance, don't answer a cell phone in the middle of a meeting. Be circumspect about using a cell phone in the lobby of offices you're visiting; don't be loud or overly zealous. Finally, when you go in to a meeting, presentation, or business meal, make sure your phone is on vibrate or in the silent mode.

Caller ID

Even if you identify a number coming in as someone you know, still use professional decorum in answering the line. Don't call out a name you think is on the other end until the caller has identified himself or herself.

Also, you should not use a number you've obtained through caller ID unless the person calling has given that number to you. Your caller ID library of numbers should not be regarded as a list of phone numbers you may automatically put into your personal or business database.

Rules for Leaving Phone Messages and Voice Mails

Always be prepared for the possibility that the person you're trying to reach might not be available. Decide ahead of time what kind of message you'll leave. Will you just leave your name, company name, and phone number? Is an urgent reply requested? Do you need to leave details about a situation? Has someone been expecting your callback and now missed you? Whatever the circumstances, have a game plan.

Phone Messages

If someone answers another person's line and is prepared to take a message, ask that person to read back your name and phone number, particularly to ensure that no numbers were transposed.

If you sense that the details of your message will end up garbled or miscommunicated, ask to be transferred into the person's voice mail, so that you have more control over your message. However, you should realize that the person taking your message verbally may also be the one checking your intended recipient's voice mail. To clarify the matter, ask if the person you're trying to reach hears his or her voice-mail messages directly.

Voice Mails

Whenever you make a call, be prepared for the possibility that you will have to leave voice mail. Know the information you'll be including in the message so that it's clear and concise, and so that you come off as professional. Don't allow yourself to blather or get off-track. Speak slowly. Include your name and your phone number twice so that they can be written down easily.

Have you ever been contacted by a rambler? These are the people who are so eager to get an item off their to-do list that they use voice mail to give you all the details of a situation, or give their view on a subject just so they can be rid of it, even when it really deserves a two-sided discussion. While it's acceptable to leave details such as addresses, phone numbers, and purchase order information, you should not use voice mail to ruminate on ideas or defend positions.

If you ever find yourself in the midst of leaving an interminably long message and have embarrassed yourself, you have two options. Many phone systems will allow you to delete the message you're leaving and start over again. If that's not the case, stop yourself, apologize for letting the message get out of hand, and take responsibility for calling again after an appropriate length of time has passed.

Guidelines for the Company's Front Gate of Communication

Many times, a company's communicative strengths and weaknesses can be ascertained directly by how a receptionist or assistant answers the phone. A cordial, polished presentation literally speaks volumes for your company. How is your company's phone answered? Take particular note of tone and articulation. Communication audit teams regularly discover that customers can't make out the name of the company they had called and thought they may have misdialed. Regarding tone or voice, no one should answer the phone at a place of business sounding tired or exasperated. At one software company, the source of the customers' ire was pinpointed to the receptionist at the company's main number. There, customers were routinely transferred incompetently and repeatedly, prompting annoying situations to become exacerbated before they were resolved.

If a caller is having trouble articulating his or her needs, the person answering the phone should help in the best way possible, not become impatient with the caller. If you field a difficult call, remember that you're the company's ambassador. Do your best to maintain integrity and, no matter how offensive the caller may be, strive to take the high road.

Finally, if a member of the media calls, the person answering the phone should take particular care to write down the caller's name, outlet name, phone number, and reason for the call. Just as important, that person should also get a deadline from the reporter that can be passed on to the proper company designee.

Make sure that you never include confidential or personal information or sensitive material in your voice-mail messages. You never know who might pick up the messages, or whether the receiver will put the voice mailbox on speakerphone, possibly exposing your words to others. (To avoid similar embarrassments on your end, be sure that you never use speakerphone when retrieving your own voice-mail messages.)

For your own voice mailbox outgoing message, state your name, the company name, and if appropriate, the date. The date is particularly important if you want to let callers know that you may be out most of the day in meetings, or may not be able to return calls immediately. If you leave a date-specific outgoing message, make sure to update it the next day. Don't use your outgoing message to take a political stance, offer a quote of the day, tell a joke, or broadcast your new favorite song. Finally, unless you have a celebrity impersonation business, don't use celebrity sound-alikes in your outgoing message.

When Not to Use the Phone

Similar to the discussion in Chapter 11 about using the phone rather than e-mail, situations sometimes warrant that you meet in person rather than talk on the phone. Just as there are times when you shouldn't hide behind an e-mail, there are times when you shouldn't hide behind a phone receiver.

The phone should not be used for these purposes:

- ⮑ Performance reviews or employee termination
- ⮑ Discussions pertaining to legal problems or ramifications
- ⮑ Most interviews (sometimes phone interviews are necessary; those are discussed further in Chapter 21)
- ⮑ Continuing conversations that have repeatedly been problematic
- ⮑ Arbitration involving more than two parties—in other words, don't use a conference call to try to solve a problem that affects several people; come together in a meeting room or office instead

Of course, particularly regarding internal matters in your company, you may also need to reach out beyond the phone if a situation has taken on grave importance, if misunderstandings have spun out of control, or if meeting face-to-face will provide a better forum for generating ideas. In fact, as integral as the phone is to doing business, face-to-face discussions are also ultra-important (and are reviewed in the next chapter).

▶▶ Test Drive

To what extent is your company dependent on the phone? How could you more effectively use the phone in your business? Consider and take stock of how these five phone areas could impact your business more positively:

1. Have you ever telephoned your office to gauge the professionalism of what you hear, whether it's from a receptionist, your assistant, or a voice-mail message? Does the way in which the phone is answered convey an image that proudly represents your company to customers and clients? How might you improve it?

2. Do you have a toll-free number? If not, are you missing opportunities to connect more with customers, or make a more lasting impression?

3. Review a few days' worth of e-mails. In hindsight, would some of the messages been more appropriately or productively conveyed as phone conversations?

4. Are there customers, vendors, or investors with whom you could make a better or more human impression if you called them periodically?

5. Analyze the messages you're receiving from phone calls. Is information routinely missing? When the calls were returned, were you caught off-guard in any way? Were these follow-up conversations focused, or did they take longer than they should have?

Getting the Most Out of Conversations

At a time when so many people are infatuated with the sheer magnitude of business that can be accomplished via the Internet, you may forget the impact that a face-to-face conversation can have. In fact, those conversations may carry even more weight today, because they are becoming increasingly rare.

Some companies revel in never having to get on a plane to meet a client or in conducting an entire meeting via instant messaging. However, the results of a study conducted by UCLA psychology professor Albert Mehrabian and discussed in *Inc.* magazine found that 55 percent of the meaning in an interaction comes from facial and body language and 38 percent from vocal inflection. Only 7 percent of the interaction's meaning is derived from the words themselves.

When company owners, executives, and entrepreneurs learn about that rather startling statistic, some change the way they do business. For instance, some enterprises institute an occasional (or weekly) "no e-mail day," which encourages employees to do business with clients, vendors, and each other, by phone or with face-to-face conversations. In other studies, such practices have been proven to actually enhance a company's productivity, as taking a break from e-mail positively impacts a company's other communication methods. In eliminating that one method, employees gain a newfound respect for communicating in general, gleaning new insights about how they relate to people in other ways, particularly if face-to-face conversations are part of the mix.

That new perspective largely occurs because, while conducting the bulk of business via e-mail may seem terribly efficient, you may be missing vital messages if you rely solely on that method. Also, more than a few situations have spiraled woefully out of control in the miscommunication, misunderstandings, and miscalculations that have resulted from avoiding conversations and completely depending on the written word.

A Conversation's Goal

To get the most out of conversations, first be clear about your goal. The goal in many conversations is simply to understand where the other person is coming from, and to use his or her perspective and information to make more informed choices, expand a project's scope, or reach a satisfying conclusion to a problem or decision. However, you may also initiate a conversation to persuade or convince, remedy a troubled situation, or inform someone of changes in a project. Follow these guidelines for the most fruitful conversations:

- ⮑ Be prepared with your topics for discussion, and your facts and figures to back them up.
- ⮑ Ground your statements and responses in facts and research, rather than emotion.
- ⮑ Don't be content to let a conversation be one-sided, with you or the other party doing most of the talking—strive for balance.
- ⮑ Be ready and willing to listen to the other party.
- ⮑ Ask questions to make your case stronger and to ensure clarity for both sides.
- ⮑ Don't enter conversations fixated on there being a "winner" and "loser."
- ⮑ Don't leave conversations confused or frustrated in understanding the other party

Know the Right Times

Realize that in business, some situations expressly, absolutely call for face-to-face conversations rather than a phone call, and certainly rather than an e-mail. A key component of sound communication practices is discerning the appropriate time for such a conversation to take place. In some of the following instances, a conversation is necessary because a situation has occurred that has unsavory elements or could have ramifications that could negatively impact business. In others, you may deem a situation appropriate for face-to-face meeting for a positive reason: to make or leave a favorable impression. Can you understand why each of these would be better for business if the discussion took place face-to-face rather than in an e-mail?

To mitigate possibly negative outcomes:

- Resolving a contract dispute
- Firing someone
- Defending your company's professionalism

To enhance positive outcomes:

- Hiring someone
- Making a case for your company to win a bid
- Meeting a potential client for the first time

Communicating Beyond E-mail

Even when you depend on e-mail, consider expanding your approach with conversational options. For instance, make sure that e-mail recipients know that you're available to answer questions or participate in discussions. If an open-door policy seems like a burden, or you fear becoming bombarded with in-person visits, make yourself available during set hours.

If e-mail has become the only way you communicate with clients, pick up the phone and schedule a breakfast or lunch to let them know how much you appreciate their business.

If you have perpetual problems with a vendor, take stock of your communication with that company. Is it solely through e-mail? Is it possible that a regularly scheduled conversation may defuse the situation, or alleviate troubles?

Are You a Good Listener?

For conversations to be their most productive, a strong set of listening skills is required for all participants. Don't be fooled: listening is hard work and most entrepreneurs, executives, and employees could enhance their listening skills at least a little. To initially check out how your listening measures up, evaluate your recollection of the last conversation you had. Is it fuzzy or patchy? Did you have a clear sense of accomplishment when it was over? Can you recall what the resolution of the discussion was?

During a discussion, note whether you're paying enough attention. Are you asking questions, giving feedback, tracking with what's being said?

You can begin to improve your listening skills by taking care to concentrate on the conversation participants at hand. That strategy should embrace the following components:

- Ignore phone calls during the conversation, and abstain from multitasking overall.
- Look at the other person, and focus on the other person's words and meanings, realizing both content and intent.
- Avoid interrupting the other person; similarly, wait until the speaker finishes to form opinions.
- Be aware that each person in the conversation may have a different agenda; don't let yours veer you off-track from listening to others.
- Offer help to others if they're having difficulty expressing or articulating their thoughts.
- Wait until the other person has finished before offering your own comment; resist jumping to conclusions, and instead analyze rather than judge the speaker's words.
- Concentrate on the flow and back-and-forth of the conversation, rather than becoming hung up on bits of information or parts of past conversation.
- Take on the responsibility of listening: being bored, not liking the speaker, or disagreeing with what he or she has to say doesn't excuse you from actively listening.
- Consider body language (which is discussed at length in the next section), and respond with both words and actions, taking into account your own body language and such traits as concern and empathy.
- Restate key points to ensure accuracy and prevent potential misunderstandings.

Looking Out for Body Language

Have you ever been talking to someone and noticed a quizzical look, furrowed eyebrows, or a grimace? Have you seen a smile, a nod, or a torso tilted forward? Body language can give you immediate indications of how you're being received by your conversation participants.

Curiously, experts have determined that if a judge and jury could accurately read body language, trials could be decided instantaneously.

Unsurprisingly, you convey a wide range of messages through your posture, facial expressions, gestures, mannerisms, and appearance. Whether it is subtle and unintentional or not, body language can foster an outstanding first impression. Just as readily, it can leave a detrimental one. In the space of only a few seconds, you use body language that could cause a prospective client to sign on or turn off.

Listening Really Counts

Some statistics conclude that three-quarters of what we hear is heard incorrectly, and within a matter of weeks, we forget three-quarters of the one-quarter we heard right.

That being the case, don't waste listening time. You can actually listen faster than the speaker can speak. While the average speaking rate is about 125 words per minute, your capacity to listen is about 400 to 600 words per minute. Therefore, your mind is freed up about 75 percent of the time you're listening. Use that extra time by staying true and relevant to the conversation: checking in with your understanding, formulating suggestions, and considering certain points.

Devoted to the benefits of better listening, and delving into instruction on improving yours, the International Listening Association offers myriad tips and techniques. You can find out more about the organization at *www.listen.org*.

Body Language: The Good

Sharpen your listening skills by noticing and giving thought to the body language you're witnessing. Realize, too, that even as you're deciphering body language, you're sending your own signals as well. In that context, understand that you can give your verbal message more impact with positive body language traits.

A handshake that is firm (but not crushing) signals confidence, as does a posture that is straight but not stiff. Eyes should be intent and focused (though not transfixed), and your face should suggest a sincere approach. Your arms should be uncrossed and, to appear open to comments, your jacket should be unbuttoned. Rolling up your sleeves usually means getting down to work.

Particularly when dealing with clients and customers, take a stance that encourages and fosters feedback and goodwill. Making eye contact, leaning slightly forward during conversations, and nodding occasionally all are mannerisms of an attentive, earnest, and interested conversationalist.

Body Language: The Bad

Conversely, you can detract or divert from a message by using body language that casts doubt, mistrust, dullness, or cynicism.

For instance, on the negative side, slouching can convey a lack of interest. Eyes that dart back and forth (or are covered by sunglasses) could signal discomfort or uncertainty. Gritted teeth and running hands through your hair may mean frustration. Fidgeting can express nervousness.

If you notice negative signs in someone you're speaking with, try a new approach in order to bring about a positive perspective. Refocus the discussion, and use your own body language to appear more open or upbeat. If you're not in an overly formal relationship with the conversationalist, you can also try a bit of humor, which can work wonders to relax tension.

Tuning In to Feedback

Feedback refers to the information you give or receive regarding a job or project done well (or poorly). Feedback is instrumental in employee evaluations, job performances, and in conducting a postmortem, which is the evaluation of an event, promotion, or project once it's finished. Constructive feedback is vitally important because it allows you to build

| Inside Track | Face-to-Face and Under Fire |

The owner of a boutique marketing agency had a presentation for a client that, while posing a significant assignment, would pay a hefty monthly retainer to the firm that landed the business. It was a hotly contested account that brought in several candidates and then whittled them down.

When the boutique agency owner, now one of three finalists, went in for the final presentation, she realized she had been blindsided. She had been told the final presentation would be for a few key executives, and that she would be laying out the generalities of her month-by-month marketing plan and the overall theme, but that there would only be time for a few questions.

Instead, the room was packed with people from across several company divisions. While she had only a few minutes to give her well-rehearsed presentation, she was peppered with a barrage of questions that lasted well over an hour, many of which had little to do with her marketing campaign.

Rather than let on that she had a growing pit in her stomach, she deftly, coolly, and professionally handled the questions posed. She promised to get back to company executives about questions she didn't have answers for or felt put off by. As often as she could, she drew in components of the marketing plan that she thought would be beneficial to the company. She purposely kept her body language in check, despite being in a definitely hostile environment.

After the meeting, she decided that she would pass on the business if it were offered to her, which it was.

Shortly afterward, some of the heavy hitters in the room moved to other companies, many of which needed a marketing consultant. The agency owner's grace under fire in difficult circumstances was so memorable during that discussion that executives now at those other companies hired her for substantial pieces of business.

on correct actions, learn from mistakes, and determine whether you are taking the right course or should alter it.

The nature of feedback is subjective; therefore, it can be positive or negative, and can often prompt harsh or hurt reactions. When you deliver feedback, be aware of the best methods to do so—even if it's negative—so that it can be learned from and considered rather than ignored and dismissed.

Feedback Outside of the Form

As corporate consultants in this area are prone to say, feedback is more than just words on a form. The best feedback incorporates a face-to-face discussion to extract the comments that will bring the most progress and best results. While a feedback form can provide an outline to start and a record for containing comments, it should not be the sole vehicle in the process.

Feedback Methods

Consider several ways to provide feedback that increase chances it will be heard, understood as intended, and accepted by the receiver, and then used in a positive way. Having extensively studied feedback, social psychologists Carl Rogers and Kurt Lewin have elaborated on the characteristics for effective feedback. Their findings include that feedback should:

Focus on actions—Don't imbue the feedback with comments or instructions regarding values or attitudes, or behavior that the recipient can't change. Discussing actions should (and will) provide the clearest, most direct link to the feedback.

Be objective in its evaluation—Steer clear of judgmental or inflammatory comments that will trigger the recipient's defensiveness and take the focus away from the issue at hand.

Be specific to the incident—Stay away from making broader generalizations, or bringing in words such as "always" and "never."

Provide alternatives—If you don't point out other, better ways to do or perform something, you deny the recipient the opportunity to parlay learning from this experience into understanding the power of considering other possibilities in the future.

Be timely—Provide feedback as close to the event as possible, while memories are still fresh.

Be mindful—Recognize that the recipient can take or leave the feedback.

Remember: feedback is different from advice. It's not supposed to espouse sage wisdom or be grounded in a mentoring approach. Feedback should be human, but objective.

Make Feedback Routine

Feedback has a better chance of being given well—and taken productively—if it's a regular part of your business communication, and not just reserved for special events or scheduled evaluations.

Plan for feedback, such as suggestions for the betterment of the company, at weekly staff meetings. Hold occasional luncheons or breakfasts for the express purpose of gaining input about different facets of the company. If possible or desired, ask questions that relate specifically to company areas that you're especially eager to evaluate or improve. During the discussions, encourage further questions and invite constructive criticism. Be sure to be genuine in your approach; in other words, don't tell others you want feedback, but be gritting your teeth while you say it. Remember, the more receptive you are to recommendations, the more likely you are to receive ideas that will help the company.

If certain input has been particularly significant to company growth or progress, find a way to reward it, both to show appreciation and to encourage further suggestions.

Great Ways to Get Your Point Across

Sometimes in discussions, people seem to be more focused on being right than on communicating well. When you engage in a face-to-face discussion, you should work to be so succinct, clear, and educated in your message that it convincingly presents the case you want to make.

Right Can Be Wrong

Don't arrive at a discussion with a presupposed position or fixed determination that you're the only one at the table who's right. That stance not only prevents fruitful discussion, but also limits your ability to understand another perspective and amass potentially valuable information that may make your case even stronger.

Realize that for your own message to be heard, you need to have been listening, taking into account other views and opinions. This openness helps you take a more well-rounded approach to conversing. Further, it steers you to choose the words and phrasing that will produce the most effective points.

You also should take time to explain how you arrived at your point or reached your conclusion. Giving others a window into that process will heighten their understanding.

Educate Yourself

When you enter into a conversation or discussion, come prepared with the facts and information you need. Do your research and have your backup. Don't assume that you can carry your point just by sounding authoritative, or being committed to your opinion. Further, when you investigate another's position, you arm yourself with information that is important to that individual and relates directly to his or her perspective, which actually helps the other person see the overall picture you're trying to present.

Exercises for Worldly Understanding

Many companies—no matter their size—have had to become well versed in cultivating relations with an international audience of customers. In doing so, company owners, executives, and employees often need help in understanding beyond language barriers, encompassing cultural differences and the way other countries do business. Created by the Center for International Business Education and Research at Michigan State University, the globalEDGE Web site (*http://globaledge.msu.edu*) connects professionals to an array of more than 50,000 resources for news and activities, including many that foster understanding. As the site's name suggests, many of its tools focus on fine-tuning skills for conducting business in the multicultural realm or with international clients.

In providing points for your cause or making your case, you should rely on an array of resources, rather than just information that you find on the Internet. Draw from and confirm your data with articles and research found in books and magazines as well as through interviews and such interactive experiences as seminars, classes, and exhibits. In addition, don't underestimate the power of personal experiences to illustrate your points. Case studies or interviews you've conducted can do an outstanding job of bearing out ideas and notions since people are often swayed by others' personal stories of success.

When you do gather information, have a specific mission in mind, with specific questions you want answered. The more exact your questions are, the more meaningful your data will be.

When your research turns up possible answers, analyze them. Ask: Are they sensible and relevant to the question asked? Do they come from an informed source? Could you get an even better answer with a follow-up question?

▶▶ TEST DRIVE

In the course of conducting business, it happens to everyone: a conversation that sputters along or ends poorly. The next time you have one that isn't going particularly well, analyze it to ensure that this discussion, as well as future conversations, will be productive. Ask yourself these questions:

- ⮩ What is your goal for the matter at hand?
- ⮩ Do both you and the other party have the same priority in handling the matter, or are different agendas clearly at work?
- ⮩ Is body language from either party indicating discomfort, tension, or frustration?
- ⮩ Are you asking enough questions of each other to clarify points and ensure that both parties are listening?
- ⮩ How can you steer the conversation away from the possible "winner/loser" scenario that may be prevailing?

What's the Point of This Meeting?

Employees, managers, business owners, investors, and vendors all have a common complaint: meetings that are a waste of time and energy. For a variety of reasons (and unfortunately, probably too often), meetings lapse into stretched-out, underutilized, inefficient time periods that leave everyone involved scratching their heads, tapping their watches, and looking for the nearest exit.

Meetings don't have to be that way. They can be productive, rousing, money-making, idea-filled, and winning endeavors that fuel sales, bolster relationships, increase output, exchange vital information, and tap into profitable new ventures.

It's important to understand the primary reason for a meeting from the outset. Meetings typically fall into one of three categories:

1. To share information
2. To brainstorm for ideas
3. To solve a problem, or make a decision

While their purposes have different throughlines and outcomes, all productive meetings have some elements in common. First, make sure that when you call—and agree to be in—a meeting, there is a clear-cut reason for it. A meeting also needs an agenda, a time limit, a goal, a direct correlation from the participants' involvement to reach that goal, and a resultant plan of action—with responsibilities assigned—that springs from attempting to achieve that goal.

To help you follow that course for a meeting with purpose, ask these questions:

- ⊃ Is the root of this meeting simply a question that needs to be answered, or is more thorough discussion warranted?
- ⊃ If it's simply a question, could that question be answered in an e-mail or a phone call?
- ⊃ What would make a meeting different than addressing this question with an e-mail or phone call?

- Do you have access to—and can you summon—all the people who can gather to make this meeting effective?
- Is there a reason why each person you would summon should be there?
- What's your hoped-for outcome of the meeting?
- Will the meeting make that outcome possible?
- If the meeting weren't held, what would happen?

The Particulars of a Productive Meeting

With just a few details, and a modicum of organization, meetings can be highly productive endeavors with positively charged environments. For starters, when the meeting begins, give everyone an approximate idea of how long you expect it to last. Restate your goal for being there, the reasons the participants have been included, and the contributions you hope they bring or expect them to make. Essentially, give everyone a road map for where you're all headed.

Before discussing the prime elements of a productive meeting, consider these characteristics of a tedious or dreaded one:

- A disorganized or unclear direction pervades it
- The participants have mismatched objectives
- A social milieu takes over, creating distractions from the matter at hand
- Decisions get sidetracked
- The time allotted is needlessly extended
- Responsibilities for subsequent actions are either confusing or not assigned at all

In a good meeting:

- A clear purpose and agenda prevails
- The host has prepared the participants
- The discussion includes dynamic, vibrant conversation

➲ The atmosphere encourages and fosters camaraderie

➲ The punctual ending results in and coalesces with defined next steps and actions

Know the Goal

When deciding to have a meeting, strive to give that gathering a goal, whether that be to set priorities in updating a computer network, to review a direct mail piece, or to decide the assembly line responsibilities for a new product.

Optimal Meeting Times

Ever wonder what the best time is to start a meeting so that it will be all it can be? A widely held belief (and certainly perpetuated by its citations on many Internet sites, including *www.effectivemeetings.com*) is that you have two options. In the morning, the best time is 9:00 o'clock, before your participants are devoting 100 percent of their attention to their daily to-do list. In the afternoon, gather your group at 3:00 o'clock, after they've emerged from the sleepiness and lethargy that lunch can bring on.

After articulating the goal, consider it. Is it too brief or expansive for a single meeting? Will you need a series of meetings to accomplish it?

Rounding up the Participants

Make a list of who you think should contribute during the meeting. Who will be directly affected by the discussion? Who has an integral role in the matter at hand? Who will make a difference in accomplishing the goal if they're at the meeting?

Communicate with each and every person who is supposed to be in the meeting to ensure that everyone knows the time, place, and purpose of the meeting. You can communicate these details in a memo or an e-mail. Don't rely on verbal instructions given either in person or over the phone.

The day before the meeting, send reminder e-mails to ensure everyone's attendance and punctuality. No one wants to wait for the one person who has the agendas, who provides the missing link, or who has the vendor in tow.

Meeting Time Limits

Meetings should have a time limit. It's unfair to you and to your participants to put everyone in a room and say, "When we're done, we're done." More often than not, the longer a meeting continues, the more likely it is that a somber atmosphere of diminishing returns will pervade the gathering, causing productivity to decline, participants to get restless, and a surly mood to set in.

Further, in setting a time limit, stick to it. Anxiety rises when meetings run longer than their allotted time frame. Have your meeting structured such that you've reserved a larger block of time than you might expect to use. That way, the meeting won't be thrown off-track by surprise topics that may arise, items that require longer discussion than you anticipated, or questions. If you use less than the allotted time, participants will be grateful. Never underestimate the goodwill that can be generated by a meeting ending early.

Evaluate

After holding the meeting, evaluate it and your performance. What worked, and what didn't? If the meeting is one that's regularly scheduled, consider handing out periodic evaluation forms to be filled out anonymously. With these surveys, you can more readily ascertain others' perspectives, and—if you receive overwhelming responses in certain areas—you can adapt your meetings accordingly, making them more streamlined and productive.

Think about your employees (that is, your particular audience). What could you do differently during a meeting that would have a lasting impact and yield better results not only for one meeting, but for all of those in the future, too?

Drawing Up Agendas

For productive meetings to take root and flourish, you have to have a game plan or your agenda. Laying out an agenda gives you and your participants the framework of your meeting and, in doing so, makes it possible to reach more actionable decisions, make more relevant comments, and create more significant ideas within the time limit.

Ideally, agendas should be distributed before a meeting's scheduled start time. Make sure the agenda includes the goal or objective; a list of people who will attend; the meeting's day, date, start and end time, and place; and a rundown of what will be discussed and who will be presenting.

Mix It Up for Meetings

Shake up the meeting status quo by considering how other companies conduct productive meetings. One CEO has everyone stand during weekly meetings. To begin a meeting on time, another executive draws an employee's name out of a fishbowl to receive a $100 bill—but only those who are at the meeting when it starts are eligible. Also consider this: a 5 P.M. Friday meeting may seem like drudgery, but participants cut to the chase much faster so that their weekends can begin.

This meeting blueprint cannot be too highly touted. With an agenda, you run less of a risk of having the meeting meander off-course as you contend with irrelevant tangents and sift through random comments. An agenda allows you to promote focus and cohesion, and cultivate a unified sense of mission.

Set up your agenda using the outline form discussed in Chapter 5, but stick with just Roman numeral headings. In other words, you don't need to have a full-on, fully detailed agenda; the participants need only the brush strokes.

On the other hand, don't be too general either. You don't want your agenda to simply state Introduction, Marketing, and Conclusion; give at least a little insight into the meeting's components.

Finally, stick to the agenda! Now that you've got it, make sure to use it.

Set a Brainstorming Scene

When I was handling publicity on the agency side for a national automotive account that was launching a vehicle conducive to Hollywood tie-ins, I set up a brainstorm session. I pulled in ten people from various departments of the agency. Not all of them were on the automotive account team; some were from our television division, working on publicity for top-ten sitcoms and dramas; some worked on a computer software account; another pair was in charge of a beverage company's publicity.

The team I assembled was informed of the mission to accomplish and the challenges we would face, and was immediately revved up by the room's atmosphere. The conference table was strewn with buckets of popcorn, and big boxes of candy like those you'd find in a movie theater; movie tickets also were sprinkled about. The walls were covered with some of our intended targets for exposure: cinema posters (to get the vehicle placed in television and film) and magazine spreads of top stars (to have the vehicle featured with models in magazines, and for stars to ride them during leisure time). The person who came up with the most ideas would receive a four-pack of movie tickets at a local theater, and money for concessions.

The brainstorm took into account changing the way the company presented its product in press materials, and crafting pitches that would showcase the vehicle in photos and layouts. Ideas flew quickly and enthusiastically. The meeting resulted in some of the company's most exciting press materials to date, and landed the vehicle in fashion magazines, a music video, and even a blockbuster action film.

Dealing with Distractions

To keep the meeting on track and all participants fully engaged, you as the facilitator have to take responsibility for running a tight meeting. Set ground rules and make sure they're followed. You must contend with both outside influences, which can be troublesome, and the myriad personalities who may be present.

Deflecting Devices

Meeting participants should not be allowed to communicate by cell phone or BlackBerry during a meeting. If possible, have your participants leave the electronic devices at their desks.

If the devices are allowed in, be wary of those attendees who may try to glance down at a cell phone as a call is coming in or, worse, try to text-message during the meeting.

The High Cost of Meeting?

According to an article in *Inc.* magazine, the Center for Continuous Quality Improvement at the Milwaukee Area Technical College surveyed its 130-person management council to find out how much time its members spent in meetings. Multiplying the time spent by members' salaries, the survey found that the college was spending $3 million per year on council meetings! Curious to find out how much your meetings may be costing your company? Calculate the per-hour salary of each participant and add up the numbers. Doing so will inspire you to trim unnecessary meeting time, and make every session have more impact.

If for some reason a participant absolutely must take a call, make sure he or she does so outside of the meeting room so that the intrusion won't continue.

Managing Your Participants

Even with those distractions set aside, you may still have to contend with personalities that may almost seem to undermine your meeting. While keeping calm and exercising a good sense of humor, follow these guidelines for helping those participants—and the entire room full of attendees—stay on task.

If participants frequently interrupt others, ask them to hold off on comments and take turns when speaking. Politely point out that the question prompting the interruption may be answered if the person is allowed to finish speaking.

If there are participants who enjoy making negative comments about suggestions or information presented, ask their input on how to turn the negative into a positive. You can also ask that, in addition to the negative, they point out the positives in the situation or idea they're commenting on.

If an attendee rambles, state or sum up the point. If the point is confusing, ask if he or she can think of another way to articulate it, or seek others' help in trying to rephrase it.

If a participant makes a habit of going off-topic, rein in that person by commenting that while his or her point is interesting (or valid or creative), everyone needs to keep to the meeting's current agenda.

Preparing Handouts

You may find that, for a meeting or brainstorm session, you need to provide information that gives your participants the necessary background and data, or inspires excitement and motivation.

If possible, prior to the meeting, e-mail the information that your attendees will need to prepare themselves for the meeting. If that isn't possible, or if you need to have handouts available at the meeting, set aside a few minutes of initial meeting time so that the handouts can be reviewed. Don't, however, devote a large chunk of time to this activity.

If the meeting has a theme, consider distributing binders or folders containing handouts that tie in with your session. For instance, if you're gathering everyone for a brainstorm on launching a new product, greet your participants with color copies showing coverage of publicity garnered by competing products that were launched well, or line sheets—photos with descriptions and prices—of possible promo items that would beneficially tie in.

Consider articles, flow charts, screen shots, "Top 10" lists, mnemonics, even advice columns and witty cartoons, as long as they're absolutely, completely relevant to the meeting matter under discussion and can foster understanding or productivity.

If you're concerned about copyright infringement, check with the source. Many sources will approve reproduction for handouts, as long as the source is cited on the copy, the handout is considered to be for educational purposes, and the material is not being repurposed for profit.

> ### Handout Help
>
> You don't have to be a graphic designer or be ultra-creative to tap into a wide array of helpful handouts that can stimulate your participants' interest and ideas in a meeting. While you don't want to be wasteful or overdo distribution, handouts can often be a tremendous help in getting participants to focus on a matter, piquing their interest, or encouraging their input.

Taking Notes During Meetings

Someone should be designated to take notes during a meeting. This responsibility includes recording important developments, listing the actions or steps that need to be taken, and identifying the person who needs to handle each one. The notes shouldn't be lengthy dissertations but they need to be concise and, above all, accurate.

These notes not only provide a record of the meeting; the facilitator should use them to write and issue a wrap-up report from the meeting. That report, which can be distributed via e-mail or internal memo or posted on the company's server, puts the notes into an official format.

That format should include a summary of the most important points discussed during the meeting, a listing of responsibilities that need to be completed, and the name of the person assigned to fulfill each action item.

Further, in assessing the value of the meeting and subsequent direction to be taken, a "Next Steps" section, which embraces a "once these are done, then we'll . . ." approach, gives participants an idea of how their accomplished tasks will move a project or plan forward to the next level. The "Next Steps" also, in turn, help set up the agenda for a subsequent meeting pertaining to the same project or plan.

Do be pithy in your approach to the wrap-up. It should be quick to read, and easily understood. Keep it businesslike. Even if the meeting experienced tense moments, the wrap-up report shouldn't dwell on emotional aspects or recount heated debates.

Be timely in distributing the wrap-up report so that the meeting is fresh in everyone's mind. Try not to make the lag time longer than a day; issuing the report as soon as possible is preferable. The sooner participants receive the report, the more likely they are to give its contents higher priority and begin accomplishing the tasks that have been assigned to them.

Meeting Minutes

In a more formal method, some organizations turn meeting notes into actual minutes that are, for instance, passed along to board and council members.

The style of minutes vary—the more important the record, the more detailed the minutes need to be. Generally, in addition to listing the time, place, and participants, the minutes should include the topics of discussion, decisions that were made, votes taken (if applicable), action items that were agreed upon, and the name of the person responsible for each action to be completed.

Keep Ideas

Particularly during brainstorm sessions, make sure to use the meeting notes to keep a record of your ideas. You never know when they can be used or built upon for a later project. During certain meetings at toymaker Mattel, for example, a technographer records everyone's ideas, entering them into a laptop, with entries either projected onto a wall or on a 35-inch color monitor for all to see. That approach keeps a permanent record that allows for a periodic review of ideas and exchanges. In some instances, ideas that didn't come to fruition on one project become instrumental to another one—or even the impetus for one—down the line.

You never know when an idea from a past meeting may be just the one you need to generate ideas for a new product or solve a current problem that you're currently meeting about!

▶▶ Test Drive

Conduct an audit of how you facilitate meetings, and commit to making them a more valuable component in your business communication endeavors. Ask yourself:

- ➲ Have your meetings suffered from either a skimpy topic or an overabundant agenda?
- ➲ Could you inject some form of excitement into a meeting, either by changing the routine, offering handouts, or ending it earlier than expected?
- ➲ Are there any meetings that would be better set up as brainstorms?
- ➲ Are distractions effectively dealt with?
- ➲ Do you issue a wrap-up report?

Recognizing Different Kinds of Interviews

Interviews are an integral part of business. During the interview process you gather information for purposes of hiring employees, selecting vendors, narrowing down candidates, or even generating ideas. You may also use an interview to collect data for prospective business, or ask for input to help you solve a problem. On the other side, you may be interviewed yourself in order to be considered for a new position, or to lend your expertise to a certain project.

Interviews may take place on the phone, in a videoconference, or in person. Face-to-face interviews are the best because they allow each party to interact, pick up on body language (discussed in Chapter 19), and get a better "feel" for the other person's personality and traits.

The Phone Interview

Now that computers are so efficient at linking people over long distances, employers and employees—and prospective employees—often are not in the same geographic area. For that reason, phone interviews have become an increasingly common way to check out candidates or interview potential vendors. Depending on the circumstances, phone interviews can be used to screen candidates and narrow down the field, or a particular interview could be the only one conducted. Because phone interviews save money, eliminating the need to fly in candidates or travel to meet possible clients, they have become even more prevalent in a time of belt-tightening.

Suggestions and Protocol

Phone interviews do put both parties at a disadvantage, since nearly 90 percent of a person's communication is accomplished through body language. So, you need to realize that your content and tone become even more important during this kind of interview.

In a phone interview, try to be as focused as you would be during a face-to-face meeting. To help stay present, consider standing, which also makes your voice more dynamic.

Preparation and Pertinence

Whether you're the person to be interviewed or the one doing the interviewing, be prepared. If you're interviewing, have your questions—and ideas for follow-ups—ready. If you're the one being interviewed, think about the kinds of questions you'll be asked, and have answers for them. Being on the phone allows one distinct advantage: you can treat the proceedings as a kind of open-book test, in which you can freely peruse pertinent notes and information to make the interview a more successful one.

As an interviewee, incorporate examples of your past work that lend credence to your answers. For example, if you're trying to land an account to furnish a company with security software, cite statistics from existing clients in your answer, explaining how their Web commerce has been burnished by using your product.

Deciding When an Interview Is Necessary

At certain times, you may need to conduct screening interviews to begin the selection process for the right person or vendor for a job. Even if a person or enterprise has excellent references, or has been recommended to you by someone you trust, you need to make sure that the candidate can fulfill the needs specific to your business.

Keep these key components in mind when deciding whether or not a screening interview may be necessary to weed out applicants or vendors you're considering:

> **Financial issues:** For example, you may have a limited budget, and will not be able to afford cost overruns. You need to verify that a prospective vendor can do a job on-time and on-budget. As far as a job candidate is concerned, you may want to make sure that your salary is commensurate with his or her expectations.

> **Time issues:** Your project faces an intense or immediate deadline. You need potential vendors to provide examples of their qualifications in meeting, and performing under, tight time frames.

For a candidate, time issues could be that you need that person to start work as soon as possible, so you have to make sure that his or her current commitments won't interfere with a start date.

Mystery issues: You have never hired an employee, consultant, or company in this area before, and need information from them on how they have dealt with (or will deal with) an inaugural venture for an organization.

Interviewing Strategies

Both in hiring to fill a position and seeking a company to be an outside vendor, a framework of do's and don'ts will add structure, cohesiveness, and a sense of cordiality to the process, and, in the end, will bring you the best person or company for the job.

The Do's

For the interview, establish a friendly atmosphere, but stick to the topic at hand. Be specific about the kind of job you're offering and the array of responsibilities that need to be fulfilled, and be ready to position those needs in positive terms. Give your search a deadline since an open-ended process is frustrating for all concerned.

Use a set of guidelines you've prepared for the interview, and take notes. Develop probing questions that get a good sense of a track record. Ask for specifics with questions that elicit more detailed answers, such as those beginning with why, how, or what. Your applicant should do 80 percent of the talking during the interview. If a "red flag" appears in any answer, make sure to ask a follow-up question to gain a better understanding of the point or situation.

Use positive body language: be interested, listen actively, and acknowledge answers to questions.

Do keep your top-tier candidates apprised of your decision-making process. Then, once you've made an offer and it's been accepted, distribute well-worded correspondence to all of the applicants who weren't hired. So many companies don't close the loop in this regard, when it's simply a sound business practice to do so, and to do so in a timely manner. (Check out Chapter 8 for pointers on rejection letters.) Above all, genuinely wish the candidates luck in future endeavors and let them know that you appreciated their time. You never know when your paths may cross again, or if and when the applicant may be a fit for your company's future needs.

More Information About the Equal Employment Opportunity Commission

Unsure of the rules and regulations your company faces when interviewing and hiring? The U.S. Equal Employment Opportunity Commission has a Web site (*www.eeoc.gov*) that can be exceptionally helpful in several areas. The site includes a manual that can be downloaded, as well as information about no-cost outreach programs. In addition, a site area pertaining to small businesses contains guidelines particularly relevant to hiring practices and operations, and details on ordering free publications.

The Don'ts

In taking a professional tack for the interview, don't use trick questions, resort to third-degree approaches, argue with the candidate, debate the issues, or monopolize the conversation.

Don't rely on close-ended questions that just require a "yes" or "no," and don't be afraid to draw out the applicant if you need more details or more information for an answer.

Of course, don't use sexist or biased language, or veer into any questions that would be at odds with standards set by the Equal Employment Opportunity Commission, or that aren't job-related.

Don't be taken in by a candidate who plays on your sympathies regarding the need for a job, one whose presentation seems too perfect or polished, or one who tries to commandeer the interview. In basic terms, you're the buyer and the applicant is the seller. So keep control of the interview.

Finally, don't settle. If you have reservations about an applicant, meet or phone that person again for more follow-up questions. If you still haven't found the right person or company for your needs, broaden your search, and seek more recommendations, or advertise more. A hasty decision will only be a quick fix and more problems will result in the long run with the wrong person or company filling the job.

Asking Great Questions

In assessing job candidates or possible vendors, your interview hinges on the depth and insights that your questions will spur.

Questions should be specific, but encourage broad responses to encourage revelations or bring up additional relevant information.

For Job Candidates

Create a question list that is ideally suited to your needs and the position you need to fill. You can use the following questions—which apply generally to all kinds of businesses—as a springboard. Of course, you may have different areas that require more information from the candidates. Still, do be mindful that questions you ask must all pertain to efforts, endeavors, activities, and positions that correlate directly to the job that the candidates are applying for.

Before launching into the questions, set up a friendly exchange, and give a positive overview of the position. Frame the questions such that they relate back to the position:

- What have been your previous responsibilities in job positions?
- How have you gotten along with coworkers, clients, and customers?
- What company culture works best for you?
- What previous experience should be considered or described that corresponds to a job with this company?
- What opportunities did you take to show initiative on past jobs?

➲ What contributions did you make to the overall success of a company you worked for?

➲ What new ideas, plans, or products did you contribute?

➲ Can you describe a particular on-the-job problem you solved, and how you reached the solution?

➲ What motivated you to seek out the job you're currently applying for?

For Outside Vendors

With job vendors, you're likely looking to an outside source to fill an immediate need that will prop up your business in some way. Once again, different needs call for different questions, but you can let the following serve as a guide:

➲ What is your previous relevant experience?

➲ What success stories can you relate?

➲ How did you contribute to the profitability of other companies?

➲ What was a situation that didn't work out, and why?

➲ How many clients do you typically have simultaneously?

➲ Which of your company employees would be specifically assigned to work on our business?

➲ What do you envision as your responsibilities?

➲ How is the fee structure set up?

➲ How will you measure your success?

Giving Great Answers

If you are the potential consultant or vendor being interviewed by a company, take care to fully weigh the questions being asked, and to give complete, thoughtful answers that will increase your chances of being hired.

Be thorough, but don't ramble. If you find yourself getting off-track, summarize the cogent point you had made—"As I said, we offer follow-up workshops for the training procedures"—and let the interviewer ask the next question.

Come to the interview prepared with examples that point out experiences rooted in facts and figures. In addition, have ideas that will be organic to and especially geared toward the company that is interviewing. Make sure to create a general outline of how your ideas can be accomplished. Go for realistic endeavors, not pie-in-the-sky possibilities that the interviewer can readily conclude would be extremely difficult to execute.

A Different Kind of Resume

While interviewing does focus primarily on talking, don't be afraid to furnish your interviewer with information that will subtly prompt him or her into asking you about specific highlights, capabilities, and strengths that you're most proud of. In essence, giving that person literature, handouts—or even better, a written snapshot of company milestones—will help inform the interview, and allow you to shine a spotlight on your organization's top attributes, particularly those that will be most beneficial to the client or customer you're trying to land. Further, while the piece shouldn't be hokey, consider incorporating your firm's attitude or spirit in it to give the interviewer an even better idea of your company's perspective.

If you've begun a new venture and are trying to get business, you won't have many experiences to draw from to illustrate your potential contributions. Instead, point to your strengths: as a start-up, you can offer a higher degree of customer service; your rates may be less expensive; the background you bring to the business may be more varied.

Depending on the situation, you also may have case studies, slides, or handouts that illustrate and back up the information you're supplying. Your resume may actually be the experience you bring to a potential client, so make sure to have a visual that shows and speaks for it, for instance, a brochure, printed Web site pages, or a sales sheet.

Check Out the Big Picture

At some point, your company may be interviewed to be a vendor or consultant. Use the interviews that you conduct to help you create a polished presence of your own. For instance, check your candidates' resumes. Are they riddled with misspellings? Poorly laid out? Incomprehensible in parts?

A resume is truly a representation of a person, and particularly offers insights into a candidate's work ethic, and what he or she deems professional. If a resume doesn't look respectable or read well, the candidate may carry over that same carelessness into his or her job performance.

When you interview vendors, depending on their occupations, examine their work: visit job sites or Web sites, review their company literature, survey their results. Find out whether their work speaks for itself, and will be beneficial to your company.

In both instances of hiring a consultant or a vendor, verify and check references. Devise a list of questions for which you need answers. Your questions may vary extensively, especially when you're hiring employees. When you deal with vendors, for example, ask about completing projects on time and on budget, delve into challenges they faced, get a sense of whether or not expectations were met overall, and assess the vendor's fit into the corporate culture.

Avoid These Pitfalls

Commonly in the business world, many have endured interviews and wish it had gone better, that different comments had been made, better experiences revealed, or a better impression been left.

Be cognizant of a few points discussed in this section for before, during, and after the interview that can help it be a winning experience. While an interview might not result in your receiving an offer to work with a company right away, you never know when the interviewer may approach you for another need, or have the opportunity to refer you to another company.

| Inside Track | You Don't Want to Win Them All |

Sure, it would be great to be offered a job after every interview you ever had, but sometimes allowing yourself a little foresight makes the process easier on everyone involved.

An entrepreneur badly wanted a contract for his company to serve as a consultant for a school district's afterschool sports programs. However, a series of interviews was forcing him to realize that his company and the capabilities actually needed just weren't a fit. The interviews were actually serving him well in the sense that he was getting an increasing amount of information about the school district's needs, but they were also giving him growing reservations about fulfilling the job.

Sometimes, after an interview, you may realize that the fit just isn't right for your company and the prospective client. Rather than hoping the client will simply never call, or that—if offered the job—you'll figure out some way to make it work, take a proactive stance.

As soon as possible, let a prospective client or employer kindly know that you respect them and their work and, because of that, you're bowing out of consideration. More than likely, the prospective employer won't be angry, but highly appreciative that you were shrewd enough to analyze the skill set requirement and to realize that, while you have your own considerable attributes, they just weren't a match in this instance.

Let interviews work to your advantage. Don't just hope for a job to come out of every interview. Use them wisely to ascertain and select the jobs that will be the best for you and your prospective client or employer.

Before and During Your Interview

Take these steps to make sure that you have a smooth and successful interview:

⊃ Send an e-mail to your contact the day before the interview to reconfirm the day, date, time, and place, as well as the name of the interviewer.

⮑ Dress appropriately. Don't head into a financial-planning office in a T-shirt and shorts (even if that's what you wear in your office), or go into a beach shop wearing a tie, three piece suit, and trench coat.

⮑ Make advance plans (including getting directions) to ensure that you won't be late.

⮑ Even if the interviewer lapses into discourteous comments or off-color remarks, don't follow the lead.

⮑ Stay on message: be prepared, follow the rules of good grammar and diction, and speak clearly.

⮑ Steer clear of conveying a "know-it-all" attitude. While you should be proficient (and possibly an expert), don't be overbearing or exude overconfidence, which can be off-putting. A confident approach is an advantage, an overconfident one is a disadvantage.

⮑ Don't emphasize the benefits you may receive: the handsome fees that this company might pay to yours, the free product you could receive, the proximity of the client to your office.

⮑ Similarly, don't emphasize problems that could arise: your view that the project has many obstacles, that the board may not approve one part of the plan, that agreements will never be reached on some issues.

⮑ Be aware of your body language: give a firm handshake, pay attention to questions, and look the interviewer in the eye.

After the Interview

After being interviewed, promptly send a thank-you note. In nearly all cases, thank-you notes make far more distinct and favorable impressions than do thank-you e-mails or thank-you phone calls. Clearly, the hirer will know that more care and energy went into sending a mailed letter, and will consider that those traits carry over into your job performance as well. However, you must also consider the company and the person doing the hiring. While some automatically discount an applicant who sends a thank-you e-mail rather than a letter, others discourage any communication that isn't electronic.

Media Interviews

Being interviewed by a member of the media is in a category of its own. Still, the ground rules of being a good interviewee apply; you just want to be careful with the information you give because it could end up in print or on television. Strive to be as professional as possible. Dress appropriately so that you will represent your company with a polished look. Beforehand, get as much information as possible about the interview itself and the outlet conducting it. Why are the media interested in talking with you? Can you get an idea of the questions that will be asked? Identify and be prepared to offer key talking points. Stick to those as closely as you can. Don't be compelled to offer information that you're not being specifically asked about. Don't be afraid to tell a reporter that you'll need to check into a matter and get back to them. They want to receive accurate information just as much as you want to give them the right facts.

Either way, the thank-you note gives you the opportunity to express gratitude for the interviewer's time, and reiterate both your keen interest in filling the company's vendor void and (briefly) your unique qualifications for the position.

 **Test Drive**

Devise an answer guide. The next time you're asked these typical questions you'll have great responses already crafted:

- ➲ What products or services do you offer?
- ➲ How is your fee structure set up? (Or, What are the costs of your products?)
- ➲ What client success stories are you most proud of, and why?
- ➲ What do you do when clients or customers aren't happy with the job's progress or completion, or are unsatisfied with a product?
- ➲ What do you predict will be your company's next milestone?

Why Would You Make a Speech?

More than likely, being in business means that at some point—during a conference, convention, banquet, or event—you'll have to make a speech. Sometimes, it could be simply introducing a keynote speaker, or it might be laying out a grand plan for a company strategy. You may need to motivate employees to rally behind a cause, or speak to a group about how your company's products fit their needs.

In all of the instances in which you might be called upon to make a speech, the basics remain constant: organizing and preparing content, mastering delivery techniques, and heeding an array of do's and don'ts.

When you are called upon to make a speech, compose a strategy to make the speech as effective as possible. Thoroughly conduct an information audit that will guide you in writing the content, appealing to the audience, and sharpening your delivery. Provide answers for the following ten questions:

1. What is the objective or goal of the speech?
2. Who is the audience?
3. In what context will the speech be given?
4. What information will you need to gather or research?
5. Do you have enough time to prepare and practice your speech?
6. Do you think visuals or handouts will enhance the speech?
7. What are the features of the room or forum where the speech will be delivered?
8. What equipment will you need to give the speech?
9. What action or result would you like the speech to bring?
10. Do you have a way or method to evaluate the speech afterward?

In answering these questions, you'll begin to shape your speech, giving it the right tone, crystallizing the information it contains, and ensuring that it flows in the most effective way possible.

Make a Speech Work for Your Company

Speeches can provide a way to boost business that you might not have previously considered (or perhaps the prospects of which might frighten you). Consider the possibilities that giving a speech can bring to your company: Within a tremendously rewarding experience, you can share information and your own expertise, enriching others and giving your company considerable exposure that could bring in customers and clients.

Start Small

Begin by finding outlets that are easy to approach and amenable to having speakers. You can start with local civic organizations, such as the Rotary Club, church or school groups, or career events at a nearby college or university.

From there, you may extend an offer to speak to business associates, customers, or clients, or they may ask you to speak. Many meeting planners rely on guest speakers to create interest in an event, or to provide valuable information.

Draw up a list of key outlets or decision-makers that you would like to have as an audience, and approach them. Once you have developed some key topics (which is discussed a little later in this chapter), you can send a letter of introduction, or make a cold call to determine their interest.

The Benefits Multiply

Can you appreciate the value of a caterer giving a speech to a meeting of special event decision-makers; a costume company owner providing a presentation at a convention for Halloween lovers; or an executive coach speaking to a room full of CEOs? While these examples may be obvious, you can immediately make the connection that having an opportunity to show your wares to those who are part of your target audience could have far-reaching, long-lasting, and profitable ramifications. Never underestimate the bump in business—or the value of public relations for your company—that giving a speech can bring.

If you could have a few minutes in front of potential customers in your target audience, what organizations would be on your wish list? Use the Internet, colleagues, and community contacts as a resource in finding possibilities. You never know what contacts those in an audience may have. Once you give a presentation that is well received, you're likely to receive several invitations to other meetings and events soon afterward. Word of mouth is particularly effective in finding speakers.

Taking the Experience Back to the Office

Of course, you also can also make the speech work for your company in other ways. Often, relating to people outside the office can give you considerable, valuable perspective. By becoming well versed in giving speeches, you'll polish your communication skills with employees, clients, vendors, and investors. When you're able to ascertain firsthand what connects with a roomful of people, you can parlay that expertise into a home-field advantage.

You may realize that in preparing for a speech outside of the office, you took extra care to make a positive impression and create an effective presentation. In effect, you were more organized.

When you make speeches outside of the office, consider how you can take what you've learned back to the workplace:

- ⊃ How did you prepare differently than you would have for a speech within your company?
- ⊃ What did this audience seem most interested in?
- ⊃ Were there points that were lost on them? If so, why?
- ⊃ Did you use visual aids? Is that a normal accompaniment to your presentations at the office?
- ⊃ Were you more receptive to questions from the audience?

Evaluate your responses, and then determine how you can use this analysis to inform and adapt the way you're communicating within your company.

Selecting a Topic for Outside of the Company

Depending on the circumstances and venue of your speech, you may be given a predetermined topic to speak about. If that's the case, you should begin outlining your content by fine-tuning the scope and giving your speech a title that directs its focus. Don't worry if you decide to change the title; it can be a temporary one at this point. Its purpose is to guide your research and organization.

In other cases, such as those in which you try to advance your business by giving a speech, you may be overwhelmed by the idea of picking a topic. Unless someone you know asks, "Can you come talk to my group about what you do?" chances are you might not have focused on subject matter you can present. But be assured, you probably have more information to share than you realize.

The Who and the What

Before diving into your possible—and certainly rich—topic possibilities, you must first assess a few key components. Who will be there, and what will they want to know? How can your presentation be effective with and valuable to them?

For instance, think about what you routinely are asked about your company, product, service, or job responsibilities. Has there been a recurring theme? If you're at a party and people are discussing the work they do, what questions are you asked when you tell others about your business? Are there common questions you often answer?

Everyone's work presents and provides several areas of interest that can provide subject matter for a speech. However, the topic must move beyond a simple description of what you do. It must be molded into an overarching speech that informs your audience and offers tips, instruction, or both, about how their lives or businesses can be better or improved.

In other words, you can't stand before an audience and expect them to be excited to hear a sixty-minute sales pitch about why they should do business with you. You need to delve into a relevant but indirect approach to pique their interest. Consider these possible topics for different businesses:

⮑ An accountant could talk about how to be organized throughout the year to prepare for tax time; the deductions people don't generally think about including in their tax returns; and setting a budget in business or at home.

⊃ A custom-car salesman could talk about the best nearby places for family vacations, and activities for kids to do in the car, or how to attract repeat business in a niche market.

⊃ A beauty supply owner could give a presentation about protecting your skin from the sun and skin cancer prevention; the best daily skin-care regimen for different age groups; or perhaps how the business got started.

⊃ A pool and patio contractor could discuss new trends in outdoor landscaping; how to avoid delays in home repairs; and even themed outdoor parties.

⊃ A Pilates instructor can tout the benefits of exercise and finding a physical fitness program that fits your lifestyle; talk about the ups and downs of teaching a dozen strenuous classes a week; or share the obstacles and benefits in setting up an exercise studio.

Make the Experience Work for You

Whenever you speak outside of your company, remember that each opportunity provides you with an audience full of potential clients. Further, each of them may mention you and your company to someone else. If the setting is appropriate, provide an extra incentive by offering everyone there a business card, or a flyer with a coupon attached to use at your place of business. If you've got a high-ticket product, consider a drawing that everyone at the presentation can enter to win.

Whatever the presentation's topic or the place that you give it, make sure the audience is left with a positive impression of what your company does, and an appreciation of the valuable information you gave them.

Organizing Your Speech

After you've selected or been given your topic—whether you're promoting your business or simply giving a speech on a related subject—you should spend some time brainstorming the different elements of your speech. To begin, determine the time frame of the speech: how long is it scheduled to last?

Then, give your topic a "stress test." State it concisely. Use it in a sentence. Jot down elements that naturally flow from the topic. Is it too broad or too narrow for the time allowed? Do the elements you just wrote down relate to each other?

After you've determined that your topic is in good stead, you should work to complete an outline, write the speech, and then flesh out the presentation with visuals, handouts, or both. In orchestrating this process, you need to remain clear about the objectives for your speech. Are you informing? Persuading? Motivating? How will your contents directly link to your purpose?

The Process Begins

Suppose you're a contractor who has been asked to speak at a homeowners association meeting in a stylish neighborhood. Many of the homeowners have been eager to embark on renovations, but all they hear from those who have completed construction are nightmare stories of over-budget, past-deadline, and unsatisfying projects. Since you have been described as a contractor who only has happy clients, you've been asked to speak about how a remodel can be done in a punctual, cost-effective manner.

Knowing that this opportunity could be a boon to referrals, you agree. You title your speech "Renovations for the Time-, Style-, and Cost-Conscious." These three areas routinely enter into conversations with aspiring renovators. Then, without giving away your trade secrets, you decide to describe a successful approach that others can adopt, no matter which contractor they hire.

In many ways, organizing a speech follows the tenets of some of the other written materials discussed in this book. You have a topic (also called a subject or main idea) and subtopics, with each section fleshed out with supporting information that flows in a logical manner.

Your first step is to draft an outline, which might look like the outline on the following page:

I. A Case Study: What Went Wrong
II. The Realistic Scope of the Project
    A. The architect's plan
    B. The time frame
    C. The budget
    D. Ground the plan, time, and budget in reality
III. Ways to Save Time
    A. Working with subcontractors who work together
    B. Linking deadlines to a payment schedule
    C. Helping homeowners realize that time is money
IV. Ways to Stay on Budget
    A. Getting deals on appliances and fixtures
    B. Ways to reduce waiting times and stop overtime
    C. Homeowners' making and sticking to decisions
V. Look Chic, Be Cheap
    A. Little-known vendors with big style
    B. Visual effects
    C. Expensive inspiration for pennies
VI. Other Considerations
    A. Pros and cons to staying in the house during reconstruction
    B. Keeping the contractor and subcontractors on your side
    C. Doing your homework
    D. The importance of referrals
VII: A Case Study: What Went Right

Now, the Writing

The preceding outline gives you an idea of how your speech might be set up. The contractor has probably fielded hundreds of questions about how to have a remodel go smoothly, so he chunked out those questions into the ways in which he would answer them in front of a large group. You can probably see in the outline that every speech, regardless of the audience, the purpose, or the venue, thrives on three components: introduction, body, and conclusion.

Linking the Introduction and Conclusion

You should always plan to begin a speech with some "Wow!" moment, or an issue that your audience is eager to learn about how to make their home or work life better. In this case, the contractor might speak first about a lengthy project that suffered from severe cost overruns, then show a picture of a dilapidated house and say, "Don't let this happen to you." He could also tease them with a picture of a stunning home he just finished and say that, at the end of the speech, the audience will know the top ten tips for a successful renovation. Just as you start with a strong opening, you want your conclusion to have a punch as well, giving the audience a key moment that leaves a strong, positive impression. The conclusion should tie in to your opening, and provide a snappy, friendly, and brief reminder of the speech's lasting benefit. The body provides the substantial bridge from the exuberant opening to the satisfying conclusion.

Banner Openings

Don't waste the audience's time with the trite clichés that are associated with speeches, such as opening with an irrelevant, poorly delivered joke, inappropriate humor, or even "It's such a pleasure to be here tonight." Write an opening that will be provocative (but not shocking), compelling, and not dull. Think about intriguing statements that may have hooked you in a speech or even in everyday conversation. People like to be let in on the best piece of advice someone ever got, an old family secret that reaped rewards, a strategy employed that averted problems or danger. Take note about what kinds of introductions you perk up to, and think about adapting one for the opening of your own speech.

Filling Out the Outline

Using the outline presented earlier in this section, the contractor can begin to write his speech. He could use a more detailed outline that provides multiple sentences for each topic and subtopic or, if he's more comfortable with it, begin writing the text of the speech in paragraph form. Remember, though, that you won't be reading your speech word-for-word. You may choose to memorize the speech, or diligently use descriptive notes as a guide.

Whichever way you choose to turn the outline into a more detailed presentation, be sure to cite examples and statistics, and provide solid supporting stories in the body of your speech. While you may be an expert or your company's leader, you can make much more effective points and be more persuasive in general by illustrating your speech for the audience. They'll be more likely to remember the points you're making, too.

In writing, stick to a "you" approach. Make sure that your speech is embracing the audience, not adopting a condescending tone or being "I" oriented. People want to hear about what's in it for them, or how they'll be affected by what you're saying, so keep that in mind as you prepare the speech.

As you develop the speech, try to keep one thought per sentence. Speeches are different from memos or letters or press releases. Since they're rooted in the spoken word, they should be written in a conversational tone. Remember that speeches are written for the ear, not the eyes. A convoluted thought or sentence could be completely lost on an audience.

Prepare the speech so that the audience can easily follow what you're saying. Take a logical approach in the presentation, whether laying out a natural progression of topics or a chronological order of events, whether moving from general to specific ideas and principles or from specific examples to general conclusions.

In many ways, creating a speech simply follows the rules of good writing: be clear, concise, and specific. Use good grammar, but be conversational. Avoid academic and professional jargon, and remember that short words are easier to speak and to understand.

Using Visuals

Even as you write the speech, you should take note of places where a visual may come in handy to drive home a point. Visuals can take various forms, including these:

- ⮑ Handouts
- ⮑ Overhead transparencies

➲ PowerPoint slides
➲ Projected photo slides
➲ Easel-bound charts and graphs
➲ A demonstration

Visuals can be particularly effective in breaking up the speech to create variety and interest for the audience. Think about speeches or presentations for which you've been in the audience. Do you remember visual aids that the speaker used? Which were the most powerful? Why did they work?

As you consider your options, remember that the visual must be relevant to your cause. Getting a laugh or just feeling that you should use a visual here or there aren't strong enough reasons for inclusion. More than likely, your research will provide a few ideas for visuals that will make sense and also help your audience learn more and understand better.

Take care to use clear, large, readable fonts for visuals, with a minimal use of colors. If illustrations are involved, avoid having them be too intricate to be seen, understood, or realized from the audience's perspective.

Make a list of the equipment you'll need. Then, make arrangements for it: either you will provide it, or the venue will. Once you have made the arrangements, check and double-check the equipment you'll be using on-site.

If you're giving handouts, have more than enough ready for the taking.

If you opt to do a demonstration, make sure you have all the tools or equipment you need. Do a run-through of it to prevent problems and accidents.

Before, During, and After Showtime

Put your speech into a format you'll be able to follow. If it's typewritten on standard-size pages, use slimmer margins so that you can add in notes on the side.

| Inside Track | Be Prepared for Words Without Pictures |

Even with the illustrative impact that visuals can add to a speech, be careful about depending too much on them. This point became particularly clear to me when I was a spokesperson for Zoo Atlanta. Zoo Atlanta presented a shining example of a city attraction that—once hampered by a moribund image and devastating controversies—had sparked a complete turnaround with a new image, amazing exhibits, an impressive lineup of corporate sponsors, and an intensely loyal public following.

Many organizations in other cities wanted to know how the turnaround was accomplished, so I made presentations that chronicled the zoo's impetus for change and ensuing progress, giving the zoo repeated, positive publicity in Atlanta and throughout the Southeast.

The speech had several visual aids: a slide presentation, enlarged maps of the park, and colorful signs. When I traveled, I typically—and without incident—checked the bulky equipment and collateral items with baggage. However, when I arrived for a presentation in Nashville, none of my visual aids had made the trip. Nevertheless, the sponsoring organization and I agreed to keep the date.

Fortunately, the speech was grounded with an enjoyable, informative script that I had committed to memory. So, while I missed the splashy atmosphere the visuals afforded, the real meat of the message and the audience's takeaway were still intact. With a good speech—more often than not—it's your way with the words that wins over the audience.

Once you've got your speech and visuals assembled, practice! You'll be so glad you did. Read the speech aloud, changing any words or phrases that may be tongue twisters. You may be surprised to find out what you get hung up on when you read passages aloud rather than in your head.

Count on two minutes of nonrushed speaking per double-spaced page, and pace yourself. Consider even tape-recording or, better yet, videotaping a rehearsal, and then listening to your speed and tone. Even consider gathering a few friends or a similar nonthreatening audience to practice in front of.

Before the Speech

If possible, survey the room in which you'll be speaking: What is the room's layout? Where will the audience be sitting? Where will you be presenting?

Double-check equipment. Be alert to any potential distractions that the room may experience: a busy street, a nearby clock tower's chimes, a boisterous session in the conference room next door. Determine whether the lighting is suitable to see slides and transparencies easily and clearly.

Arrive a half-hour early, and have the contact person's cell phone number and other information handy.

When you are ready to take the podium, or head of the conference table, make sure your cell phone is in the silent mode or turned off, and that you aren't wearing a watch that beeps at certain intervals.

Alleviate Anxiety Before a Speech Begins

Before giving a speech, you may feel tense or anxious, which is perfectly natural. You can call on several recourses to contend with those preperformance pressures. First, you'll definitely help your cause by being extra-well rehearsed. Solidly knowing the material will be a boon to your confidence and will ease at least some of your worry. Second, give yourself ample time before you give the speech; don't rush in from someplace else. Allow yourself a few moments before your speech begins to take some deep breaths and appreciate a calm feeling. Last, strive to remember that you're really engaging in a conversation with an audience. While you'll be projecting to be heard by a number of people, try to focus on a friendly one-on-one approach.

The Delivery

Even though you shouldn't read your speech word for word, you can certainly rely on your detailed outline, index cards with message prompts, or other clearly printed notes to guide you. While you shouldn't be too rigid or formal, you also shouldn't be so relaxed that you go off-topic, make off-the-cuff comments, or bring up anecdotes you didn't plan to. Adhere to the script's outline.

Work the room. Don't be afraid to move from behind the lectern or podium, which can sometimes present a barrier between you and the audience. In general, move around; be active but not distractingly so; be cool-headed, confident, and engaged; and make eye contact.

Convey a controlled enthusiasm. Be excited about your subject or topic, but not overwhelmingly so.

Additional Publicity for Your Speech

Realize that when you make a speech, you may have additional opportunities for positive exposure for you and your company, in the way of media coverage. Depending on the speech's subject matter, location, and purpose, you should consider having a media advisory distributed, having a photographer present, and being available for interviews afterward.

Further, you can summarize key points from your speech in a release that is distributed to appropriate media outlets, such as your industry's trade publications. Of course, you should include that information on your company's Web site, too.

Pay attention to the speed of your words. Don't speak too fast. Check in periodically to ensure that you're taking a measured but natural approach with your delivery.

If you use visual aids, don't read them word for word either. Treat them as supplements to your presentation, not mainstays.

After the Speech: The Question Session

More than likely, you should be prepared to take questions after your presentation is finished. In doing so, keep control of that session with a one-at-a-time approach. Don't allow one person to dominate the proceedings and give everyone a fair chance to get a question answered. You should limit the time allowed for questions, and let everyone know, near the end of that limit, that you "have time for two more questions" so that you can cleanly wrap up your presentation.

If a question is confusing, paraphrase it to ensure accuracy. If you don't know an answer, don't be afraid to say, "I don't know, but let me get back to you on that." An honest approach engenders goodwill and actually lends credibility to all else you say. Do be sure to write down the questioner's contact information so that you can follow up with a response promptly after the session.

If possible, use questions to reiterate points you've made, and use the last question you take to segue into an overall but quick summary.

Providing Your Biography

When you agree to give a speech, you may be asked to provide a brief biography (bio). You want to make sure that the information included in it is particularly relevant to the topic of the speech you will deliver. A bio is simply a two- or three-paragraph snapshot of your current position that, in this case, illustrates why you're ideally suited to present the speech.

You may already have a bio in your company's press materials or on your Web site, but if you don't, you can use your most recent resume, if available, as a guide. (Do not, however, send your resume in place of a bio.)

The bio should begin with your current post and title, your company's name, and—if it's not obvious from its name—what your company does. Briefly elaborate on your experience, but don't include experience that isn't relevant. For instance, the contractor giving the renovation speech would include his past jobs as an apprentice architect and as the foreman for a corporate headquarters construction site, but exclude his experience as a shoe salesman.

If you've received awards or other recognition, include those, too.

If someone else is introducing you, give that person bullet points listing your experience, drawn from your bio. That way, you'll have pointed out exactly the details that person should mention about you and your background.

Getting Input for Effectiveness

Follow up with your contact the next day, if possible, to ascertain how the speech was received.

If possible and if appropriate, depending both on how often you give a speech and the audience involved, consider handing out evaluations afterward. These questionnaires can be immensely helpful in getting feedback and determining which content should be jettisoned, what information should be added, and which components were most effective.

Questions could be answered on a numerical scale (5 being most enjoyable, 0 being the least), or allow for more open-ended responses. Sample questions could include these: Did the introduction attract your interest? Were visual aids relevant? Will you use the information presented? Were questions answered completely? Was the conclusion sufficient?

If you're interested in obtaining more extensive feedback, consider questions such as these: What information or points could have been covered that weren't? What other visual aids would have been helpful? What related topics would you be interested in hearing or learning about?

▶▶ Test Drive

Develop an idea for a speech that promotes your business. Think about the following areas:

- ⊃ **Consider your work and your background.** What ideas do you have that might have the most play in your community or with your target audience?
- ⊃ **Consider your community.** What venues do you know of that would be receptive to your making a speech?
- ⊃ **Consider the outcome.** What positive impact could the speech have on your business outside of increased sales?

What Makes an Impactful Presentation?

PowerPoint presentations have become a ubiquitous component of many meetings and conferences. As such, you should become familiar with the best methods—and the ones to avoid—in creating an effective presentation.

If you're not accustomed to the terminology, a PowerPoint presentation is a computer-generated slide show that effectively blends words with cohesive images and illustrative graphics, which could be photos, charts, graphs, or simple illustrations. As you deliver your presentation, the PowerPoint slides give a brief summary of what you are discussing in greater detail.

At their best, these are seamless presentations that allow the audience to easily follow with your discussion, provide lively visual support, and offer key summaries to accompany longer or complex points.

At their worst, they become disjointed, one-sided monologues that prompt the audience to think that they're getting all they need up on the screen and, subsequently, tune out your words.

Your first step in making a PowerPoint presentation as strong as it can be is to resist the urge to merely consider it a vehicle for dumping information. Instead, truly home in on the reasons for giving the presentation in the first place:

- Who is your audience?
- What will giving this presentation accomplish?
- Why are you using this method to communicate with them, rather than another?
- What benefits does a PowerPoint presentation give your cause?
- After the presentation's over, what's your next step?

Defining the Purpose

Your first step in tackling a PowerPoint presentation is the same as in other business communications—to clearly delineate the reasons behind it, and determine your audience.

Defining your objective, audience, and also the arena in which you will make your presentation will help you to create and make the most effective presentation possible, one that will complete your goals and connect with your audience in a space that is conducive to, and fosters, a productive program.

Answering these questions will help you to craft a sharp and strong PowerPoint presentation:

- ➲ Where will the presentation be given?
- ➲ How many people will you be speaking to?
- ➲ What is your relationship to your audience?
- ➲ What is your topic?
- ➲ Will you be informing or persuading?
- ➲ Is the topic one that will be met with excitement, reticence, or both?

Take the Tutorial

If you never have before, take a moment to open up the PowerPoint application, which is probably in your applications folder or already on your navigation bar. Once you do that, you'll have the opportunity to open up a lesson and learn about such PowerPoint capabilities as creating templates; navigating toolbars; adding text, images, scanned photos, charts, and hyperlinks; running a slide show; troubleshooting; sharing files; incorporating special effects; and discovering more about such Power Features as transitions and keyboard shortcuts. Arm yourself ahead of time with this information and you'll instantly get a better idea of how to make PowerPoint achieve its highest potential for your needs.

How PowerPoint Can Help Your Cause

You may be unsure of how you can use a PowerPoint presentation to provide information and meet your goal with your intended audience. To that point, consider the benefits of a well-designed and well-executed presentation.

PowerPoint presentations are often considered effective because they provide the audience with a visual outline of content. Those words on slides (or cards) help an audience to focus their attention.

Further, hard-to-explain concepts can be more easily grasped or enhanced when accompanied by a visual image such as a photo. That's because, in addition to the words, visuals offer the chance to present content in diverse, even entertaining ways. Graphics, pie charts, bar graphs, and snapshots are all standard inclusions, but you can also incorporate video, audio, animation, and sound effects. These words, visuals, and sounds coalesce to capture the audience's attention in a most impressive way, and allow them to comprehend and logically follow the information being presented.

Selecting the Perfect Words and Visuals

Don't be intimidated by PowerPoint. The application is exceptionally easy to open, learn, and operate. Your PowerPoint presentation boils down to two main components:

1. **Content,** or the words and messages that will be relayed
2. **Design,** or the visual framework and images that will accompany the content

The Content That Counts

Your presentation absolutely must begin with an outline (outlining is discussed at length in Chapters 4 and 22). An outline provides focus for your presentation and lays out your information in a logical format.

Once you have your topic in mind, your outline should flow from this question: "Where am I taking this audience with this presentation?" Each slide that you write will be a natural progression, continuing to build on the information that was previously given.

However you best write outlines—in complete sentences, fragments, with a mind-mapping method (which is discussed in Chapter 4), or even using PowerPoint—dedicate yourself to taking a detailed approach in addressing your specific topic.

Remember that this outline isn't the one that you'll put up on the screen during your presentation. Rather, this one will provide a comprehensive, step-by-step format to follow. With it, you'll draft and attach detailed notes that will accompany your presentation. The detailed notes, in effect, become your script.

With a lengthy, detailed outline in hand, you can begin to prepare your deck of PowerPoint cards. You'll break down the presentation according to your outline, tackling one subject area per slide. For each slide you create, type in the bulleted points that pertain to the area within the topic you're covering. For each slide's words, you can extract potent points from the outline, or draft the copy from scratch.

Below each slide that you're providing bullet points for, you'll find the "Comments" section. In this area, write all the information that elaborates on each bullet. The "Comments" sections will not show up on the screen in your final presentation. Instead, they essentially serve as your slide-by-slide script, and can be printed out separately for you to use as a reference during your presentation. (Do make sure to follow the application's instructions so that your "Comments" sections do not show up when you give the presentation, whether directly on your laptop or projected on a screen.)

With Design in Mind

Your design elements encompass the font size and style that you use for the presentation's words, the background color of the slides, any framing or borders for the slides, visual images or photos in the slides, or such other components as animation or video.

As you write your outline, you should also jot down ideas that readily come to you regarding graphs, charts, or other visual components that might beef up, elucidate, or elaborate on the slide's contents.

Don't feel compelled to include a graphic on every slide. Quite the contrary; use them only to illustrate important points. For instance, you can incorporate a table that shows budget line items, a bar graph that shows an increase in media coverage since a product launch, a pie chart that carves up the duties and percentage of time for each person in a certain job position, and so on.

However, don't be afraid to break up the text with images. That is, take a cue from the saying "A picture is worth a thousand words." If you can find a photo, graphic, or clip that provides a literal snapshot of your text, use it.

The size of the fonts you use for your bullet points should be no less than 24 point. Stay away from frilly, curly, or thick fonts that could be hard to read. Remember that your presentation will be seen by a group, in a large format, at a calculated pace, not read by an individual who can spend time examining it closely or at his or her leisure.

Use colors, but use them judiciously. Vivid colors can certainly add interest, but when used excessively or inappropriately, can distract from your message. Stick with a few well-chosen, complementary colors rather than several loud ones. Once you pick them, be consistent. Don't shock the audience by switching to neon-colored backgrounds, or suddenly bringing in checkerboard, two-tone patterns.

Templates and Clip Art

PowerPoint makes available several prepackaged templates for setting up your presentation, and a library of clip art choices to incorporate. However, by virtue of them being readily available and easy to use, they have become overexposed. You probably have seen them in a variety of other presentations and flyers.

Even if you're new to PowerPoint presentations, you should strive to take an original tack in crafting your presentation. If you can, rely on your own images. In most cases, you'll be able to find a photo or graphic that's more appropriate for your use and more specific to your cause.

Bells and Whistles

While you may want to dabble in sound effects or animation, keep it simple if you're a novice. For your initial efforts, concentrate on getting your primary message across with simple text and clean design. As you become more comfortable with the format, with audience reaction, and with the vast options that PowerPoint can provide, you can get more creative with your presentations. To that end, several Web sites, including *http://office .microsoft.com* (which explains how to add sound and video to a presentation), give tips and pointers on more elaborate elements to include.

Educating PowerPoint Presentations

The sheer capabilities of PowerPoint are astounding. Studying applications of it outside the business world can sometimes give you ideas for your own presentation. You can take a look at some amazing endeavors and facility with the program, particularly in the realm of education, at *www.loyola.edu/education/ PowerfulPowerPoint*. There, you can click the "Examples from Real People" link to survey such efforts as a presentation that examines living in colonial times, and another that offers guitar lessons.

Analyzing Your Text and Images

To ensure that you'll be giving a memorably rich, vibrant, and exceptional presentation, ruthlessly review the words and images that form your slides and accompany your script. Too often, PowerPoint presentations become meandering exercises that leave audience members confused, or offer little more content than what the slides themselves are saying. (In the latter case, the slides could just as well have been presented in an e-mail or memo.)

Take time to give your presentation a rigorous, thorough analysis. In doing that, you will:

⤵ Expose gaps in information
⤵ Keep logic and flow in check
⤵ Evaluate whether the content maintains interest
⤵ Assess whether the images are relevant or match the words
⤵ Decide whether there are too many/not enough visuals
⤵ Appraise readability and comprehension
⤵ Gauge whether or not the presentation will connect with its intended audience
⤵ Determine whether the presentation meets its purpose and can achieve its goal

Know Where You're Headed: The Introduction

Your introduction will include your presentation's title page. Make sure that the title of your presentation is clearly delineated and is congruent with the content that follows. Save a clever pun or humor for later in your program (if you use it at all). You want your audience to immediately grasp the matter at hand, in the proper context, and be ready to receive the information that will follow.

Visually, a background is fine for this slide, but avoid an illustration. After the title slide, do segue into a table of contents, which will provide your audience a brief overview of the information to follow, allowing them to share your vision for where the presentation is headed.

The Rest of the Story: Words and Pictures

The slides that follow your table of contents should be ordered logically as they build up to the answer to the question that you initially asked: "Where am I taking the audience with this information?"

As you progress through your presentation, does each slide relate to the one preceding and the one following? Do any need to be reordered? Does each slide present succinct bullet points? Does any one of them contain too much information—or more than one point—that should be broken out into additional slides?

Offering a Bridge from Bullet Points

One book that has attracted both fans and controversy regarding PowerPoint presentations is *Beyond Bullet Points*, by Cliff Atkinson (Microsoft Press, 2005). The book delves into ways to completely avoid the bullet point format in creating a presentation. Instead, you use the decks in a PowerPoint presentation to build momentum and tell an overarching story to communicate your key messages. The book's key premise is that you can throw out bullet points and, instead, combine the concepts of classic storytelling with projected media. Using a step-by-step approach, complete with an explanation of the three-act storytelling structure, this strategy strives to replace a show-and-tell of information with an engaging, involving "experience" for the audience.

A Case of Information Overload

One client came to me frustrated that the PowerPoint he had created to win a *Fortune* 500 account didn't win over his audience. He said the worst insult was that the potential client had been "overwhelmed" by his company's capabilities. In giving his presentation a once-over, I realized what had happened.

He truly had conveyed a wealth of potent capabilities, creative ideas, and dramatic initiatives—all in a seeming avalanche of bullet points that literally tumbled from the top to the bottom of each slide.

Some of the most common mistakes I've seen in analyzing PowerPoint presentations for clients might strike you as the most basic. Many times, kinks in the program flow, or in an approach that veers into the uninteresting, relate to or boil down to a simple, central problem: too much information on the screen, packed unrelentingly on slide after slide.

Sometimes, presentation organizers are so eager to get all their information on the laptop or big screen that they cram several bullet points onto each slide. Often, those points would be better regrouped under different, simpler, and more descriptive headings; broken out onto individual slides as standalone information; or even scrapped from a slide to become part of the presenter's script.

Further, the words that do make the cut should be attention-grabbing. When there are too many words, or they just repeat from one slide to the next, your audience members' eyes glaze over. They lose interest, and allow their minds to wander on to the other priorities in their day.

Analyzing that client's PowerPoint gave him the tools to streamline future presentations, using sparing but vibrant words, incorporating some of his messages into the script rather than on screen, and breaking up the text with more images.

Take Another Crack At Editing

Edit both your words and images with zeal. Make sure that your bullet points sparkle; that your wording is crisp and clear; that your messages are easily understandable; that each slide has its own distinct message; that images are instantly recognizable.

Then, run through the presentation. Make sure that the details you're offering or explaining are timed with the slides that are appearing. Determine whether any words, messages, or images unintentionally relay double meanings.

Delivering Your Presentation

No matter how big the audience, resolve to be comfortable, relaxed, and enthusiastic. Make sure that you've rehearsed so that you're aware of the particulars of your delivery ahead of time, and can replace any words you may mangle, correct any grammar glitches, and repair confusing text.

Once again, don't read your slides word for word. The audience can do that for themselves. Your job is to explain and expound on the contents to present a complete picture that informs, persuades, or does both.

Handing out Handouts

You may decide to provide handouts with your PowerPoint presentation as a takeaway of the information you've presented or reviewed. Plan to wait until after the presentation is over to hand them out. If they're offered beforehand, handouts tend to take the attention and concentration of the audience away from you as they become engrossed in what they're reading, or as they decide that they can refer to the handout at any time for anything they need to know.

You can create handouts from your presentation slides, or you may opt to offer complementary information in addition to or instead of what appears on the slides.

Be Prepared for the Unexpected

Make sure your equipment is functioning properly. If possible, and depending on the presentation's importance, run through an equipment and computer check. Companies are brimming with stories of accounts that were lost, investors that pulled out of projects, and press conferences that went awry because a PowerPoint presentation was delayed, malfunctioned, or never was presented at all due to technical difficulties. Don't let that happen to you.

If you can't check the equipment and room beforehand, and even if you can, have a backup plan. Know your material, and rehearse it in front of others. In case all else fails, be prepared to entertain a room with your knowledge, even without slides.

▶▶ Test Drive

Can you think back to recent efforts at spearheading a meeting or orchestrating a bid for business that could have benefited from a PowerPoint presentation? For a future meeting, answer these questions to determine whether PowerPoint will serve your purposes better:

- ⮑ Do you need to do an impressive job of drawing people in?
- ⮑ Do you need to explain complex components of a program?
- ⮑ Would chunking out information into several projected slides promote understanding?
- ⮑ Do you need to give a large audience a view of a Web site at the same time?
- ⮑ Would displaying images spark interest in the topic you're presenting?

Communication in Charge

What Constitutes a Crisis?

Statistics show that the average company will face a significant crisis at least once every four to five years. Yet, more than half of all companies don't have a crisis communications plan in place.

A crisis is any event, situation, or matter that threatens the integrity of your company and could subsequently harm your reputation, cause a decrease in market share and revenues, and irreversibly damage how customers or clients perceive your company. Your preparedness, competence, and responsiveness in assessing the situation and acting upon it quickly will determine whether the crisis will take your company down with it, or build trust with the public and actually improve your standing.

Crises come in many shapes and forms. In just the past few years, high-profile companies and huge conglomerates—such as Enron, MCI, Disney, and Wal-Mart—suffered crises that have attracted enormous media attention, which usually made the situation worse.

As you survey recent company crises in the news you'll quickly notice that—depending on how they deal with it, some businesses rebound, and some collapse. The key to surviving a crisis is not often a secret: analyzing how a company handled the situation can reveal the rejuvenating or debilitating result.

Connection and Recollection

Even when a company survives a crisis, it may have to endure a lingering detrimental effect. A seven-month grocery-store strike in Southern California crippled three chains; two years later, the stores were still trying to win back shoppers, regain market share, turn around earnings, and stave off new competitors.

Media reports during the strike were constant. Many shoppers were disappointed when they learned how the chains' management teams chose to deal with the workers' union, and believed that their patronage was unappreciated. (Later in this chapter, you'll learn more about how the media can present a company's message and, in effect, hurt or help its case with consumers.)

With each crisis that occurs, customers link a company to how it handled the situation. While people generally understand that some crises are unavoidable, they realize that a company does have control over how it chooses to deal with the subsequent fallout: explain and rectify it, or ignore it and wish it away. Therefore, you must do your part to ensure that the public's perception and ensuing recollection of the crisis are both positive.

What Does the Government Advise?

The press office pages at *www.usinfo.state.gov* take a cue from two presidential quotes: "A popular Government, without popular information, or the means of acquiring it, is but a prologue to a farce or a tragedy; or, perhaps both" (James Madison), and "Let the people know the facts, and the country will be safe" (Abraham Lincoln).

In that spirit, the site offers these "five best tips" for crisis communications, which can readily apply to any company's operations: have a crisis plan; in a time of crisis, go public immediately, but only with what you know; get top management to the crisis site; inform your internal publics; and update frequently and regularly.

What Could Really Happen?

Probably the most common crises relate to companies enduring tough times, such as layoffs, downsizing, or poor financial reports. Common crises regarding employees could include discrimination and harassment. Consider other crises that could crop up as well:

- A natural disaster that affects business
- A boycott by a national group
- A product recall
- A serious injury sustained by an employee on the job, or by a customer on-site
- An insider trading scandal
- A major technology snafu or interruption of service
- The death of a senior executive or celebrity spokesperson

⟳ A holdup or other crime committed at your place of business
⟳ Embezzlement or misreported company earnings
⟳ Fraudulent advertising, or fake positive news
⟳ Being subjected to damaging rumors
⟳ Exposure for sharing customer/client information that was released without permission

Getting the Right Message Out Quickly

First, to examine how best to deal with crisis communications and devise an effective plan, you need to understand the importance of an immediate, responsible, and well-orchestrated response.

A crisis so often worsens because the business experiencing it doesn't initially have enough information, or doesn't have any message in place to begin disseminating. While some information may not be readily available, your business should be able to get at least a basic statement out to show sensitivity and responsiveness to the situation. That action alone would typically bode well for your company in the short run. Most people will cut a company some slack when a potentially devastating crisis hits. However, they won't tolerate silence (which becomes thundering in its continuation) or falsehoods.

Unfortunately, when a crisis occurs, some company owners and executives almost unfathomably opt to press the "ignore" button to completely avoid the matter at hand. However, simply hoping no one will notice the crisis and that all will return to normal is not only naive but it also takes precious time away from tackling the problem and shoring up negative consequences. In some crisis counseling circles, this practice is known as the ostrich effect: essentially, bury your head in the sand and hope the problem will go away. This no-response approach is rarely (if ever) a good idea.

In most cases, if a crisis is drawing attention, it will continue to draw increasingly more until it's recognized by those in charge. Further, even if you don't take the lead in providing information, details will still be uncovered. Worse, when they are, you'll be in a reactive mode when you answer to them, rather than a proactive mode in discussing them as you see fit.

If you don't initially own the crisis and seek to remedy it, you'll be in an increasingly difficult position. When you do finally decide to comment or release a statement, and you're playing catch-up with swirling stories or media coverage or internal anguish, correcting the situation will be like changing a tire on a car that's traveling at 60 miles per hour.

Proactive Preparations

Obviously, your best option in dealing with a crisis is having a plan in place beforehand that will guide, outline, or dictate your actions both internally (within your organization) and externally (with the media and your customers).

In the crunch of everyday events at your company, thinking about the possibility of a crisis may seem like a time-consuming and energy-draining headache you'd rather not put on your schedule. To get you motivated, do a quick mental survey of your company. Are there areas that seem vulnerable to a crisis? For instance, if you own a restaurant, a patron could get food poisoning. In this litigious society, a disgruntled employee could sue you, as could a customer who slips in your store and gets hurt. A hacker could infiltrate your Web site and steal customer information.

Don't be caught off-guard. Devise a crisis communications plan before your company faces a problematic scenario, rather than trying to draft a game plan in the midst of a heated and worrisome predicament.

While you can't predict the exact details and ramifications of a potential crisis, you can take steps to form loose but actionable guidelines.

Name the Possibilities

List the vulnerabilities your company may have: aging equipment, an employee who routinely offends customers, a product that has been repeatedly returned. First of all, right now, can you do anything to prevent any of those from turning into a crisis? Make a list of steps you can take to eliminate or lessen the risk such a vulnerability poses, to prevent it from becoming a full-blown crisis.

| Inside Track | Forewarned Is Forearmed |

The publicity team for a *Fortune* 500 beverage behemoth of which I was a member was charged with laying out a comprehensive crisis communications strategy long before the company's introduction of a new soft drink. That plan delved into several components that may seem obvious, from possibly bad reviews for the product and consumer distaste for it, to demand for it outpacing production and incurring negative feedback from grocers and other sales outlets.

However, one further crisis was a definite consideration: the soft drink was top secret. Its name, taste, branding, and other characteristics had not been announced, and the company was vested in keeping the beverage completely under wraps until advertising for the product was to begin in a print and broadcast campaign, which was months away. In other words, leaking any details about the beverage at this point would have been a crisis, too.

At every turn, and in all aspects of the crisis plan, we considered the media, keeping in touch with them and considering how different reactions from them would need to be taken into account.

To that end, the publicity team leader even made further suggestions in warding off potential crises. In Los Angeles, commercials showcasing the product would soon be shot. Even though television and film shoots are routine events in the city, we devised a game plan in case the shoot unexpectedly attracted unwanted attention. During each commercial's production days, a member of the publicity team was present, equipped with talking points should a member of the press appear without warning and ask questions about the commercial being shot.

The press never appeared, but if they had—and had we been unprepared—an unplanned-for crisis would have been in the offing: we would have been playing catch-up, re-engineering publicity plans for a top-secret product that was suddenly out in the open.

Basically, this exercise gives you the framework for what you would need to do if a crisis happened today. Even if one of these crises isn't the one that materializes, having thought about these scenarios better prepares you to battle any that may happen. You must get into the take-responsibility-and-remedy mode: What will you do to correct the problem, and stop the crisis from continuing?

Assemble Your Team

A large company has several staff to draw upon to form a crisis communications team: representatives from legal, public relations, operations, and so on. While you might not have that benefit, consider who you would want to contend with and solve a crisis. Most likely, you need to have a lawyer, and the top executives from your company. You also might want to make arrangements with a media specialist who can be called in should his or her services be needed.

You need to be able to keep in contact with everyone on the team, at all times. For this purpose, gather the team members' home phone numbers, cell phone numbers, pager numbers, and e-mail addresses.

What to Do When a Crisis Comes

Realize that some crises are either not newsworthy or handled so deftly that they don't appear in the press. Even so, when a crisis does occur, realize that your crisis communications plan must embrace a two-pronged approach.

Internally, you'll be working to solve the problem that has arisen within the company, rectifying the situation, and communicating progress, changes, and improvements to the employees.

Externally, you'll be communicating with your customers and clients through oral and written forms of communication. Depending on the scope and seriousness of the crisis, you may embark on large-scale communication attempts through the media who will, for better or worse, serve as your mouthpiece.

Mistakes When the Crisis Happens

You can learn from a litany of mistakes that plague organizations facing a crisis. In addition to taking too long to respond and failing to have a plan already in place, the most common mistakes a company makes are:

- ➲ Giving a "no comment" to the press
- ➲ Ignoring calls asking for details about the situation
- ➲ Refusing to make necessary changes or adjustments

➲ Taking a misleading tack when dealing with inquiries
➲ Resisting input from trusted experts
➲ Failing to provide written materials regarding the business

What You Need

When the crisis occurs, recognize what has happened, and draw up a plan to deal with it. While you may not have all the information you initially need, you can start taking action toward fixing the problem at hand. Shortly after the crisis surfaces, you'll need to ask these three questions:

1. How will you deal with the immediate problem?
2. How will you communicate with employees and other internal groups?
3. How will you communicate with the media?

Communicate with Employees

This sometimes-overlooked group can be your first line of defense in keeping a crisis from spiraling out of control. Don't assume that your employees will catch on or simply trust that everything will work out. Also, don't become preoccupied with communicating to other groups that may initially be deemed more important or influential than your employees. Keep employees abreast of developments. During a crisis, plan for question-and-answer sessions with them at regular intervals. You can meet with employees in person, and also communicate with them via voice-mail messages, e-mails, and Web postings. When you don't keep your employees informed, they understandably may feel frustrated, and worried that the situation may worsen and that their jobs may be at stake. Sometimes, employees have even been the catalyst for a crisis becoming worse for a company because they revealed their frustrations or the internal lack of information to the press.

Don't Avoid the Media

When a crisis is unavoidable, and particularly if it's attracting attention, some enterprises seem initially bent on keeping the media at bay, treating them as a foe, and believing that the media's only goal is to bring devastation to the company.

Taking that stance is dangerous to a company's well-being for several reasons. While the media are eager to cover stories that they believe the public wants—and has a right—to know about, they also want to provide audiences with accurate reporting. If they fail to do that, they then face a crisis of their own: audiences will think that stories reported by the news organizations are unreliable or contain falsehoods, prompting the audiences to shrink.

In all likelihood, if you have a story the media is interested in, they will find a way to get the information they need to file a story, whether or not you provide details. Your company is much better off taking the initiative. You get a better shot at controlling the story and customers' perceptions if you take a proactive stance, and make the media an ally.

Your crisis communication efforts should be prompt and open. You can start with the media list that may have initially been created for your publicity efforts. However, depending on the crisis, your media contact efforts may need to be significantly broadened.

Presenting the Communication: What to Include in Your Message

While you may be waiting for details about the situation, you should start as soon as possible to frame your position for the crisis, and take ownership of the story. Determine the message points that you will distribute, and decide who will be the spokesperson for your company—ideally, someone who is poised and comfortable with talking to the media. If necessary, prepare that person with talking points, as well as answers for possible questions that may arise.

In taking the media's questions, stick to the facts and the information that you know. If a question is posed that you don't feel comfortable answering, or simply don't know the answer to, reply by saying that you will get back to that person.

Don't issue a "no comment." Doing so almost always leaves the unfavorable impression that your company is trying to cover up the crisis.

What to Draft

You can start your communication by writing a succinct statement about the crisis, and explaining the steps your company is taking to handle the situation. Even if you're not clear on the most recent developments, you can issue a brief release that covers the who, what, when, and where, leaving the how and why to further analysis.

For example, suppose your store was robbed during business hours, and someone was injured. The initial release would give the specifics of the robbery: that someone was injured during an armed robbery at an indicated time at your store's location; the injured person's current condition; and the current efforts your company is conducting to monitor the victim's progress. You would also include that your company has efforts in progress to investigate current security measures at the location; to collect information as police reports are available and their investigation continues; and to work on beefing up security so that customers can always feel safe shopping at your store.

In drafting your communication, make sure to show care and concern for afflicted parties. In addition, adhere to the facts; don't speculate, guess, or hypothesize on how it happened or what might happen next. Release only the information that you definitely know.

The release can be read as a prepared statement, or distributed via e-mail or fax to news outlets.

As additional information becomes available, you can draft statements that keep the media and other external audiences posted.

Meanwhile, as mentioned previously, keep employees informed of initiatives so they understand the situation, what the company is doing about it, and how they may be affected. When employees aren't informed, they may begin to gossip about what they think is going on, which is usually worse than the actual events. With their attention devoted to thinking about and discussing possibilities with coworkers, employees are likely to grow restless and discontent, and they're also less likely to be committed to the work at hand. If you withhold information from your work force, your company will suffer both in perception and in production by its employees, who often are a company's biggest group of supporters.

Other Materials on Hand

With your company in the spotlight—unwanted or not—you will probably be asked to provide additional materials about your company: recent press releases, corporate brochures, executive bios, and the like. Be prepared to supply media-friendly information about your company. Do give all the materials a once-over before you distribute them; don't be caught off-guard by content that unintentionally points out the vulnerability that has prompted the crisis currently in motion.

If you don't have materials available, carefully but promptly draft a fact sheet that gives at least a few key specifics about the company.

Other Avenues

To keep employees, customers, and the media posted on developments, you might also consider a phone line dedicated to either taking calls about the crisis, or providing a prerecorded message that gives the latest update.

In addition, some companies have "dark pages" on their Web sites. These are pages already built in to the Web site that can be quickly activated and can serve as an electronic source of information about the crisis.

Do make sure, though, that you vigorously keep your Web site information about the crisis completely up-to-date. Once the crisis has passed, include only the information that would currently impact customers.

For instance, a national quick-service chain had to recall an ice cream flavor that had been tainted and caused some customers to get sick. The ice cream was pulled, with plans for it to be reformulated and then reintroduced. With those plans intact, the site put up a page announcing "Alert Me When the Flavor Returns" with an explanation about its temporary unavailability. Months later, the flavor had been reformulated and could be ordered again at stores nationwide. However, the "Alert Me" page was still on the site, with the same outdated explanation about temporary unavailability. If the site had been correctly updated, it would have had a page that said "Our Popular Flavor Is Back!" instead. Not keeping up with the Web site was needlessly drawing attention to an embarrassing matter that had been responsibly resolved.

> ### Bnet.com
>
> At *www.bnet.com*, you can find a treasure trove of crisis communications case studies that offer in-depth looks at media coordination and strategy, action plans, and checklists for success. Nearly 300 white papers—such as "When a Plant Closes: Using Crisis Communication to Save the Day," "Ford Motor Company: What Went Wrong," and "Lessons Learned from the Top 10 Crises of 2002" (regarding those that ensnared Nike and Martha Stewart Living Omnimedia, among others)—let you in on invaluable techniques, information, and hard-won experiences to carry over and use in your own crisis communications planning. The site's tagline is "Get Smarter About What's Working at Work," which you can start doing simply by signing up, free of charge, to read the site's content.

How to Determine Your Success

Once the crisis has passed, orchestrate a plan that will allow you to gauge your success in handling the situation, by checking in on such areas as the effect the crisis had on sales and customers' perceptions.

To begin, track media coverage, if that played into the crisis. You can sign up with a news media monitoring service (such as BurrellesLuce at *www.burrellesluce.com*, VMS at *www.vidmon.com*, or Bacon's at *www.bacons.com*) that can furnish copies of the articles and clips to you. Your company should also keep a running log of media calls that come in, and then follow up with the service to see if that outlet covered the story.

Additionally, you can sign up for a Google Alert. With that tool, you supply the search engine with key words regarding your company and the crisis. Then, Google automatically e-mails you back with stories posted on the Web that contain those keywords.

To determine how the crisis affected customer support and loyalty, you can chart sales increases or decreases, and conduct focus groups to gather opinions.

Learn from the Crisis

Once the crisis is over, make sure to thoroughly conduct an internal audit to determine what the company learned from the crisis. Give thoughtful answers to the following questions:

- How will your enterprise do business differently?
- What changes implemented during the crisis will stay in place?
- What vulnerabilities should you start troubleshooting now?
- If the media was involved, did their stories hurt or help your cause?
- What did the crisis tell you about your company's operating procedures regarding the flow of information, how you deal with employees, and how you handle the media? Were there instances in which the information distributed was wrong or given too soon?
- Should technology play a bigger role next time? Was your Web site well equipped to handle a page or more devoted to the crisis, as well as additional traffic? Were additional phone lines needed?
- Did you have written materials ready?
- What will you do differently the next time your company faces a crisis?
- Are contingency plans necessary the next time? For instance, if the crisis affected shipping, do you know how you'll plan to ship product if a crisis occurs again?

What Can Go Wrong—or Right

Remember that when a crisis is mismanaged, your company may suffer from a damaged reputation that can take years to repair, or may even lead to the demise of the business. A poorly handled crisis can also prompt employee malaise, a loss of customer confidence, depressed productivity and sales, and investor backlash.

A crisis that ends badly could also have ripple effects that take the company away from doing business and tie up resources in legal proceedings and staff changes.

Conversely, a deftly handled crisis can strengthen your company's connection to those who contribute to its success, including employees, advisers, and customers; heighten visibility; increase profits; and demonstrate your company's aptitude in showing "grace under fire" by taking responsibility and excelling in challenging circumstances.

▶▶ Test Drive

If you haven't already done so, take the time to outline a crisis communications plan for your company by elaborating on each of these key suggestions:

- ➲ Pinpoint potentially problematic areas, people, or concerns
- ➲ Analyze the vulnerabilities presented
- ➲ Devise scenarios to cope with crises that could occur if those vulnerabilities caved in
- ➲ Assemble a crisis team
- ➲ Establish communication plans with employees and the media
- ➲ Decide which basic information about the company should be available

PART **6**

Communication in Charge

Communication Mistakes to Avoid

To ensure that your business thrives—to keep customers loyal, employees productive, investors informed, and vendors helpful—you need to avoid mistakes in communication. If you take stock of even a few recent mishaps, problems, or unfortunate situations, you probably will be able to trace the incidents' origins back to miscommunication.

As you have delved into the modes and methods of business communication, you've learned that you need to be acutely aware of content, tone, and audience; take a professional tack; and pick the best way to present your message.

Shun Disparity and Inconsistency in Messages

Be committed to the motto that—in all of your communication endeavors—content matters. You should strive to have your business communications manifest a unifying theme for your company. In other words, it should always seem that your communications could only have come from your company. While your company may not be wholly original in any one area, you should still work toward putting forth a singular point of view that is distinctly your company's.

A part of staying on track in that consistency and uniformity is ensuring that each message has a predetermined goal: What do you hope to accomplish with that specific communication piece? Give meaningful consideration to the goal and content.

Make sure that this regard for consistency and its resultant approach run across all company correspondence and materials. In doing so, bring all your communications "under one roof"—make them match. With those efforts, you'll present an enterprise that's organized, polished, and worth doing business with.

Beware of the Indistinguishable Audience, Indifferent Tone Syndrome

In drafting your content, you must know which audience you're communicating with—and know about them. Too often, companies consider the audience to be an indistinguishable mass that is simply there to take in a message. Rise above that thinking: you must weigh in with the purpose of your communication, and how it should be geared to resonate with your intended audience.

Will the message attract business or remedy a vendor relationship? Are you appealing to an investor or dealing with an employee? Is the message in a memo or an advertisement? Is it spoken or written?

Before you begin crafting your message, have the image of your audience firmly planted in mind. That focus lends itself to adopting the proper tone. You never want your tone to incorporate a one-size-fits-all, generic flavor. The proper tone in the right context with the right audience lends power and credibility to your message and makes it so effective that it will yield the action or results you're trying to achieve.

Mistakes in Web Site Communication for Your Audience

According to ClickZ.com—which presents ideas for marketers—the top five biggest mistakes in design for attracting an audience with sound Web site search engine optimization are: being lax about the content and components that will most appeal to and satisfy your target audience; lacking content that relates directly to the keywords and phrases that will attract an audience; not considering key words in the initial stages of design; becoming preoccupied with splash animation pages to open a site rather than a page that emphasizes keyword-rich text; and not striking a balance of text and graphics. Not surprisingly, Internet Marketing Chronicle's list of the worst Internet marketing blunders almost all concern how you relate to your audience. The offenders include not asking for, and acting on, visitor feedback; not managing e-mail communications effectively; failing to create and build an opt-in mailing list; sending out inappropriate advertising, such as unsolicited e-mails; and forgetting that marketing to your target audience is the key to your success.

Switch from the Wrong Communication Channel

Once you've dedicated yourself to refined content and a defined audience, don't reach for the improper way to deliver your message.

In many, sometimes regrettable, ways, e-mail has made doing business just too easy. Why write a thank-you note when you can send an e-mail? Why get on the phone when you can send an e-mail? Why set up an interview when you can have an applicant answer questions in an e-mail?

While e-mail certainly has distinct advantages in numerous situations, it's not the be-all and end-all. Always keep in mind that you have a variety of communication options at your disposal. Don't automatically open up your desktop e-mailbox to draft a new message just because it's the easiest alternative. Choose the method that will truly create the intended effect with the most impact to help you reach a stated goal.

Similarly, commit to using the best platform—direct pieces, publicity, advertising, or a combination thereof—for your marketing messages. Each has distinct advantages and disadvantages. Carefully weigh the options of each before taking the approach that will assuredly bring the most significant results.

Slow Down: Steer Away from a Rushed Approach

In the communication decisions that you make, don't get caught up in an "I needed it yesterday" mindset. Absolutely, deadlines are important and everyone's in a hurry to make progress. The instant transmissions of e-mail, the speed of overnight delivery, and the rapid-fire returns of a messenger mean that you can often wait until the last minute to accomplish a task. However, there are two reasons why you should not wait until the last minute to craft copy or choose a communication method. First, waiting until then leads to rash decisions that you might regret. Second, in being so eager to get the mission accomplished, you may neglect to proofread for grammatical mistakes, or press the "Send" button before you've really had a chance to consider what you're about to send.

Enlivening Your Communication

While you guard yourself against making communication mistakes that will cost your company, resolve to bring three other commitments—to plan well, to think big, and to embrace technology—into your fold to enhance your correspondence, meetings, marketing materials, and other endeavors. These additional commitments are also certain to contribute mightily to your bottom line.

Have a Plan

Don't chart the course for business success without a map. Make sure that you have given your company the tools for success in several areas: an overall business plan that delineates your mission, points out your unique sales positioning, and finely details other cogent points about your company; a marketing plan that strategizes across several formats to get out the word about your company to the clients and customers who may patronize it; and a crisis communications plan to ensure that your company won't suffer needlessly and lengthily when a mishap hits.

Realize that these plans are never meant to stay confined to their initial draft. They should be considered living documents that change with your business. Schedule to revisit them often, update them as your company undergoes changes and developments, and refine their content on an ongoing basis.

No Matter Your Company's Size, Think Big

Small companies fall into an (un)easy rut, thinking that, because of their size, they're not held to the same standards as a *Fortune* 500 company. While your organization may not have the budget, resources, or staff of a conglomerate, you should think and act as though you do, presenting strong communication materials and adopting expert procedures to help you relate to and keep in contact with clients and customers.

Make sure that your materials all have a professional sheen and a unifying theme and that your correspondence is crisp and worth reading. Exude the respectful, knowledgeable attitude of a company that has a large, loyal consumer following or client base, and act accordingly. Don't think that being small means you can hide flaws. Think of it as your opportunity to stand out and shine.

Embrace Technology

In the realm of the latest advancements in technology, keep pace with—or charge ahead of—your competitors. Get a sharp Web site up and running, and update it frequently. If you're out of the office, have your phone answered via voice mail that you routinely check, and put your e-mail on an auto-responder. Alternatively, remain constantly available with a BlackBerry. Don't hand over a written proposal to a potential client if a PowerPoint presentation will get the job done—and win the new business—more impressively and more easily.

The whiz-bang elements of technology can seem maddening to master, and they just keep coming with new components, methods, and equipment. Your business will benefit, however, if you stay ahead of the learning curve. Most customers and clients want you to know more than they do, and part of that commitment is conveying the most up-to-date information and techniques by using the most up-to-date devices and programs.

Mistakes Vendor Companies Make in Communicating

Newmarketbuilders, Inc., a retail trends advisor and management-consulting firm, devised a list of the Top 10 mistakes suppliers make that give their competition the edge. While the study that was completed to compile this list specifically pertained to retail businesses, you can quickly notice how it stresses problems that could thwart the way all kinds of companies do business. The list includes poor communication, bringing the wrong people to meetings, dropping innovation, hiring the wrong people, not observing buyers' patterns and preferences, and not keeping up. You can hear a free audio presentation about the list at *www.newmarketbuilders.com.*

Checklists for Clear Messages and the Right Methods

Guidelines for disseminating clear messages dovetail with doing the work necessary to avoid mistakes. To that end, answer the upcoming three sets of questions in this section so that you can more fully examine and evaluate both your company's prime attributes and areas of deficiency. In the section after this one, you can consider suggestions and possibilities for the problem areas you pinpoint.

For Unity and Consistency

This area provides a vantage point that positions your company as being professional, a pleasure to do business with, and one that offers a unique advantage over competitors. Consider the following questions, which relate to your company's proficiency in this category:

- Do you have professionally printed and designed letterhead, business cards, and mailing labels?
- Does your logo clearly convey your company's name and essence?
- Can you state the edge your company has over its competitors?
- Is your brand unique, vivid, and simple?
- Is your mission statement readily recalled?
- Do your employees know the mission statement?

For the Right Audience and Tone

How well you know your company's audiences—who they are, the characteristics of each, and the best way to communicate with them—comprises and contributes to your strengths in this domain:

- Do you have regular meetings with employees?
- Is there a system in place for communicating with investors?
- Do you have avenues for customers to weigh in with comments about products and service?
- Do you have a feedback system in place for each of your different audiences?
- Before distributing information to any audience, do you analyze the piece to ensure that it has adopted the right approach in tone; that it's not condescending; that it more often than not is conversational; and that it's always respectful?

For "Big" Matters

In portraying and positioning your company as one that takes its business and customers seriously, consider these questions, which pertain to your enterprise thinking big, even if it's small:

➲ Do you proofread all written materials (correspondence, RFPs, ads) that are distributed?

➲ Does your company have a Web site that meets its fullest potential?

➲ Does your company ensure that visual materials look professional (even if you haven't chosen the most expensive option)?

➲ Are calls and e-mails returned promptly? Is correspondence answered or responded to in a timely manner?

➲ Does the company have a designee for fielding inquiries, suggestions, or information from certain audiences, such as investors or the media?

➲ Do meetings have agendas?

For the Right Methods for Your Messages

As you know, picking the right forum for your communication involves several areas. Answer these questions to determine whether you know the advantages, disadvantages, and other guidelines that influence the choices you make for various methods of communication:

➲ Do you know when a memo should prevail over an e-mail? A phone call over a memo? A face-to-face conversation over a phone call?

➲ If you want to run an ad, would it be for broadcast or in print? If you think print will be most effective, are you leaning toward newspapers or magazines? Why are you choosing the one you are? If you're considering broadcast, will it be radio or television? Do you know the advantages and disadvantages of each?

➲ What occasions provide the impetus for a press release?

➲ Is a direct mail piece a possibility for your organization? If so, do you already have a recipient list that would be targeted enough to yield a high response rate?

How to Remedy Poor Communication

Perhaps your business isn't reaching the pinnacle of success you had hoped. Or maybe you're finding lapses and voids that, if filled, could bring profitability. In either case, a thorough examination of your communication methods (in content, audience, tone, and mode) could ferret out the culprit and allow your energy to be directed toward fixing it. So, whether you feel that your organization is riddled with poor communication or suffers intermittently from its effects, be assured that you have plenty of options to improve it.

When large companies experience the same problems repeatedly, or endure a significant downturn in business, they often hire an outside firm to conduct a communications audit. This across-the-board examination delves into communication and marketing activities and policies, turning up problematic procedures, wayward modes, or incongruent messages that hamper communication with intended audiences and affect productivity and profitability.

The goal of the audit is to identify how a company interacts with key audiences, such as customers, employees, vendors, and the media, with the tone it conveys and the messages it distributes. Once the information is researched, formal recommendations for preserving or enhancing the processes are presented.

If your company is dissatisfied with its investment in a media relations program; if it wants to refocus corporate initiatives; or if it is having trouble finding the time to keep employees informed, or suffering from poor visibility of products or services, you might consider a review of your communications.

Oftentimes, your best recourse in correcting poor communication is an obvious one that—perhaps—wasn't so glaring until your attention was called to it. Deciding to conduct an audit aside, this section allows you to glean information to ascertain where your communication might be breaking down, and how to strengthen it.

Analyzing Your Communications

In the first step, gather up materials that you rely on to get your job done every day. These could be memos, your company's Web site pages, letterhead, or a recent proposal for new business.

Scrutinize each one individually. Standing alone, does each make a strong, credible, enticing impression? Does it point out your attributes? Does it convey quality and professionalism?

Now, look at them collectively. Do the pieces, in essence, "get along" with each other? Does one stand out as not fitting in somehow? Are the messages contained in each one consistent and particularly relevant to your company practices, tactics, and attributes?

Next, consider the messages in the communications themselves. Are the messages brief and concise? In them, can you find unnecessary words or sentences? Is the copy engaging? Does it speak to the audience's benefit, or is it self-serving? If someone didn't bother to read the words, does the communication itself still convey a sense of quality and professionalism? Are there grammatical mistakes or typos?

Further, in the overall scheme of these pieces, is it clear that you strive for an "ambassador effect" with employees, customers, clients, vendors, and investors?

In your general practices concerning communication, are you prompt in returning calls and e-mails? Are your letters and memos professional? Is your follow-up with them consistent?

Checking in with Your Customer Audience

Is your correspondence with your customers or clients respectful and inviting, and reminiscent of how you would want to be approached (and dealt with) by a company who wants to have (and keep) you as a customer? With your customers, are you clear and concise with instructions? For instance, are forms to be filled out for an order easy to follow, or are shipping instructions on your Web site confusing? Do the materials that customers see have a cohesive look and sense to them?

Engaging Your Employees

Though they work with you the closest, your employees may unfortunately be the farthest from your mind in terms of communication. Do your employees act on your behalf, or the company's, in the best way possible? Do they know what it means to do so? Are your employees informed when they need to be? Are they working in accordance with clear job descriptions? Do they have a sense of where the company is headed, in terms of its vision? Do you strive to keep their loyalty by keeping them abreast of company news and developments, particularly those that impact their individual jobs? Are you receptive to their suggestions for changes?

Mistakes in Communicating with Employees Can Start with Hiring

Make it a point to showcase your company's strong communication skills right from the start during the hiring process. That will allow the candidates to realize the company's belief in solid communication, and encourage a potential employee to continue the trend if hired. Some miscommunication-based hiring mistakes outlined on *asktheheadhunter.com* include relying on written job descriptions that are too narrow in scope and severely limit candidates to be considered; failing to prep a potential candidate before the interview with the job and its responsibilities, and company information that will give the interview a better, more visionary, more successful context; talking too much during the interview, rather than hearing what the candidate has to say; and keeping your team out of the loop to get feedback on a candidate's expected impact on the company.

Surveying Your Opportunities

Finally, in analyzing and gathering the most information possible, take the time to survey others regarding the way you communicate for your company and its products or services.

For instance, select twelve to fifteen friends or industry insiders who can give you the most insight into your communication modes and methods. Create a questionnaire that encourages their frank opinions and honest assessments about the way you do business, and concentrate on areas that you've determined may be problematic. If you receive duplicate responses that surprise you, don't ignore them. While one unexpected response may be an anomaly, you should pay attention to similarities that crop up in the surveys—even if you don't agree with them. Depending on your relationship with your respondents, check in with them as follow-up to ascertain whether they can give you more details and feedback on an unexpected area of concern. In some cases, you may have phrased the question wrong.

Alternatively, you could ask six to eight people to convene for an organized roundtable discussion (with a time limit and with an agenda you've prepared, following the meeting pointers in Chapter 21). People are often eager to help, they just need to be asked. If you've pinpointed individuals for a survey, they most likely have credible, exciting insights that could be invaluable to your enterprise.

Similarly, you might gather specific groups, such as employees and highly regarded customers, for focus group questionnaires or meetings. You'll take a different tone with them than you would with friends or colleagues, but you'll also gather different types of helpful information from these other perspectives.

Ensuring that Communication Is Making a Difference in Your Business

This book has surveyed a wealth of different communication formats, and the best techniques to use them—all at your disposal to bring efficiency, profits, and, ultimately, success to your business. Becoming proficient at relating to your audiences, being the architect of banner business and marketing plans, mastering avenues of correspondence, implementing expert ways to go after and win new business, engaging in sparkling conversation and interviews, and creatively producing sales pieces and Web sites all are robust, heady ways to get ahead in an ultra-competitive business world.

Relaunch: It's Never Too Late to Reassess and Regroup

In analyzing your communication methods, you may decide that you need to change course, redirect your efforts, and reshape your endeavors. You may want to redesign your logo, change your Web site, initiate new ways of dealing with vendors and investors—and those would just be for starters.

The fact is that you can look to hundreds of recent examples of companies that have taken new directions in trying to appeal to new or more customers by relaunching their brand. Obviously, the bigger the company, the more visible the relaunch. National chains, companies that have enjoyed public offerings—and their ensuing publicity—and businesses with products that are available at multiple locations all face much more substantial work in relaunching a brand.

Still, to get an idea of the process involved, consider this example.

In a dramatic and highly visible relaunch, Kentucky Fried Chicken abbreviated its moniker to KFC in 1991 to avoid its connection to the perceived unhealthful effects of fried foods, and to appear more youthful with a shorter, catchier name. However, in 2005, the chain seemed to have another relaunch afoot. It returned to its roots when it opened a restaurant under its original name—Kentucky Fried Chicken—tapping into the nostalgia and Southern connection still positively associated with the company. That relaunch has proven to be so successful that plans for dozens more are now in the works.

Yet, even as communication can assuredly be a boon to your organization, you must take on the continual challenge to harness and refine it in a variety of areas. Constantly look for ways to improve and build upon your efforts. Get feedback from trusted sources. Be open to improving your approach and trying new methods. Finally, always evaluate and gauge your success.

Despite our increasing reliance on technology, you'll always have to do business with other people to succeed, which means that communication will always be a necessity! Be continually ready, eager, and dedicated to embracing and enhancing your business communication. The correlation between your proficiency and your profit will be exciting, measurable, powerful—and will change the way you do business for the better!

▶▶ Test Drive

What's your most problematic area in business communication? Is it in looking more professional, or being better at thinking big? Are you generally unsure of your target audience? Do you have materials that seem completely out-of-sync with each other? Whichever the case, resolve right now to start addressing it.

You can begin by taking stock of your company's best communications asset. What is it? Is your business plan a winner? Does your Web site routinely win raves from customers? Is your follow-up with clients superb?

Now, what's one step you can take to make the weakness stronger, bringing it more in line with the attribute?

Appendix A
Web Sites

www.allbusiness.com: Brimming with advice, forms, agreements, and other helpful materials, this site bills itself as "Champions of Small Business."

www.bnet.com: This site offers resources—such as case studies—that delve into the principles behind thinking about how to make a business work better.

www.businessplans.org: Studying the wide range of business plans offered on this site can help you write a plan for your own company.

www.dailycandy.com: Check out a weekday array of quick, snappy ideas regarding product positioning and branding, and communicating with your target audience.

www.entrepreneur.com: Look into a bevy of tips, tools, and ideas for starting, running, and growing your business.

www.fastcompany.com: Want the lowdown on hot trends in the workplace? Fast Company covers it for "people who believe in fusing tough-minded performance with sane human values."

www.inc.com: A comprehensive array of topics relating to a wealth of small business matters.

www.office.microsoft.com: The place to turn to for PowerPoint news, how-to articles, updates, and even training.

www.sba.gov: This is the official Web site for the Small Business Administration. Visitors can learn about myriad services provided by the agency and its partners.

http://online.wsj.com: The Wall Street Journal in its online format includes business stories pertaining to all sectors.

Appendix B
Further Reading

Collins, Jim C. *Good to Great: Why Some Companies Make the Leap . . . and Others Don't.* New York: Harper Business, 2001.

Griffin, Jill. *Customer Loyalty: How to Earn It, How to Keep It.* San Francisco: Jossey-Bass, 2002.

Hamlin, Sonya. *How to Talk So People Listen: Connecting in Today's Workplace.* New York: Collins, 2005.

Hughes, Mark. *Buzzmarketing: Get People to Talk About Your Stuff.* New York: Portfolio, 2005.

Laermer, Richard. *Full Frontal PR.* Princeton, NJ: Bloomberg Press, 2003.

LoCicero, Joe, Richard J. LoCicero, M.D. and Kenneth A. LoCicero, Ph.D. *The Complete Idiot's Guide to Clear Thinking.* New York: Penguin, 2005.

Morgenstern, Julie. *Never Check E-Mail in the Morning: And Other Unexpected Strategies for Making Your Work Life Work.* New York: Fireside, 2005.

Post, Peggy, and Peter Post. *Emily Post's The Etiquette Advantage in Business: Personal Skills for Professional Success.* New York: HarperResource, 1999.

Sandler, Corey, and Janice Keefe. *1001 Letters for All Occasions: The Best Models for Every Business and Personal Need.* Avon, MA: Adams Media, 2003.

Stewart, Martha. *The Martha Rules: 10 Essentials for Achieving Success as You Start, Grow, or Manage a Business.* Emmaus, PA: Rodale Books, 2005.

Strunk, William Jr., and E. B. White. *The Elements of Style Illustrated.* Illustrated by Maira Kalman. New York: Penguin, 2005.

Wendt, Lloyd, and Herman Kogan. *Give the Lady What She Wants! The Story of Marshall Field & Company.* Chicago: Rand McNally & Company, 1952.

Williams, Robin. *The Non-Designer's Design Book.* Berkeley, CA: Peachpit Press, 2003.

INDEX

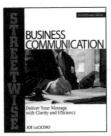

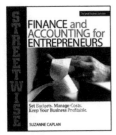
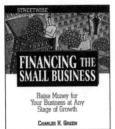

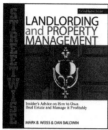

Streetwise® Landlording & Property Management
Weiss and Baldwin
$19.95; ISBN 10: 1-58062-766-8

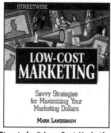

Streetwise® Low-Cost Marketing
Mark Landsbaum
$19.95; ISBN 10: 1-58062-858-3

Streetwise® Low-Cost Web Site Promotion
Barry Feig
$19.95; ISBN 10: 1-58062-501-0

Streetwise® Managing a Nonprofit
John Riddle
$19.95; ISBN 10: 1-58062-698-X

Streetwise® Managing People
Bob Adams, et al.
$19.95; ISBN 10: 1-55850-726-4

Streetwise® Marketing Plan
Don Debelak
$19.95; ISBN 10: 1-58062-268-2

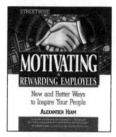

Streetwise® Motivating & Rewarding Employees
Alexander Hiam
$19.95; ISBN 10: 1-58062-130-9

Streetwise® Project Management
Michael Dobson
$19.95; ISBN 10: 1-58062-770-6

Streetwise® Restaurant Management
John James & Dan Baldwin
$19.95; ISBN 10: 1-58062-781-1

Streetwise® Sales Letters with CD
Reynard and Weiss
$29.95; ISBN 10: 1-58062-440-5

Streetwise® Selling on eBay®
Sonia Weiss
$19.95; ISBN 10: 1-59337-610-3

Streetwise® Small Business Book of Lists
Edited by Gene Marks
$19.95; ISBN 10: 1-59337-684-7

Streetwise® Small Business Start-Up
Bob Adams
$19.95; ISBN 10: 1-55850-581-4

Streetwise® Start Your Own Business Workbook
Gina Marie Mangiamele
$9.95; ISBN 10: 1-58062-506-1

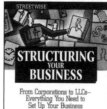

Streetwise® Structuring Your Business
Michele Cagan
$19.95; ISBN 10: 1-59337-177-2

Streetwise® Time Management
Marshall Cook
$19.95; ISBN 10: 1-58062-131-7

About the Author

As a Los Angeles–based writer, marketing consultant, and master of communication for the past fifteen years, Joe LoCicero has been integrally involved with the marketing strategy for hundreds of cable and network television programs, as well as numerous consumer products. In his vast experience, LoCicero has created and developed communication materials for such clients as The Coca-Cola Company, Discovery Channel, Paramount, Disney, Marriott, Sony, Turner Broadcasting, Fox Sports Network, Time Warner, and Hallmark. He has put his marketing, publicity and advertising skills to work launching his own lifestyle brand company, Practical Whimsy, while also consulting with other small stores, firms, Web Sites and startups, including candy company Good Karmal (which has been featured on Oprah's "O List") and Donum, a nationally-recognized celebrity gift service.

As part of his own company's efforts, he currently writes the monthly column "Practical Whimsy: Southern Hospitality, Hollywood Style" for *Y'all: The Magazine of Southern People,* and keeps commerce and communication thriving on his company's Web Site at practicalwhimsy.com. The site offers reversible styles for baby and home, recipes, and tips for entertaining, and supplies select retailers with Practical Whimsy goods. He's also a regular columnist for momready.com.

LoCicero and his advice have been featured in such media as *Cosmopolitan* and *Woman's World* magazines, daily newspapers in the U.S. and Canada, and on Sirius' Martha Stewart Living Radio. Tenets and exercises for clear communication are a linchpin in his book *The Complete Idiot's Guide to Clear Thinking* (Penguin/Alpha 2005). His next books include *Streetwise® Event and Meeting Planning* and *Cake Decorating for Dummies.*